# LIFE LIBERTY HAPPINESS

## SUBURBS ARE BUILT TO SELL CARS

## VILLAGETOWNS ARE BUILT FOR LIFE

## BUILD YOUR VILLAGE

*A journey from Blandville to a VillageTown*

By Claude Lewenz

© 2010 Claude Lewenz – All rights reserved

Jackson House Publishing Company
Tucson Arizona USA and Auckland New Zealand

ISBN 978-0-958-2868-4-8 (Hardbound)
ISBN 978-0-958-2868-2-4 (Paperback)
ISBN 978-1-44143843-0 (CS Paperback)

2 April 2010

Except by a reviewer who wishes to quote brief passages in connection with a review, no part of this publication may be reproduced or transmitted in any form or by any means, electronic, mechanical including photocopying, recording, or by any information storage or retrieval system, without written permission from the Village Forum.

Having said that, the publishers strongly recommend you ask the Village Forum for written permission since the whole idea is to spread the word about VillageTowns.

Post: The Village Forum - RD1 Church Bay
Waiheke Island, Auckland, New Zealand
Web site: www.villageforum.com
E-mail: info@villageforum.com

Author: Claude Lewenz
Photographs & drawings: Claude Lewenz

With Cameos by and written by:
Stewart Udall, Chairman Emeritus of the Village Forum (1920-2010)
Dr. Elisabet Sahtouris, www.sahtouris.com
Michael Henderson, www.valuesatwork.org
Richard Hollingum, www.departmentofdoing.com
Andrew Blake, www.villagetowns.net

The Fine Print: Neither the Village Forum nor the various businesses associated with VillageTown projects are tax-exempt or charitable organizations. Building a community involves real estate development, and it's easier to pay taxes than try to convince the tax department that sale of a book or 4,000 homes and 1,000 workplaces is an act of charity. Proceeds from the sale of this book will go to the company that sets up and secures funding to build VillageTowns. That company or companies are intended to build, or cause to be built, as many VillageTowns as are needed, world-wide. If it becomes wildly successful, as we hope it does, we would like to ultimately set up charitable trusts as the beneficiary of that success. That is our dream.

# This Book is an Invitation

Sometimes the clearest way to explain a good idea is by telling a story. We need good ideas nowadays, ideas not just worth spreading, but ideas worth doing. This book is about one of those ideas, a do-able idea, told in a story form. The problem? Something has gone terribly wrong with our communities; so wrong we need to start over. The good idea? Build a VillageTown.

What is a *VillageTown*? It's a 10,000 population town made up of about twenty side-by-side villages intentionally designed as socially & culturally enriched. Its foundation is a strong, durable local economy that enables its citizens to protect themselves from national and global systems failing to deliver on their promises. Its continued purpose is to enable its citizens to enjoy what Thomas Jefferson called *life, liberty and the pursuit of happiness*. Aristotle called it *The Good Life*, consisting of *conviviality, citizenship, and artistic, intellectual & spiritual growth*.

In story form, we join Ed Rice, ex Blandville town planner, who devoted his whole career to approving Blandville's suburban explosion – the place that looks like everywhere else. When Ed loses his drivers licence, he realizes what an absolute mess his suburban sprawl spawned. In the first chapter Ed is leaving Blandville, on his way to his only option: a retirement home. As he passes mile after mile of strip malls, car dealers, gas stations, motels, office blocks, apartments and big-box stores, Ed talks to his driver like a blind man first given site. With eyes that see, Ed is appalled.

They stop for lunch; Ed's driver choosing to dine in a VillageTown. Fascinated with what he sees, Ed asks if he can take a tour of the VillageTown, a tour on foot as the town itself is car-free.

With a charming and knowledgeable guide, Ed and his driver walk from one village to another, meeting its people, hearing their stories, learning how a VillageTown works. Some of the characters in the book are imaginary. Others are real people, some of whom use their own words to tell their story, to give their viewpoint. The eldest of these speakers is senior statesman Stewart Udall who honored us with his words in Chapter 12. Ed learns how the people who live with the result become involved at the beginning. It's your life, your community and your money, so why shouldn't you control it? This way of building is not a new idea; America was founded by ordinary (and extraordinary) people who called themselves citizens not consumers, and acted accordingly.

Each village in each VillageTown will be as different as people are different. For this reason, we use storytelling to give a sense of what it might be like. When we set about to build real VillageTowns, they will have character and authenticity that comes from the citizens who will live there. This is different than conventional development where we call their people consumers.

If you like this idea, we invite you to read two other books. *How to Build a Village* and *Villagetowns - The Next Step*. We invite you to go to *VillageForum.com* and enroll. Become involved as we organize future VillageTown citizens to plan and design their own community, combining their purchasing power, and then provide them both tools and professional guidance to enable them to create their own vision of the good life. This book is not written to be a good read but to be an invitation to act.

We hope you enjoy the story and we hope by the time you finish, you are inspired to change your life. Build your village. Build your life.

*The Village Stewards*

## Dedication

This book is dedicated to the memory of the Village Forum's Chairman Emeritus Stewart L. Udall 1920 - 2010 who died peacefully on the equinox, March 20, 2010 at his home in Santa Fe, among family. This photo was taken two months earlier at his table.

Stewart came from a small town where neighbors looked after each other; where there was a low tolerance for crime; where they valued education so they taxed themselves to pay for it... there was a direct connection between governance and the citizenry that today we seem to have lost. After active military service in World War II – where he bombed Nazi oil refineries, he went on to study law and then serve in government. He first served in the US Congress where in 1956 he voted for the landmark Interstate Highway Act that changed the face of America and, by extension, the world – a vote he later said proved to be a colossal mistake that occurred with very little debate. In 1960, newly elected President Kennedy invited Stewart to join the Cabinet as Secretary of the Interior, a position he held under Kennedy and the President Johnson. Stewart loved the land, and devoted much of his life to preserving land, water and air for future generations.

Stewart came from a generation that had less and gave more; from a time when politics was more about service and less polarized than it is today.

On June 20, 2009 (coincidentally, the summer solstice), he generously gave us time to record his message for future generations in a video that became Chapter 12 of this book.

Stewart loaned his name and his stature to the Village Forum, giving us the moral support to work for the good, and giving us the inspiration that comes from an elder who succeeded.

We will miss him.

"After we provide for the essentials of life, the purpose of continuing the existence of our VillageTown is to provide for *the good life*, meaning the social desires of conviviality, citizenship, intellectual & artistic growth, spiritual fulfillment. We built for life, liberty & happiness, not to sell more cars. We are citizens not consumers."

\* \* \*

This book intends to reach millions of people about the idea of VillageTowns. If a million people decide they are no longer satisfied to be passive consumers, no longer accepting the banality of what planning authorities, developers, designers and architects offer in lieu of the basic purpose of why citizens seek community, then this book serves a good purpose.

If they decide to act, to come together as citizens to build their VillageTown, then this book succeeds.

Thus, the first intent of this book is to start a new conversation about how we live. To help it, we offer the Village Forum, found at www.villageforum.com.

The other intent is to raise funds to build the VillageTowns. We are not satisfied with talking, we want to live in a VillageTown and link up with other VillageTowns around the world. To do that we need to start a business, and in today's economic climate raising capital is hard. Writing a book is an unusual way to raise capital, but it can work.

If you like the idea, please buy the book.

\* \* \*

**The authors of this book will collect no royalties, and the publisher no fees. After printing and distribution costs and taxes, all income from book sales goes to establishing and building VillageTowns.**

# Contents

**Leaving Blandville** ............................................................................................. 9
    *The Desperate Life - Jared* ................................................................ 13
    *The Escaped Life - Liz* ........................................................................ 16
    *The History of a Bland Town* .......................................................... 19
    *End of World War Two - The Origins of Suburbs* ....................... 20
    *Senator Gore's Highway Legislation of the 1950's* ...................... 21
    *Commercial Sprawl* ............................................................................ 25
    *The Fragile and Vulnerable National Economy* .......................... 28
    *The Science of Malls* .......................................................................... 28
    *Big Glass Office Blocks and Flat Industrial Parks* ....................... 30
    *Bedroom Suburbs* ............................................................................... 32
    *Schools and Youth* .............................................................................. 34
    *Aging Sadly* .......................................................................................... 35
    *Character and Politics* ....................................................................... 36
    *Crisis, Crisis, Crisis* ............................................................................. 37
    *Transition to a VillageTown* ............................................................ 41

**Welcome to Villageton** ........................................................................................ 42
    *The Design - A 100:1 Scale Model* ................................................ 44

**The Idea of VillageTowns Explained** .............................................................. 53
    *When Money Buys Freedom* ............................................................ 54
    *Purchasing Power* ............................................................................... 55
    *People or Citizens?* .............................................................................. 57
    *Consumers or Citizens?* ..................................................................... 59
    *Why We Build Communities - For the Good Life* ...................... 62
    *Money* ..................................................................................................... 65
    *The 80/20 Local Economy* .............................................................. 67
    *Conviviality and Citizenship* ........................................................... 69
    *Artistic and Intellectual Growth* .................................................... 70
    *Spiritual Development and Fulfillment* ....................................... 71
    *Green Architecture* ............................................................................. 72
    *Alarmists vs Skeptics - Who's right about Climate Change?* .... 74
    *Left and Right Wing Politics* ........................................................... 74
    *Corporatism* .......................................................................................... 75
    *We Hold These Truths to be Self-evident* ..................................... 80
    *The Meaning of Liberty and Freedom* ......................................... 81
    *VillageTowns Are Not Utopia* ......................................................... 84
    *How Design can Protect Liberty* .................................................... 84

**Sophia – The Tour** ................................................................................................. 87
    *New Urbanism* ..................................................................................... 88
    *The Role of the Village Coordinator* ............................................. 90
    *The Village Mortgage and Savings Bank* ...................................... 91
    *About some of the Villages* ............................................................... 92
    *Pets, Bikes and Rules* .......................................................................... 93

- *The Prancing Pony or Having Fun Building Your Life* ........................................ 94
- *The Film Set Plaza* ........................................ 95
- *Sally's Village - Friends & Relations Take Care of Their Own* ........................................ 97
- *Medical Care* ........................................ 99
- *Care for the Elderly and Infirm* ........................................ 101
- *Bulk Building Material - Variable Density Concrete* ........................................ 102
- *Slow Food* ........................................ 107

**A Village Coordinator's Story** ........................................ 110
- *Grandmother's Insight* ........................................ 111
- *Building Our Village* ........................................ 112
- *Gentrification v Parallel Real Estate* ........................................ 115
- *Dynamic Engagement Design Process* ........................................ 118

**Suvies** - *Single Unencumbered Villagers* ........................................ 124
- *The Priest* ........................................ 126
- *Youth* ........................................ 127
- *The Lone Eagle* ........................................ 130
- *Divorce and Children* ........................................ 132
- *Human Damage* ........................................ 134

**The Creative Class** ........................................ 138
- *The Guild Halls* ........................................ 141

**Entrepreneurs & Pioneers** ........................................ 148

**Education - The Teachers' Story** ........................................ 160
- *The Parent's View* ........................................ 167
- *Passion* ........................................ 174
- *The Village as University* ........................................ 177

**The Baby Boomer's Story** ........................................ 179

**The Politician's Story** ........................................ 188
- *Becoming a Politician* ........................................ 189
- *Approving Villageton* ........................................ 191
- *The Farmers Who Feed Villageton... Every Day, Forever* ........................................ 194
- *Zoning and Plan Approval* ........................................ 196
- *Construction* ........................................ 196
- *Race vs Tribe* ........................................ 198

**Stewart Udall - The Conservationist** ........................................ 201

**The Many Faces of the Greenbelt** ........................................ 207
- *Alcohol Production and Permaculture* ........................................ 211
- *Solid Waste Avoidance and Recycling* ........................................ 212
- *The Industrial Park* ........................................ 215

**The Last Chapter - The time is now** ........................................ 219
**This is Not a Drill** ........................................ 223
**Build your Village** ........................................ 223
**Checklist for the Stewards and Future Citizens of a VillageTown** ........................................ 225
**About this Book – About the Vision** ........................................ 226
**Twelve Principles for a VillageTown** ........................................ 230
**How to Build your Village** ........................................ 232

# Chapter 1

## Leaving Blandville

Ed Rice opened the front door of his empty ranch house. Suitcases and a few cardboard boxes stood in the hallway. Along with some portable memories of a lifetime, the bags held the all possessions he would need for the rest of his life. He was sad to have sold his library, but he would not be working anymore and books are awfully bulky for his future home, a single room in a retirement village. Parked in the driveway, he saw a large metallic-gold sedan with a dent in the rear door. The word *pseudo-luxury* popped into Ed's head. A young man in a limo driver's dark blue polyester suit greeted him. "Mr. Rice? I'm Michael; here to drive you to Heathcliff Manor. Are these all your bags?"

Ed locked the door, put the keys in an envelope and left them in the mailbox for the buyers. No one came out from neighboring houses to say goodbye. At 10 a.m. during the work week nearly all the other houses were empty; almost everyone else was gone. Ed just shrugged; it was a solitary ending to the prime years of his life.

Michael the driver held the back door with the dent open for him, but Ed said he would rather ride up front. "Call me Ed" he said, and then "I thought all limos were supposed to be black", he added with a smile.

Michael was a friendly, chatty sort, asking Ed about his future plans, his home and family, his work and his life. Ed didn't mind. Having no future, he had plenty of time. He was moving out of Blandville.

He lived in a suburb called Blandville Heights, one of the first developments based on the model invented by Bill Levitt. Ed explained to Michael that after the Second World War, Levittowns offered a new way of living that promised to be the ideal for America's growing middle class. Ed was a retired urban planner with a degree in architecture. His first job, right after graduating, was with the Blandville Council. He was responsible for reviewing the developer's proposal for the Heights, as they called it. Forty years later, after retiring as head of Blandville's Planning Department, he kept working part-time, filling in when the Council was short-handed. During the real estate boom, or bubble as they now call it, he was sometimes busier than before his retirement. He enjoyed it; but since the bubble burst, they didn't much need him.

Unlike most of his neighbors who moved in and out with job transfers that cleaned out the neighborhood every two to five years, Ed had lived in the same house in the Heights all of his married life. They called it a raised ranch house, but that was 1950's market-speak; it had nothing to do with ranching and would have made no more sense out on the prairie than a chihuahua running with coyotes. It was cheap, mass produced and looked like every other house on the street. He should have sold it when his kids grew up, and certainly after his wife died. An old man has no place in the suburbs. Now, he had no choice. He had to leave.

Michael smiled, thinking about the chihuahua and coyotes, but at the same time feeling sad for Ed, who had said he did not feel old, but the world said he was. A couple months ago, a nice young judge had taken Ed's drivers license away. It wasn't his fault. A punk had run a red light and Ed had hit the car. But the judge said Ed's reflexes were too slow, he could have swerved and missed it. The examining doctor agreed. At least the judge did not fine him. His car was totaled. The insurance company paid him and cancelled his policy. No one was hurt. It was Ed's first insurance claim since he started driving at age 16. Michael was impressed.

Ed tried living in the Heights without a car, but soon concluded it was too hard. Taxis were expensive, the place was never designed for walking, and it was clear he was imposing on those acquaintances and neighbors who gave him rides. Ed had only himself to blame. More than anyone else in Blandville, he had been the one to set the standards and approve a design where to get anything done, you had to drive. Of course, these were not his ideas; the whole country shifted to suburban housing, freeways, commuting, bussing to schools, driving to malls. Even though he was the head of planning, he never really thought about what he and his department were doing. In the two months he lived in the Heights without driving, he saw it in a completely different light. While they called it a community, it was the opposite – a non-community. During the week, it was dead, as nearly everyone except himself emptied out to go somewhere else. In the evenings, every home had flickering blue lights as first television and then computer games substituted for social life.

Weekends were for chores, as the drone of lawn mowers filled the air. People were friendly, and social life tended to revolve around parents whose children were the same age, but even this was forced: Mom driving kids to practice, Dad's two hours on Saturday playing ball with the boys. Teens hung out at the mall or killed time pushing joy-sticks on electronic game-boxes or keystroking on-line.

Ed took a taxi to the pack-and-post store at the strip mall where a young man listed everything Ed owned on an auction web site. Some things sold for prices he found astounding – *who would pay prices like that for such junk?* Ed wondered aloud. Some of his treasures sold for a pittance. His books did not sell at all until the young man re-listed the whole library at a one dollar reserve. An architectural book dealer in Connecticut bought the bulk lot for the reserve and the pack-and-post made a bundle on boxing and shipping. Decades of pristine architectural magazines with photographs of his colleagues' prize-winning designs ended up on the curb for recycling.

Two weeks later, all the possessions that marked the stages of his life were gone and his bank account had three months extra rent for Heathcliff Manor. He kept his bed so he had a place to sleep until the sale of the house closed. He arranged with the buyers to have the downtown Salvation Army pick it up.

Surprisingly his home sold within a couple of weeks – although that was because he took the advice of the real estate agent on pricing it, at far less than it was worth in 2005. "But that depends on what *worth* really means" he had said to the agent. He figured that given the times, he came out OK. Some of the houses in his neighborhood had been vacant for over a year – bank foreclosures with peeling paint, un-mowed lawns, and drained swimming pools – the kids pumped the water out, and then trashed the pool walls with their skateboards. "Where were their parents, to allow that sort of thing to go on?" Then Ed chuckled, "I'm beginning to sound like an old grump, but the decency I knew when I was that age somehow got lost over the years, as if the whole country turned bad."

He kept one design book. Published in 1995, his daughter Liz gave it to him, but he never read it. Pulling it off the shelf to take down to the pack-and-post, he flipped it open to Chapter 5, where the author wrote *"We all sense that something has gone terribly wrong with our communities. Hamlets and cities, slums and suburbs, all lack a sense of cohesion. Not only is there no centre there – there is no there there."* Ed took the book out of his battered leather briefcase and showed it to Michael.

"I don't know why I opened to that page, or why I even chose to look at the book except my daughter cared enough to give it to me, and I felt it wrong to sell it without even having a look at it. When she gave it to me, the title *The Green Imperative* was enough to put me off, but in the last two months those words have haunted me. I began to look at my life's work and kept hearing the same words *there is no there there.*"

"The author Victor Papanek asked *why do people build communities?* It's a fairly basic question that I confess in my whole professional career, I never asked. Let me read his answer: *City planners of former times – of ancient Greece, of medieval city-states, of the heart of Amsterdam, London, Paris or Vienna – did not pursue different aims as their age changed, but instinctively always worked toward the one unchanging purpose that has always made people desire to live in urban centres in all human communities. Aristotle said that men form communities not for justice, peace, defence or traffic, but for the sake of the good life. This good life has always meant the satisfaction of man's four basic social desires: conviviality, religion, artistic and intellectual growth, politics."*

"I'm old enough to have been schooled in the classics, so I went to my Aristotle to check it out. I found while the translator used the word *politics*, citizenship would be closer to his meaning; and since Aristotle wrote before Christianity began, *religion* also meant something different, more like spiritual development and fulfillment. In discussing the good life, Aristotle actually wrote: *When several villages are united into a single complete community, large enough to be nearly or quite self-sufficing, the City-State comes into existence, originating in the bare needs of life and continuing for the sake of the good life."*

"In other words," Ed explained, "once the economy is sustainable, the reason to build communities is so people may pursue the good life."

Michael interjected, "That's an interesting phrase, *the good life.*"

Ed replied, "I have to admit, I found it a bit strange at first, as if it was some sort of cliché or a TV show, so I looked it up. I was surprised to find the good life was part of the inspiration for Thomas Jefferson's *the pursuit of happiness*, as in *Life, Liberty and...* That got me thinking about why he chose to substitute for *Life, Liberty and Property* his original formulation, our familiar *Life, Liberty and the Pursuit of Happiness*. Life, liberty and property are how our society keeps social control. Break the law, we fine you, jail you or hang you, depending on the severity of the crime; the state takes away your property, your liberty or your life. But Jefferson transformed it into a higher principle. He saw that while property provides for the bare needs of life, above that comes community for the sake of the good life, what Papanek defined in four terms as:

- *Conviviality* – having fun with others,
- *Citizenship* – being a part of society,
- *Art & Intellect* – that which sets apart humans from other life forms, and
- *Spiritual experience* – that which gives us hope and fulfillment."

"So having gone down that wonderful and inspiring path, I then began to ask myself, why did we build Blandville? How had I and my department contributed to life, liberty and most importantly the good life or pursuit of happiness? As I reviewed my life's work, the answer was profoundly disturbing. We built it to create a consumer society – an ever-expanding economy pumped on steroids, and we designed it for traffic. I would say half of my career was obsessed with traffic and how to deal with it."

As Michael waited for the next red light to turn, he did not know how to respond to this, so instead he asked Ed how he had selected Heathcliff, their current destination, instead of a retirement village closer to Blandville.

Ed's face saddened as he explained. "There were closer retirement homes, but they were either full or too expensive. Heathcliff Manor is about a four hour drive. It's not a manor, and despite its pretentious British name there are neither cliffs nor a heath anywhere to be found – the name was recommended by the branding company hired by the retirement home chain. From experience I knew few friends or relations would come to visit me after a couple of months, so location was not important. With my life savings, I figure I could pay for about seven years at Heathcliff before I went broke and become a ward of the state. That gives me seven years to die and not much to do while waiting. I never took up golf, and kept working after retirement because I enjoyed the company of younger people. In my world, losing my license was the end of my freedom."

"I put my own father in a home twenty-nine years ago. I hated the idea of turning him out that way, but saw no other options, just as I see none for me now. Four years ago, my wife Helen died of cancer; that was hard. I met her when I first came to Blandville; she was a temporary typist hired by the town when the first real estate boom started. She was funny, and a great dancer. We married, and bought a new home in the Heights. Now, she's gone and my children live their own lives many thousands of miles away."

The mention of children prompted Michael to ask Ed about them. Ed pulled out his wallet and passed over some worn photographs of his children and grandchildren.

## THE DESPERATE LIFE - JARED

"My son Jared is on his second marriage with alimony kids to show for the first. I never hear from those grandchildren – their mother does not like me – it was a bitter breakup and I come from the wrong side of the family. Jared struggles as a middle level marketing manager with a computer software company. He lives up north in a three bedroom suburban house now worth less than the mortgage held on it. He is working for a company where he survived the first round of cutbacks but fears he will be tossed out unless the economy turns around. Both he and his wife Debbie work; two children – one, Ashley, a six month old girl, in day-care until 5:30 every day; the older boy, Ryan is bussed to the local public school and then to the after-school center until one of his parents pick him up after work. There was no place for me there."

Michael handed back the photographs and asked why. "I tried." Ed replied. "After the car crash, Jared invited me to visit for a few weeks, but the visit saddened me. During the week, the family woke up early when the coffee-maker's alarm clock beeped like a trash truck in reverse. On the kitchen counter Debbie lined up boxes of cereal and set out frozen packaged waffles to be heated in the microwave. The family ate in shifts, the boy at the kitchen table, the parents standing up at the counter. It reminded me of fueling up the car; so different from my own childhood when meals were an important family time."

"Like mine, their home is a rancher, fancier than my 1950's house, and loaded with consumer goods. A massive plasma TV dominates the lounge, another TV was installed in an overhead cabinet in the kitchen and they had a third in their bedroom. The whole time I was there, Ryan watched cartoons in the lounge. In the kitchen TV blasted out the morning news and weather. The broadcasters' intensity seemed overdone when I actually listened to what they were reporting. The weather was worse than the news – reporting an approaching storm like the coming of the Apocalypse. I noticed televisions left on every waking hour when someone was in the house. For much of the time, it seems they provided an artificial replacement for company – or a way of avoiding it – the equivalent of family and friends talking in the background. Ryan glued himself to the big set every evening until bedtime, while Jared and Debbie occupied themselves on office work brought home on their laptops. Debbie would set the baby, Ashley, in an electric swinging chair next to her desk while she worked."

Michael looked sad. "Sounds like an awful visit. What did you do with yourself, since it does not sound like you are a big TV watcher?"

"After the first day in their empty house, and walking lifeless cold suburban sidewalks, I asked Jared to give me a lift to the library on the way to his office. Of course he agreed, and I helped him put Ashley in her car seat to drop her off at day-care. I was surprised – no, I can fairly say I was shocked – to see that the day-care was another rancher in the same suburban development. It was an overheated house with steaming windows. Inside there must have been 20 or more children including babies younger than my granddaughter. As in my son's home, the television was on, and several children sat transfixed in front of it. As a parent from a pre-TV world, I never got used to the unnaturalness of motionless children. I have to admit TV was effective in keeping them quiet, but I am fearful of what the long term effects will be."

"The day-care woman looked haggard." Ed went on. "She was divorced; she needed the money, because all she got out of the divorce was the home. 'Besides', she told me 'these children's parents had no one else to look after them and I'm close enough that they can pick them up after doing shopping on the way home from work.' I wondered how she got the permit to run such a business in a residential zone." Ed mused, "I wonder what sort of adults all these children will become, deprived of normal contact with family and a functional community."

Michael sighed, "I take your point Ed, it's a deep worry. What happened next?"

"The library was near Jared's office, so we arranged to meet for lunch. At noon Jared collected me by car and we drove to a franchise restaurant specializing in Mexican food with an American decorator's idea of a fiesta theme. The food was mediocre, the service chirpy but rehearsed. It felt as if the franchise owner never ate or worked there. Debbie had to work late that night, so Jared picked up the kids and I offered to buy them all dinner. The boy opted for McDonalds. I never said anything to them but I see why Jared, Debbie and Ryan all have an extra layer of fat in their faces. It's a strange world, Michael, especially the expanding size of ordinary people. I have worn the same sized shirts most of my life. I remember the day I went to my usual store and the salesman told me my shirt size was now *trim*, and the ones that used to be *husky* were now *regular*."

"Everything I ate with my son's family was laden with fat, sugar and salt. It took me a couple of weeks to readjust when I returned to Blandville since I usually buy and prepare my own food from fresh. Michael, we human beings are a strange animal. We slowly poison ourselves with the food we eat, then spend billions on medicine trying to heal the damage."

Michael nodded ruefully. "I'll remember that when we stop for lunch, today."

"That night Jared and I talked, or rather he talked and I listened. Michael..., my son and daughter-in-law have no savings. They struggle under mounds of credit card debt that bought the gadgets in their home and the fast food they eat. The 20% equity they put down on the house when Jared got the job was wiped out in the housing crash. With both salaries, they are just able to cover the mortgage and the payments on the cars, the furniture and the credit cards, but all of this will come unstuck if Jared loses his job. No one was hiring in Jared's industry, and when he tried to explain to me what a marketing manager did, I could see why. When times get tough, companies stop investing in their long-term future; middle-level managers like Jared get the chop."

"No such thing as company loyalty anymore is there Ed?" replied Michael.

"No, there isn't Michael, but after a week with them, what amazed me the most was the constant sense of desperation amid apparent affluence –certainly far more affluence than I knew as a child during the tail end of the Depression – and the extent to which they were so busy that there was very little family life."

"It's sad, Michael." Ed said.

"We were so proud of our boy, Jared. He was the responsible one, the one to make us grandparents. We were always disappointed with our younger daughter Liz, and yet now Jared's life and everything he stood for is turning to custard. For the life of me, I can't figure out how he went wrong, except that they spent too much – buying things they can't afford and probably don't need. Thank God Helen's not alive to see this, it would break her heart, seeing her boy in such a mess."

Michael was a good listener, and Ed appreciated it, as he half-told stories and half thought out loud, trying to work out this jumbled ball of tangled threads causing so much heartache in people's lives. For the first time in his life, after the car crash and visiting Jared, Ed had begun to think about the effects of the suburban planning he had overseen in his professional career. He had been so caught up in roads, shopping malls, subdivisions and infrastructure he had never noticed what effect these designs would have on the people who had to live with them. In a curious paradoxical way, by making life easier, it became entangling, complicated and eventually, toxic.

## The Escaped Life - Liz

Ed continued his story. "Our daughter Liz chose to live overseas, having rejected her middle-class upbringing as boring, banal, hollow and pretentious. I argued with her about this when she came on those infrequent visits, but when I look at the legacy of my life packed in my boxes in the trunk of your car, I begin to see her point." Turning the sedan onto the commercial strip that now defined Blandville's economy, Michael nodded, making noncommittal noises that expressed neither agreement nor disagreement with Liz's view.

Ed kept talking, glad to finally have an opportunity to speak his thoughts out loud. It did cross his mind that he was disclosing some very personal thoughts to someone he hardly knew, but he felt safe, and besides, where he was going, sensitivities like these did not matter anymore.

"When I was Blandville's planner, much of my job was to develop the very way of life Liz rejected. I was born in the Great Depression... no money to speak of, little food except what we grew or canned, and patches sewn over worn patches on my pants. I swore my children would never face the deprivation that my family faced. It baffled me how Liz could reject it all and move to an island in the Mediterranean where they have broadband but no cars – they walk, use bicycles and transport goods on hired donkeys. She's doing well, I have to admit, writing books on leaving the rat race and finding Paradise. Liz invited me to move over, but immigration law made it difficult – too hard at my age anyway, and I doubt I would enjoy living as a foreigner dependent on my daughter to translate. I like to talk with people, to share a beer or a cup of coffee. The idea of living in a place where I cannot understand the locals turned me off."

Ed opened his leather bag and pulled out one of his notebooks where he kept some albums of pasted photographs. He opened it to a page and passed it over to Michael as they waited for another traffic light. "Here's a photo she sent me from her home. She says this is their shopping mall."

Michael looked at it and smiled. "Looks pretty idyllic," he said.

"Yeah," Ed replied. "And have a look at this postcard she made up for me using her computer. She took the top photograph when visiting home, but I have to say it could have been anywhere." Ed handed the postcard to Michael.

*Dear Dad, How can you live in Blandville when you could be living like this? This is my daily commute – why don't you move here? Love, Liz*

Michael laughed. "She sure knows how to make her point, doesn't she?" He then shifted the subject by asking Ed about his career and Blandville's development. Ed knew his local history well. When he became the senior manager of the Planning Department, he was expected to give reports to the Council, so he joined Toastmasters and learned how to tell a good story so the Councillors would understand his message of the day. Ed was on comfortable ground with this question, and he started at the beginning.

## The History of a Bland Town

"Blandville was a sprawling jurisdiction founded in the 19th century when they first laid the rail tracks. Nothing distinguished the site except the need to keep the railroad's steam engines fired with coal. Before the rail, it was open, flat grassland with pockets of ancient forest; if there were any indigenous natives, they would have been passing through or following the buffalo."

"The carrying capacity of the railroad's smallest coal car determined Blandville's location. The railroad brought coal in hopper cars, piled it into black, dusty mountains next to the tracks to load the coal tenders of the trains passing through. The rail brought farmers who grew grains – mostly corn and wheat on the flat, then-fertile land. Every week with their large families, the surrounding farmers drove horse-drawn wagons to Blandville to stock up on provisions and socialize. The town merchants saw their fortunes rise and fall with the market price of grain. Few of the farmers understood how fragile the land's ecosystem and how cyclical the weather was. Over the years a lot of good topsoil blew away or washed downriver."

"After World War One, Blandville became a state highway town with a couple of intersecting commercial streets surrounded by picket-fenced, wide-porched homes built on narrow streets. In planner-speak, they classified Blandville as a country town – it was about 25 miles north of Metropolis, a large city along the river. While the citizens of Metropolis used to eat food grown around Blandville, increasingly after the war, the supermarkets sold food trucked in from other parts of the country or shipped from overseas. Blandville's economy suffered. The Depression almost killed the town but since the whole country suffered, they say it did not seem to be as hard."

"Then things got better. After the Second World War, people began to move out of Metropolis because of increasing crime, the decline of quality education and higher property taxes. These were code words for racial tension. The real story had to do with race and money. It had to do with business greed detached from any sense of what is right or good. It was driven by short-sighted urban government policies and a national plan to reinvent how people live by zoning land so people had to drive cars to accomplish their daily chores." Ed explained.

"The racial part began when the invention of better tractors and farm implements almost eliminated the need for farm workers. Most unskilled farm workers were black, and they found themselves unemployed and unemployable. Many moved to the cities where some found work in factories, but others ended up on welfare – a strange term," Ed observed, "since people do not fare well once they are caught within a system that encourages single parenting and loss of family control within a community. Anyway, those policies provided the capital to fuel a massive urban demographic shift as blacks moved in and whites fled. They called it *block-busting*".

Michael was unfamiliar with the term, and asked Ed to explain. Ed was agreeable but said he needed to digress a bit. Michael replied they had plenty of time, having not yet crawled past Blandville's city limits to reach the freeway entrance.

So Ed continued. "Cities like Metropolis grew with the industrial revolution as manufacturing and trade needed many workers to run the massive machinery required to make and move things. When the local labor market proved insufficient, factory owners looked overseas, especially to Europe, and whole communities of workers sprung up... Irish, German, Polish, Italian, Greek and so on. They tended to segregate themselves by city block in the two and three story row brick houses, some occupied by extended families, others broken up into apartments. For the most part people walked or took the trolley train to work, shop and socialize. When World War II broke out, many of the civilians who enlisted came from these working class communities. Mothers, wives and sisters took over their jobs as the factories shifted, almost overnight, from producing civilian goods to delivering war materials under government contract."

### END OF WORLD WAR TWO - THE ORIGINS OF SUBURBS

"Toward the end of the war, America's leaders began to plan for peacetime. If millions of soldiers returned home looking for work just as the government contracts dried up, it might trigger a relapse into another depression. I bet you didn't know this Michael, but the war had been won on lead. Not lead in bullets, but lead in gasoline – tetraethyl lead that increased the octane of gas. American war planes, tanks, trucks and jeeps all ran on a single fuel, gasoline; not diesel, and octane gave their engines more power."

Michael admitted this was news to him; "Never thought about it before" he said.

Ed continued. "The companies that won the war were transport related companies... companies like Standard Oil, DuPont and GM. Those three companies owned the Ethel Gasoline Corporation that held the patent for a poisonous fluid compound containing lead. That fluid when mixed with the gasoline to fuel high compression engines, added greatly to their efficiency. In war that meant American planes and vehicles could go further and faster than the enemy's. The owners of these companies worked with the political leaders of the day; Presidents Roosevelt, Truman and Eisenhower, Senators Gore and Bush and many others to develop a plan to keep the post-war American economy stimulated."

Michael interrupted him, "Gore and Bush? They're not that old are they?"

Ed laughed, "Sorry, Michael, I should have qualified that; they are dynasty families where generations pass on the tradition of public service. No I'm talking about their daddies and granddaddies. But to continue, naturally, the business leaders who helped win the war favored stimulating businesses that would maintain and increase their profits. They proposed to invent new ways for Americans to live by building what later became known, disparagingly, as suburban sprawl. Personally, I'd always objected to that disparaging term because I saw the value in the plans developed to keep the country from relapsing into another Depression. *We won the war overseas, but now we must win the peace at home* was how they sold the public on the idea." Ed said. "It's only in the last two months that I'm beginning to rethink my opinion on the whole question."

## Senator Gore's Highway Legislation of the 1950's

"Federal legislation was the key and it took about ten years of politics before the new economic engine shifted into high gear. The Interstate Highway Act of 1956 was the capping legislation that changed the direction of American life. In one of those almost forgotten ironies of history, the chief Senate sponsor of that bill was Senator Al Gore Sr., father of the man who now says that a mobile society based on continued burning of oil, gas and coal may doom civilization as we know it."

"GI legislation provided returning servicemen with low cost mortgages and the opportunity to return to school to pursue a college education. Federal highway funds provided states with money to build highways like the Eisenhower Interstate Highway System. On the local level, zoning laws were enacted that separated homes from offices, factories, schools, and shopping. Millionaires were made – their money coming from subdividing farms into suburbs. In local government, politics began to change as competition for road contracts produced new lobbying, campaign funding and in some cases, new corruption."

"Moving those white families out of the cities had its own complications. While the President called for millions of new homes to be built, it was not due to an expanding population – the Baby Boom came later. It appealed to the returning soldiers' desire to upgrade from an apartment in the city to their own home in the country, with a car in the garage and all the modern conveniences. What would happen to those surplus city residences?"

"The answer turned out to be bloc- busting. A Block-buster would buy a home in the middle of a white, working class community, and then would move in a poor ex-rural black family on welfare. Rather than welcome that family into the neighborhood, the block would sprout *for sale* signs in front windows – white flight tinged with anger and bitterness. With no buyers other than the block busters, home prices plummeted. In the end, the block buster owned the whole city block, and instantly converted it to rental units for poor families on welfare. The welfare department assured the block buster of a constant stream of revenue, and a tidy profit could be made provided he spent nothing on repairs and maintenance – that is allowed the area to deteriorate."

"It was shameful." Ed confessed. "I remember someone passing on a newspaper story to me back in 1958, where a journalist, from Baltimore I think, wrote *"Experts and laymen can agree that slums breed a hopelessness in people's hearts. Amid the piles of rotting garbage, tumbledown porches and junk-filled backyards, the human spirit seems to wither away."* I came across that clipping when I was packing. It made me ashamed of my profession, especially since our cities are still teeming with those slums, now in their third and fourth generation. "I saw it happening. This is when I came of age, so now I'm not reporting history anymore, but giving you eyewitness reports. Over time the buildings, without maintenance, deteriorated until finally the city condemned them. The landlords stopped paying the property taxes and Metropolis ended up owning blocks of abandoned, rotting shells; a foul rats-nest of drug addicts, homeless derelicts and the squalid smell of a city dying, as the more affluent whites fled."

Ed opened his bag again, and took out another photograph album. "This is not a particularly good photograph," Ed explained, "because it did not feel safe to stop and get out of my car. I took it while driving down the street, rather than stopping. These are slum buildings today, where the city has gone from boarding the ground floor doors and windows to filling them with concrete blocks to keep them from being totally destroyed. If you look at the details, you see that when they were built the masons took a lot of care to add beautiful details."

"The first of those white-flight suburban developments in Blandville was the Heights, and for me it was a great opportunity for a young man on the way up. I not only worked on the zoning approvals; but when I got married, I bought one of the new houses in it – the very same house you came to today."

"Then about four decades ago, south of town, the state built a freeway, part of Senator Gore's Interstate Highway system. Around the freeway exits, land prices rose as my department planned new zones for more suburban residential tracts, shopping districts, larger public schools serviced by fleets of school busses, and office & industrial parks." Ed swept his hand in a wide arc, and said "If we were not going somewhere else, I could show you development after development where I walked the land, worked on their plans and played a part in what you would see today. Of course, the Blandville Council was happy to approve the changes in land use because it increased their tax revenue and the developers made generous campaign contributions to help them get re-elected. We thought we were building the ideal society, never asking ourselves what that really meant."

"Not all of Blandville did well. With the farmers struggling and travelers bypassing the town, central Blandville went into decline. Saltzmann's Clothing store closed, the diners went bust, the owner-operated shops held closing down sales – everything at

70% off including fixtures. Today, what's left is the welfare office, strip joints, rough bars and sleazy shops clustered near the bus depot. But the cops do a good job containing it; protecting the suburbs from Blandville's low-life and riff-raff. The only problem they can't seem to contain are middle class kids – and adults – driving to old Blandville to buy drugs and contraband."

Ed flipped the page in his photo album and showed Michael another picture. "This is an old factory that used to make clothing. It provided about a hundred jobs. Now it is abandoned, and everyone knows that's where the drug dealers are, but for some reason I could never understand, the police never shut it down. I had to inspect it for the council at one point, and I was surprised to see how solid the walls were. They used to make buildings to last, and that one has foot-thick, double-walled brick."

Michael handed it back as traffic began to move again, and commented, "In other towns such places are being restored as people go back to the old towns, which they say feel more authentic in a way developers can never match."

"That's true," Ed replied, "and I've often wondered if it will happen to Blandville. It seems that they let places get very bad, then politicians demands a clean up, all the riff-raff gets picked up on various charges that bring prison terms, and someone makes a huge profits buying up all the abandoned buildings at just the right time. The taxpayers end up paying for more prisons, and people who in prior generations would have been working in the factories now enter the predator-prisoner cycle. So while it does make for nice historic districts, I wish it could be done without so much social damage."

As he spoke, Ed was listening to himself, and he found himself surprised by what he was saying. He never had thought much about how deprivation and depravation affected society, and his explanations to Michael made him feel ashamed. He remembered when he was a student and they talked about how planning would solve the world's problems. Now he was seeing how his department had divided Blandville into winner and loser areas, and how not protecting blue collar jobs had resulted in the children of those factory workers turning to dishonest occupations that weakened his community and his country. He put his album back in the bag.

## COMMERCIAL SPRAWL

As Michael drove Ed out of Blandville for the last time, he commented to Michael that in a strange way, he felt as if he was observing the now not-so-new commercial strip in its entirety for the first time in his life. In the past, he had usually driven this highway with half a mind on the traffic and the rest on work. Now, as he realized he would never see this place again, he looked at it differently. As an urban planner, he had been the boss of the staff recommending town approval of the development of all this commercial development on the strip.

He had never realized how many franchises there were in the endless strip malls that bordered both sides of the wide street. Most were in various shades of beige and browns with large parking lots in front of all of them. He wondered how much land Blandville had given over to parking cars. He thought about the word *store* meaning a place to store goods, and wondered if there were any goods in those stores that had been made in his county or even his state anymore.

Ed took out a digital camera his daughter gave him for his birthday. Realizing he would probably never come back to Blandville, he took a few snapshots as he spoke to Michael. He rolled down the passenger window and as they slowly proceeded through the start and stop traffic he pressed the button and looked at the display.

Today with no car to drive, he viewed the fruits of his career along the wide thoroughfare formerly known as State Highway 44, now known as Blandville Boulevard. As they drove slowly in heavy traffic, seeming to hit all the red lights, Ed said to Michael "I've never really looked at the Boulevard this way before. Each of these buildings, surrounded by hundreds of parking spaces is built for one reason only – to sell things. Look at this... fast food outlet next to gas station, next to strip mall. Then a lifeless motel with nothing to do but watch TV or plug in your laptop and keep working. Next a huge big-box electronic store with people carting out more stuff that either break or become obsolete. The sheer number of car specialty stores is amazing. Look over there, a drive-in that just sells batteries, and next to it a muffler shop and across the street a place that does nothing but change engine oil. Michael, I'm looking at these buildings and then begin to be haunted by the words that are in Liz's book, *There's no there there.*"

Michael replied, "There is not a lot of spirit to them, that's for sure. Looks to me like they were built to serve a purpose – to make money for their owners, provide jobs for their employees and provide goods and services to consumers."

"That's exactly the point, Michael," Ed continued. "Where Papanek wrote *City planners of former times worked toward the one unchanging purpose*, the purpose he called the good life, I'm beginning to realize that as a city planner, I – we – did not work toward any purpose, any conscious ideal purpose, so much as churn out approvals to feed one massive, consuming machine. We reduced *Life* to consuming and earning so we could consume more. We reduced *Liberty* to the freedom to choose Chevy versus Ford, and *Pursuit of Happiness* to a two week vacation at Disneyland, Vegas or a cruise."

The car stopped at a long traffic light by the enclosed shopping mall that had killed off the remaining downtown stores. Looking to the left of the mall, the parking lots were almost empty, and the mall was reporting an alarming number of vacancies. Ed pointed it out to Michael and remarked. "It's not just the tough economy hitting the malls. They are losing a lot of business to internet shopping which can offer lower prices by shipping goods from central warehouses direct to the buyer. People come into the mall, try out the clothing sizes or look at the electronic gizmos, then buy them on the Internet for less and no sales tax."

They drove by an empty Wal-Mart building along the highway with weeds growing in its parking lots. Ed commented, "This is the second time this has happened. A new, much larger Wal-Mart just opened on the other side of the freeway, and this property is up for sale. As you can see, there is not a lot selling."

Behind them, an ambulance's siren caused Michael to squeeze the car over to the side. The state widened the highway three times since 1945, and now has four lanes in each direction. In rush hour speeds drop to a walking pace, but there is no more room to add a 5th lane unless the breakdown lane is removed. Ed told Michael about the state planners' promise that all would be solved when they went from two lanes to three. Michael laughed as they crawled through traffic.

## The Fragile and Vulnerable National Economy

"It was during the last big price spike in gasoline," Ed said, "that I realized for the first time how fragile and dangerous an economy my department had approved for Blandville. It was utterly dependent on cheap and abundant fuel for survival. I looked it up and read the average American meal travels 1,500 miles to get on the plate. While the web site presented these facts to argue the case on global warming, I wondered what would happen if trucking were to stop. I looked into it, and found that within two weeks, the supermarkets would be stripped bare. Take away their food, and civilization would break down awfully fast. Where our regional farmers used to grow a full range of local foods, now they all are industrial farming, mostly planting grains for cattle feed and biofuel. The kids today do not know how to plant a garden or can food. At least in the Depression, people knew how to take care of themselves. We have built one of the most vulnerable systems in the world."

"But as we saw, even with mild price rises in fuel, affordability of suburban living diminished. It exposed the fatal flaw in our planning regime. What would happen to this spread-out infrastructure when driving from 3-car garage to 4,000-car mall parking lots no longer could be supported? What would happen to the billions of dollars invested in the mega shopping malls?"

"Did you know that most of the mega-malls are funded by pension funds? Too many mall failures could mean those pensions get into trouble. Should that happen my son's generation is in even worse shape. My generation took the profits, my son's would suffer the losses, my grandchildren will pay the cost."

## The Science of Malls

"Michael, do you know the science behind shopping malls?" Ed inquired. Michael shook his head no, so Ed continued. "It's a bit scary, I have to say. When they were seeking permits to build, I had a meeting with the prime developer of Blandville Mall, our largest – the one we just passed – and its managing director told me some of the science behind its plan."

"As I recall his story, they hire brilliant social scientists who study human behavior. Everything is designed to induce the highest level of spending by consumers. They determine that the maximum consumer shopping tolerance is 3 hours, so they design for a three-hour experience. Anchor stores are placed at the ends... three, four and in large malls, five big-brand stores that sell clothing, shoes, houseware, jewelry, make-up and perfume. The entrances cater to women not men – men are expected to hunt out their section, and at the entrances, they have women offering free samples or even help applying makeup. Brands play heavily in the anchor stores and they typically have one store for budget products, one for midrange and one for pseudo-luxury. They sell identity, not things we need."

"The connecting pedestrian 'streets' are designed to keep you moving so you look at all the side stores, stopping in to make spontaneous purchases. The kiosks in the middle of the 'streets' are to break your stride so you look into all the shops, not walk by too fast. The seating is enough to provide rest, but not comfort."

"Try it sometime. Go shopping in a mall, but also observe everything. Observe how you are drawn to certain stores and what motivates you to buy. Listen to the music, see where they place the water features and how they manage light coming in from the sky – just at the intersections. If you're married... are you married Michael?"

"Nope." Michael replied.

"OK, then take your girlfriend, sister or a female friend and observe how they shop – note how they shop differently than you. Note which way they turn when going into a store – usually they turn right. See how long they stay in the store, how they make purchase decisions. Ask them what drew them to specific places, why they stopped to touch certain goods, then note how they designed those places for women. Based on research and studies, everything is planned to, as the managing director said, *maximize individual purchase decisions of goods the consumer did not intend to buy when they drove to the mall* or as the pastor would say *lead us into temptation*. To accomplish this they design a large, windowless, self-contained space in which consumers shape their identity through the consideration, selection and the purchase of brands. *Pēnsō ergo sum. I shop, therefore I am.*"

"It's all carefully controlled and the mall has strong controls on behavior it does not want. While it looks like a public space, it is not. Free speech or public assembly is not allowed, for example. Take a professional camera to a mall and try to take photographs of the stores or the shoppers... a security man will appear out of nowhere to say the mall is private property and requires written permission of management to take a picture. I know this because it happened to me when I took the audit pictures for the Town records. The managing director regarded these things as good. 'Malls are safe, sparkling and fun!' he told me."

"At the time I did not think much of it. It was only after reading those lines, *something has gone terrible wrong* that I began to wonder what our founding fathers would have thought of my mall director's view of the perfect world; it's intent is to make consumers out of citizens The fact is that the mall is a well-oiled machine to maximize consumer spending. However, it is also a machine literally dependent on oil. Gasoline has to remain affordable, and consumers have to continue to have discretionary income to spend. Turn off either of those two taps, and the system grinds to a halt. The whole thing is based on consumption, cheap oil and cheap credit. In today's world, it's a house of cards."

### BIG GLASS OFFICE BLOCKS AND FLAT INDUSTRIAL PARKS

As they drove past ten city blocks solely devoted to new car dealers called AutoMile, Michael asked Ed "Where do all these consumers work to earn their money to buy things, and where do they live?"

Ed opened his notebook, showing a photograph he recently took of a vacant office building in the executive office park near the other freeway exit. "This is, or was, one of the buildings where Blandville white collar workers worked. Essentially, they are big glass and steel boxes to house computers, telephones and conference rooms where people do what passes for modern work. It's strange. All of the productive work is done by wire, or now sometimes wireless. Buying, selling, talking to customers, coordinating warehouses, even engineering design, all is done on the telephone or using a broadband-linked computer. When I retired and did consulting work for Blandville's Planning Department, I found I was more effective working at home, linked to their office computer than if I sat in their offices. People sit side by side in little cubicles, with the bosses getting private rooms with views of the parking lot, but almost all work is done by wire. Even face-to-face meetings are now starting to happen using video links. My daughter got me to load Skype on my laptop and I can see how video conferences will eventually replace that awful office ritual, the business meeting." Ed explained.

"The problem for places like Blandville comes because networks and the Internet free business from what is called the *tyranny of distance*. The current generation of business leaders are pre-technology people who still feel we need to have offices to have such people work effectively. However, the upcoming generation born after computers became a part of life will see places like this vacant office block as costly dinosaurs, and they will then seek out places to live that offer more than the expensive blandness that is our well-named Blandville. The good jobs will be moved to beautiful places that offer people high quality of life, and the awful jobs will be moved offshore to low-income countries. For example, they used to run a call center in this "now leasing" building I photographed. The call center was relocated to the Philippines. It drives me nuts when I call those places. They are so polite in not understanding my questions." Ed said with crackling frustration.

Michael smiled at this comment and told Ed his experience when he tried to get customer support when he installed the GPS navigation system in the limo. "They had me re-install the software three times before they finally passed me on to their level two American team that figured out the database they packaged with it was programmed for England! But to expand on my prior question, do they actually make things in Blandville or just buy and sell products made somewhere else?"

Ed thought for a moment and answered, "Not far from here you'll find three industrial parks mostly used for wholesale distribution businesses and some executive blocks that are presently half empty after many of its tenants went bust when the economy collapsed. Not much is actually made in Blandville anymore. For the most part, the consumer goods now come from low-wage countries in Asia or Latin America. There used to be a sock factory downtown, but the two brothers who ran it took to arguing with each other when competition from Asia cut into their business. To spite each other they shut it down. They auctioned the machinery; I hear it ended up in Asia as well. My own socks used to say *Made in USA*, but now the same brand now says *Made in China*." Ed added, "It seems everything productive went to Asia."

Michael considered this, and then said "I suppose I need to be a smart economist to understand the business foundation of what you described, because it sure does not make any sense to me. I always thought that to create wealth in a community you need to either extract something from the earth, like iron or convert energy from the sun, like farming, and then make something. But what you describe sounds like the foundation of the economy no longer exists here."

"I'm afraid you may be a smarter economist than you think, Michael." Ed replied. "From what I can figure, there was a major shift in America that occurred sometime in the 1970's or 1980's. It was as if the captains of industry got fed up with America and decided to abandon it. The unions were becoming very effective in negotiating a bigger share of the products their workers made, and the cost of running a factory floor grew. Some of the cost was due to increasing regulation as the government began to require business to clean up its messes, not dumping their wastes in the rivers, the air and on the land. Other costs came as unions negotiated a higher standard of living, better pension benefits and the cost of medical care kept rising. At the same time the business schools stopped teaching any sense of morality and patriotism, and the new graduates bought into the doctrine that maximum profits was the only measure of business. So Americans started moving their factories to countries whose factory floors cost less; places where workers put in long hours for low pay, and their governments did not worry about pollution. The result of all this is that China is emerging as America's biggest manufacturer, something that could become a major problem if China did something as simple as change the exchange rate so their products were no longer so cheap. I fear the day when it's time to pay the piper."

"Not a great future, is it? Michael commented. "But where do the people live who work in all these glass boxes and warehouse distribution centers?"

## BEDROOM SUBURBS

Ed explained. "Housing choices include gated communities at the high end, with huge houses on small lots, designed in a mishmash of various ostentatious styles. Upscale architects, not hired to design such homes, disparagingly coined the word *McMansions*, as they saw them built along similar sameness principles to those of the fast food franchise, McDonalds. Even though I am an architect by training, I had no opinion on McMansions. Developers offered them, people bought them. Now they are in trouble. They built one of the gated McMansion communities with its own golf course but recently it had to open its greens to the public to stay solvent. The final stage of that development lost its financing and collapsed. Twenty half-finished homes with studs and plywood exposed to the weather are slowly rotting away. Others are finished but in this climate if you don't keep the heat and air conditioning on, within a year they will be so damaged by moisture and mildew, they will be unsalable. Right now this country has millions of homes like that and many will never be sold."

"Medium priced housing in Blandville's suburban rings offer smaller homes along curvy roads with cul-de-sacs. These developments came with ten different building designs taken out of a national high-volume construction catalog that offered fixed-priced, ready-to-move-in units built in at a rate of 2,000 a year. These developments were named after some rural farmer, feature, bird or wild animal whose memory or presence was obliterated by the development... Deatrick Village, Willow Run, Pheasant Ridge and Antelope Valley."

Ed flipped his photo album again, and showed Michael an example, explaining: "This was a lovely farm five years ago; good soil and protected from the prevailing winds. We approved it as a staged subdivision, and the first stage was built just before the credit crunch hit. The second and third stages have now gone back to weed infested fields divided by paved roads and empty street signs pointing to nowhere. I wonder if eventually it will go back to farmland, or stand there long enough that Nature returns it to forest land. It's unlikely to ever have a market for more homes."

"At the bottom end of the market, there are numerous developments of tightly packed town houses; some with small fenced back yards and most with parking spaces in front of each home. We made a real goof on those. My planning department required spaces for two cars per home. We presumed couples would live there. We were wrong. Tenants would fit as many roommates in as they could to share the cost of rent – causing all sorts of parking problems. Most of these homes are rentals, and some of their tenants include people who walked away from mortgages they could not support in the Antelope Valley subdivision when the Executive Park businesses started to fold. One of the first of these cheap developments, not far from the old town center is now a slum – crime and drug ridden with frequent police call-outs."

"We're coming up on one of the worst recent developments in Blandville. For the life of me, I cannot figure out what the developer was thinking when they built it. This is the busiest road in Blandville. They built all those townhouses right along the road. You have to live with windows closed all the time if you want any peace or quiet. The developer went bankrupt." Ed pointed to it and then took a photograph with his camera. "The crazy part about it is that my department approved it." He said. "I begin to wonder why we called it a planning department; we were the sprawl department."

### Schools and Youth

"Tell me about the children," Michael asked. "Tell me about the schools."

"Decades ago, Ed replied, "the school department closed the brick and stone pre-war school buildings from an era when people valued education differently. I remember when I first went to school in one of those magnificent brick buildings. Even though I was only six, it left a lasting impression that my education was important to adults. We walked to school, and we were in good physical shape."

"Now almost all students are bused to large sprawling school campuses with cheap single-story classrooms connected by covered walkways. This architectural travesty emerged from a funding formula for new schools in the days when no one paid much attention to heating and cooling costs. The high schools merged until now they are the size of small towns – although I have to qualify that by saying a part-time town since they use the campus less than 15% of the 24/7 year. Westside High School alone has over 4,000 students."

"I wonder what my grandson thinks today, walking among those low-budget shoe boxes connected by breezeways. Of course, maybe he has been so numbed by television that he does not notice; for him this is all he knows."

"Many children now start attending day care when they are a few months old, and they spend most of the working day under the supervision of an institution. Both parents, or their solo parent, work – no one at home or in the neighborhood to look after them."

"A while back, our local TV station did a feature story on teens after another student shooting spree occupied the national news for a day or two. Our teens were almost unanimous in their feeling that life in Blandville's suburbs was utterly boring. *If it was not for television, computer games and hanging out at the mall, they might just kill themselves* they said, and in fact some do. Drug abuse is a major problem. A number of our Blandville young people report a new addiction, playing computer games for days on end, only breaking for food and sleep. Virtual reality is taking the place of living experience. With their fast-food diet and passive indoor life, it is no wonder we have new illnesses and an epidemic of obesity." Ed let out a sigh and shook his head.

## Aging Sadly

"You've lived in the same suburb a long time, Ed. Is that unusual?" Michael asked. "Did you leave many friends in the Heights?"

"Yes, it was unusual and no, all the folks who became friends moved away a long time ago. When I was a boy, families lived in the same village or town for generations. If a family moved in from somewhere else, they were considered newcomers for a long time, sometimes for generations. Folks would take you to the cemetery on

Memorial Day and show you the graves of their ancestors, some going back to when that place was settled. All of that changed with the new suburbs. The husband worked for a corporation, and those on the way up took transfers every few years. The children learned how to make friends fast, and how to leave them when dad got transferred. For them the job defined their life.

I was the only one my age left living in the Heights. I was an oddity; the old man next door. During the work and school day, the homes emptied out, rendering the neighborhood lifeless rather than tranquil. Most older people moved to retirement villages, either voluntarily as I am doing, or because their children pressured them. I visited a few of my former neighbors, but found it depressing… no children, no young adults and no one living an active life. When they became ill, it went from dull to dreadful as they moved into nursing homes that wiped out dignity as well as any remaining savings. For my generation, ending life on welfare was shameful. I see it coming for me, and I'll end my life before the money runs out. How, I don't know, but the odds are in my favor."

"When adult children came to visit their parents in the nursing home, those children vowed it would not happen to them – sitting with nothing to do during the day but wait to die; those retaining their mental faculties enduring the dementia of those who have not. Despite their vows, I met none who had a plan how they would avoid such a fate. And now as that time is fast approaching for me, I have to admit I too have no plan. I know some old people hoarded fatal doses of prescription medicines. My mother's aunt had always said she would take her own life before it became unbearable, and a few days after the doctor said she died of natural causes after suffering a stroke, a postcard arrived from her that made it clear the doctor failed to report the true cause."

## Character and Politics

Michael shifted the conversation; this line of thought was turning too morbid for comfort. "Tell me about the character of Blandville" he inquired.

"That's an oxymoron" replied Ed with a wry smile. "The only visitors to Blandville are business people there to conduct business or relatives visiting family. While millions of visitors flock to those wonderful ancient cities, towns and villages of Europe – designed and built when urban planning meant something different,

Blandville offers no such attraction. What visitor intentionally goes to visit modern suburbs – to see tract home after tract home on a wide street with its empty front lawns and sidewalks devoid of pedestrians? There is nothing about Blandville or its sprawling residential and commercial zones that offer any character that would attract people for the experience. It was first a railroad town, then a farm town and now it is a suburban town. I moved there because they offered me a job. That's pretty much everyone's Blandville story, I reckon. We made an OK life of it, with family, schools, the clubs and church, and it was a whole lot better than life during the Depression."

"All of the places of natural beauty and history are long gone; the thick grasslands gave way to huge farms a century ago; the last stands of old forest cut down by the 1940's, and they re-channeled the river to prevent floods – its banks now made of concrete. The few remaining Victorian buildings of the old town are run down, butchered over time and the area is unpleasant during the day and unsafe after dark. The only reason people visit Blandville is to shop, and yet now the stores on the boulevard and in the mall are the same stores found in all the other satellite towns around Metropolis. They even run the same sales at the same time. Sometimes I wonder how Blandville's economy actually works, given that it seems to be nothing more that circular consumption. It's as if they are living off of wealth created in earlier times, and credit borrowed from their grandchildren or, as I should say, *my* grandchildren."

"In order to attract more people and make Blandville more interesting, a few years back, the Blandville Council began to look at various ideas. One group of councilors pressed for construction of a sports stadium, and another group of upstanding citizens said a Hotel and Conference Center would be the ticket to bringing life into the community. A third group began to lobby the legislature to approve a casino. My department was asked to review the options."

## Crisis, Crisis, Crisis

"Before any of these ideas could progress particularly far, however, the state environmental management agency organized local showings of Al Gore's film *An Inconvenient Truth* and the elected officials split along party lines in response. The left wing, holding a one-seat majority, voted to bring in consultants to come up with a plan whereby Blandville could become carbon neutral. Given the spread-out nature of the sprawled post-war development, the consultants reported that the town would need to become a Transit Oriented Community (TOC), and to adopt strict building codes to achieve a 70% carbon savings in terms of heating, cooling, hot water and lighting. This was greeted by howls of derision from the industries associated with construction and transport who increased their political contributions to the right wing party. I have to say, Michael, I have my doubts about arguments on both sides, but it was still at a policy level using consultants, so the directives did not make it to my department."

"However, before these ideas could be moved forward, the Council began to realize their economy was in trouble. When the price of gasoline hit its peak, many commuters found their suburban lives were becoming unaffordable, too expensive to drive back and forth from home to work, schools and shops. The very basis of Blandville's suburban footprint and infrastructure was becoming untenable – it was based on the presumption that gasoline would always be cheap and abundant. At the same time, housing prices began to fall, in too many cases like my son Jared's home, with values dropping below the mortgage balance. People began moving out, posting the keys to the bank – they even had a word for it: *jinglemail*."

Ed opened his bag again, showed Michael a photograph and then explained. "This is one of the unfinished houses that is now sitting exposed to the weather. It's not even clear who owns the mortgage on it. It will probably have to be condemned."

"Where do you think it will all end?" Michael asked.

Ed stroked his chin for a moment and then answered. "If it gets worse, the tax base will erode and the town will struggle to keep the roads paved and the utilities operational; just like in the old days when the highway would be paved by the state, and then turn to gravel going through the town because they lacked funds for paving. I'm not sure if it will get as bad as all that, but when it hit, anxiety, fear and then panic took hold as ordinary citizens found the life to which they had become accustomed began to fall apart. At the next election, the left wing party lost three seats, and the new right wing majority repealed all the energy and transport initiatives adopted by the prior regime. One of the newly elected representatives, a radio talk-back host who commuted to Metropolis every day, commented on his show that he believed the Global Warming scare was bad science promoted by liberals to take away freedom and raise taxes. He did not have facts to go on, but that did not stop him from shouting."

Ed shook his head sadly. "As a professional planner with the conservative bent that seems to come with age, I don't know what to believe anymore. I fear Al Gore's message may be like his daddy's – producing undisclosed adverse outcomes and I suspect the science is no where near as wrapped up as the alarmed side says. But on the other hand, I fear that the talk-show councilor reflected how pandering and polarizing politics had become, and how dumbed down the average citizen was to accept it. In some regards I'm grateful I no longer was needed to provide the answers."

Michael replied. "Are you not being too hard on yourself, Ed? I mean was it your job to come up with all the right answers?"

Ed thought about it for a minute and then pulled out a notebook, where he wrote down quotes he found interesting. Let me read you this quote from a famous architect named Christopher Alexander. He wrote this in 2002 in a book called *The Nature of Order*. It's harsh but I think it may answer your question:

*"In the 20th century we have passed through a unique period, one in which architecture as a discipline has been in a state that is almost unimaginably bad. Sometimes I think of it as a mass psychosis of unprecedented dimension, in which the people of earth – in large numbers and in almost all contemporary societies – have created a form of architecture which is against life, insane, image-ridden, hollow. The ugliness which has been created in the cities of the world, and the banality and pretentiousness of many 20th century buildings, streets, and parking lots have overwhelmed the earth. Much of this construction is caused by developers, housing authorities, owners of hotels, motels, airport authorities. In this sense architects might be considered blameless, since in some degree the ugliness of what has been created is caused by new relations between time, money, labor, and materials, and by a set of conditions in which the real thing – authentic architecture that has deep feeling and true worth – is almost impossible.*

*But architects are not blameless. For the most part, architects have stood by, content to play their role as part of the 20th century machine. In many cases they make it worse. They guild the lily of commercial development with pretentiousness. Many architects have raised the designer-consciousness fashion of building to new levels, have invented absurd ways of thinking about architecture, have altogether poisoned the earth with an abundance of terrible and senseless designs which have few redeeming features."*

"Whew" said Michael, "that fellow sure does not pull any punches does he?"

"No, he doesn't," Ed replied. "And I have to say I took this one in the gut, because I was trained to do better. Just because I may have been part of what Alexander calls a mass psychosis does not make me feel better about it. The fact is that almost every building on this boulevard is ugly with some aspiring to banality and pretentiousness. The same goes for the subdivisions and industrial parks. But worse than that, it is this very architecture that now threatens the wellbeing of my son, his family and our whole country. It was built on the assumption that petroleum is abundant, cheap and harmless. And by this I don't want to sound like some greenie Chicken-Little saying the sky is falling. That may be true, and it's beyond my pay-grade to decide, but the social impact alone is devastating. As Papanek said *There is no there there*."

"When I first read that, I took it personally. But then, having lots of time and nothing to do, I began to use Google Earth and look at the street views of freeway exit boulevards like Blandville's. I would zoom in from the sky, where major portions of our country are now grids of streets, subdivisions, malls and industrial tracts, and look at their major streets. It was both scary and appalling to see that no matter what the city or town, they all looked almost exactly the same as Blandville Boulevard. The names of the businesses were the same, even the building designs were the same. The only variation was in the backdrop... the mountains, sky color or the climate and its types of vegetation. Everything was dependent on cheap, abundant petroleum and massive consumption of electricity to run these artificial environments. The whole of the country seems to be one big Blandville." Ed concluded with despair in his voice.

As the limo entered the interstate, Ed finally felt talked out, but not for the better. Ed felt his life's work had turned to custard; his dream that life would be better for his children and grandchildren was turning into a nightmare. As he headed out of Blandville with Michael driving, he asked if his life was a failure. At least his daughter Liz was happy and doing well, but she rejected everything he stood for. What was his life about? What legacy had he left for future generations? What would happen to his son and grandchildren? He felt tired.

## Transition to a VillageTown

Ed and Michael drove on the freeway for several hours, and somewhere along the way Ed must have drifted off to sleep, because when he awoke, Michael had pulled into a covered parking garage with many cars. Looking at his watch, he saw that it was shortly after noon. Michael said it was time to get some lunch.

Michael had stepped out of the car and was waiting for him on the raised walkway where people were transferring packages from golfcart-sized vehicles to the trunks of rental cars. Michael seemed to Ed somehow taller than when they first met, more present than before. "Curious" thought Ed.

Together they walked out of the garage; the sign called it *The Motorpool*. They followed a footpath alongside a high, soft adobe-type wall, arriving at an elegant large gateway carved in a classical style, over which the words read *Welcome to Villageton*. Ed had never heard of Villageton, but it looked inviting, and he was hungry. As they walked in through the gateway, he noted the beauty of the framed view and he took out one of the grid-notebooks he always carried with him since his student days, to do a quick sketch. The gateway reminded him of his studies of old towns in Europe or colonial America, places built when planners designed on different principles than today.

"Welcome indeed", he thought. "This promises to be interesting."

# Chapter 2

## Welcome to Villageton

The street sign read *Village Parade*, and it was certainly wide enough to hold a parade that could be watched by thousands of people. Below the street sign was a smaller sign that read *no cars or trucks beyond this point*. To reinforce the point it had locked, shiny painted black cast iron posts in the road wide enough to let a golf cart through, but not an automobile or truck.

Most of the people he saw were walking, some arm in arm talking and laughing. Others pedalled on slow, single-speed bicycles with baskets laden with food, packages or babies strapped in. A number of people drove by in small electric vehicles loaded with goods... boxes of food for the shops, a boy making deliveries of packages with addresses written on them, and a family driving to the motorpool with sports equipment to be transferred into one of the VT Rental Cars he had seen. They caught Ed's eye and said they were off for a week in the mountains. Nice.

On both sides of the Village Parade, Ed noted the shops and stores catered to visitors. While this place had a main gate, it was not a gated community. Visitors clearly were welcome and could come and go as they pleased. The shops near the gate suggested the economy did well from its visitors, and he noted the products appeared to be high quality and locally made. It appeared there was a strong local food industry, more resembling the boutique foods of Europe, but with surprisingly reasonable prices: Pears and apples stacked high in shades of red, yellow, gold and green, all looking crisp and fresh off the tree. One proprietor had dangled mouth-watering blue-purple grapes from hooks, complete with grape vine and green leaves. He would have to remember to stock up on his way out to take with him to Heathcliff Manor. Signs told Ed the foods were local, and organic with many from heritage stock.

The buildings were stunning. Instead of wall-sized plate glass windows, many used divided panes of glass, reminding him of buildings in his Christmas model train set his father helped him build when he was a child. One masterpiece of window design set curved glass in a half-round display to give the shopper a walk-around view of the clothing within.

It was too good to miss, so Ed took out his pencil and pad to do a quick sketch. He marveled at the detail of each shop's door. Framed in what appeared to be carved stone, each door presented a delightful welcome to its customers – not a single utility door in sight; each one hand-made by artisans who clearly understood what makes a great door. As an architect, his professional eye also noted the high insulative design of the doors and windows – no high heating or cooling bills for these businesses.

The walls were over a foot thick, with irregular exterior surfaces appearing not painted, but coated in pastel slurries with a soft finish no paint could ever match. The hanging shop signs, mounted on wrought iron frames jutting into the street, were works of art – fine lettering and clearly done by hand. They must have a blacksmith in this town, he thought, as the workmanship was both masterful yet clearly new. In fact, they must have a number of such masters, given the different details he kept noticing.

The street lights appeared to use energy saving bulbs mounted in elegant, black painted, cast metal poles with fine gold detail lines. At their base, he noted the streets paved in what looked like cobblestone, but with a more stable walking surface. Ed always liked using pavers – when the street crews needed to tear up the road to access cables or pipes, they always left a horrible black patch that never matched the rest of the street. When workers lift pavers and put them back, they leave no evidence the road was ever broken.

As he looked, he listened. Ed sensed an absence of the background roar he had lived with for many decades. There was no white noise from traffic, no fan or compressor roar from air conditioners or restaurant fans. Instead he heard the chirp of birds, the clap of shoes as people walked – Ed saw many wore quality leather shoes, not the ubiquitous trainers of suburbia. He heard conversations and shop doors opening and closing with jingling bells announcing the arrival or departure of customers. Peaceful.

Ed noted a certain strategy to these first shops. Many appeared to be made not for people arriving, but people departing. He saw a picnic shop that sold bag lunches, traveller's meals and fully stocked picnic baskets for a day out. The baskets could be purchased, or borrowed with a deposit refunded on return. Artisan stores sold handmade goods, not the usual crafts-fair products, but outstanding works with great utility and beauty. One store sold hand garden tools, replicas of 17th and 18th century tools, with a sign indicating these also could be ordered on the internet and be shipped anywhere in the world. He saw, of course, the usual memento shops, except these seemed not to offer the typical tee shirts and toys, but locally made products. They must have a thriving music industry, Ed thought, noting the extensive collection and variety of local CDs on sale. Next to it, the windows displayed a wide range of soft home fabrics – towels, tablecloths, blankets and rugs – all made in Villageton and reasonably priced. This strategy made sense to Ed, as visitors would pass these stores on entry, but would be able to do their final shopping when close to their cars parked in the motorpool. Finally, not far up the street, they came to the Visitor Center where Michael directed Ed inside to inquire about a good place for lunch.

## The Design - A 100:1 Scale Model

Agnes, the visitor center's volunteer hostess was about Ed's age – a friendly person who recognized Michael the driver. She saw Ed had never been here before and had no clue where Michael had brought him. Instead of providing a list of eating places, Agnes came from behind the counter, introduced herself and invited them into the next room to view an orientation scale model of the town to get a better idea of the different villages where he might prefer to have lunch.

Agnes said to Ed, "What you see here is the actual planning model used when they designed Villageton. Each of us ordered a scale model of our home and we selected the village and street where we would live. We defined the theme and look of our village, and on this scale model, we designed our future."

"While everyone was invited to participate in the design process, I would say it was five different groups of people who drove it:

- Baby boomers concerned about their future facing uncertain retirement
- Parents of school age children worried about their safety and education
- Single working adults looking for a socially, culturally-enriched happening place
- What they call the Creative Class; the artists, musicians, scientists and inventors looking for a critical mass to support creativity
- Young people starting out on their own.

Of these, Boomers and Parents were the strongest drivers. Look at what is happening in the world today, and you appreciate why they were so motivated."

Ed looked to her to elaborate, so Agnes explained: "Baby boomers need to reinvent the next stage of their lives or face a very difficult time. Boomers have a lot of money, a lot of talent, and hold positions of power in many institutions. However, they see how all that will change as they grow old. The competition they knew from the day they were born will become competition for limited resources to support them. As it turned out, during the enrolment process, Villageton had to allocate housing to various sectors of society and, because of the extreme oversubscription of boomers, had to decide who would get in. Some village coordinators held a lottery while others examined what businesses they would bring, and chose the best economic mix to ensure a strong local economy."

"That's different," Ed said. "Usually developers struggle to sell homes. Are you saying that here they had to ration homes?"

"Well, yes," replied Agnes, "although I had never thought about it that way. A similar thing happened with parents of school age children. Parents are finding it extremely difficult to find a safe community with good schooling for their children. Families will move to get into a good school zone. Here, when they understood how it worked, and the extent to which they could be involved and actually know what kind of an education their children would receive, they were kicking the doors down to get in. In some cases, the village coordinators just went on a first-come-first-serve basis, while others used the lottery or the economic mix analysis. In the end, there were a substantial number of people on the waiting list, and I understand that many have gone on to form the core of another VillageTown sponsored by the Village Forum."

With Ed's professional eye, he reckoned the model was about 100:1, almost twice the scale of the popular HO model train set. It was a remarkable design, a technical masterpiece and at the same time, Ed saw how useful it would be to orient first time visitors. The town had no grid – that right-angle street design so beloved of surveyors, road builders and military suppressors of 18th century insurrection. Instead the streets turned and twisted, some very narrow. The design almost resembled a labyrinth with many winding streets and foot paths with multiple connections to the many village plazas. It reminded Ed of communities built not only before cars but before large horse drawn freight wagons came into fashion. In his student years Ed had studied such places in old Europe, South America and in indigenous parts of Asia, but it was an utter surprise to find such a design within two hours of Blandville.

Ed noticed that some of the streets were narrower than anything Blandville had ever approved. He asked Agnes how they secured approval from the fire officials. She laughed. "In an on-line op-ed story called *Design by Fire Truck,* Virginia journalist Jim Bacon asked *Why can't developers today create walkable communities like the small towns of the 1920s? Go ask your fire marshal.* He makes the point that it is the size of fire trucks and the power the fire marshall has in setting the rules so fire trucks can get to house fires. We separate people in the name of fire safety. Of course, we all agree that safety is the number one concern, but we noted that the great cities of the earth all got smart after they had their 'great fire', as in the great fire of Rome in 64 AD, the great fire of London in 1666 or the great fire in Chicago in 1871. After their fire, they rebuilt using noncombustible materials. If you look over here at this card on the side of the table, you will see you are not the first to ask the question." Agnes explained.

Ed picked up the card and saw that it contained the building codes for what is called Masonry Noncombustible IBC Type IIA. Ed was familiar with the terms, where IBC stands for International Building Code. It is a model building code developed by the International Code Council adopted throughout most of the United States. Much of it addresses fire prevention. "So, the standard for Villageton is not fire resistant, but completely non-combustible?"

"Yes," Agnes replied. "In Villageton buildings the walls, floors and roofs are all completely non-combustible. This means that all that can burn are things people bring in, such as furniture. The rooms have sprinklers, and the streets have strategically located pressure hoses, so fire fighters only need to get themselves and portable equipment to the fire, which they do using specially built small electric trucks. Thus, Villageton is made safe through prevention, not through fire fighting. If something in a room catches fire, the fire will stay in that room and probably be put out by the sprinklers long before the fire department arrives. I should note that Villageton has a unified public safety department, where the same people are trained as emergency medical technicians and police, since having a dedicated fire department would mean a very lonely and boring job. We have only had one fire call a year since we opened, and most of those were people leaving things on the stove."

Ed contemplated this information, and then said to Agnes, "I'm impressed both by the logic and by the fact you convinced the fire marshall to accept it. In my town, those fellows had pretty strong ideas about what is needed to fight fires, and also had what my daughter would call a very narrow comfort zone."

"Yes." Agnes answered. "It was helpful that we began at the political level where the elected officials were able to see the big picture. In the end, however, the fire officials came around. They saw that requiring a single bulk material that is entirely non-combustible and that has a five-hour burn rating provides a higher level of safety. I have to say though, it was interesting how they got there. As the Village Organizing Company team was walking them through the details, one of their younger fellows suddenly had one of those light bulb moments. He said 'Chief, what if we looked at this like a big shopping mall, only instead of just stores, it's mixed use? When we get a fire call to the mall, we don't drive the trucks down the streets inside the mall, we park outside and run in. And we do that because the mall is completely Class Two, noncombustible construction.' The others considered this and then asked 'But how do we know someone won't tear down one of the existing buildings and construct using a more flammable class?' Our team answered that once built, the whole of Villageton within the village walls is designated as a historic district, which means there are very strict controls over future construction. It's a *what you see is what you get* approach."

"But, what about young families starting out who can't afford to build what they will eventually need?" Ed asked. "In most places, they get to add on over time."

Agnes appreciated Ed's mind, and she smiled as once again, she had an answer for him. "Because of how the buildings were constructed, the extra cost of the upper floors is negligible. The forms and molds are set in place, and the cost of the bulk material and the extra exterior windows is a small percentage of the final cost of construction. So the whole house is constructed at once, but the upper floors are left sealed off and completely unfinished. The major cost of adding on to a home is in the finishing – this is delayed until the family can afford it. You will also note that many of the homes have an old fashioned pulley-and-post at the top that allows construction equipment and the odd piano to be winched in through the upper balcony door rather than tracked through the home. Most homes have a staircase with a door that faces the back so construction workers can have access without tramping dust through the living room." Ed shook his head in admiration, impressed with the attention to detail.

Ed turned back to the model and looked carefully. He saw the architectural styles varied considerably; that around each plaza there was a consistent theme, but each plazas and its surrounding streets was completely different. One plaza was clearly a Chinatown, similar to those found in many cities where Chinese immigrants settled in the 19th century. Another evoked a feeling of a Tuscan village, ocher yellows and earthen reds. A third was modern, bright metal and glass and a fourth evoked a cottage feel vaguely reminiscent of English or Irish villages. Near the motorpool, outside the Villageton walls a large area was marked *Industrial Park*, and close to it were two plazas, one marked *youth zone* that appeared to have a bandstand for outdoor dancing in the streets. A sign indicated a noise overlay, with a higher noise level near the industrial zone that explained why youth housing would be near that end.

"Agnes, how is it that each village cluster is so different? I have been in cities where there are ethnic neighborhoods, but except for the Chinatown district they usually are similar buildings with different signs. Here it looks more like what would happen if I hopped a jet and flew from country to country."

Agnes brightened. "That's the best part of it. When I said we selected the village and defined the theme, we began with a choice of 21 themes, and each of us would decide which suited us best. I picked the Celtic village because I come from Irish ancestors who came to America in the 1820's and founded a little town on what then was the frontier. Just about everyone in that town descends from four Irish families. Years ago I went on my own to Ireland for a week, leaving my husband and daughter at home. It felt like a homecoming. Even though I'm 7th generation in the New World, I felt such a deep affinity for the Irish land, the buildings and the people. So when my daughter and her husband decided to move here, they wanted to build me a granny flat in their village – what I call the Genius Village… my son-in-law is an inventor – but I said no. I was going to have the time of my life in the Celtic Village, and they could walk over to see me. My granddaughter comes over every Saturday for Irish dancing lessons, and the two of us take the classes together. But to answer your question Ed, they are so different because we wanted them to be different. It adds spice to life."

Ed replied with a wry smile "I'm beginning to see how appropriately named the town I helped to build is. I cannot recall one single meeting in Blandville where we considered *spice* to be an important design criterion." He continued to examine the details of the scale model of Villageton. He saw that some patterns were consistent. In all but the largest central plaza that looked like the town center, the buildings were two and three story, and almost all were attached, connected on the sides, but not like urban row-houses. Instead of the narrow, deep and dark attached housing found in prewar cities, these homes were turned 90 degrees, so they received lots of light and people did not live cramped together. When Ed was a young planner, he advocated such an approach to building for Blandville's low-cost townhouses, but the developers and town managers made clear this required longer streets to accommodate the cars. Neither elected officials nor private investors were prepared to foot the bill for additional road costs, so residents got dark, cramped homes. Looking at this model, Ed was delighted to see someone had the sense to do it right. Remembering the sign prohibiting cars and trucks from within the village walls, he saw how they overcame the financial obstacle... eliminate cars and you can make streets narrower and longer while staying within the same or lower road-building budget.

Ed saw the Village Parade led to the town square, where there was a prominent clock tower, town hall and what appeared to be a cathedral. This latter building surprised him, because religious institutions no longer built such classical anchors of urban architecture. Instead they built acres of parking around a sprawling building – warehouse with steeple, or a neoeclectic over-the-top monstrosity lit at night by blue and pink spotlights – fantasy temple on steroids. In contrast, here the cathedral and town hall formed perfectly balanced bookends that defined not only the square but Villageton as a whole. Whoever designed those buildings was an outstandingly trained classical architect who understood the difference between timeless design and slavish copying of yesteryear. "Is this a religious community?" Ed asked Agnes.

"If your asking if this is an intentional community built by a religious group, no" she replied. "However, as in any normal town we have those who are church-going. The central cathedral is non-denominational. It's available to any religious or non-religious group for sacred events or rites of passage such as large weddings or funerals. We call it a cathedral because of its size and shape rather than to imply a particular religion. Having said that, some religious denominations that wish to use it require space that is blessed in accordance with their teachings. These groups paid for wings off the main building to serve their purposes. If you visit it, I think you will find it inspirational no matter what, if any, spiritual beliefs you might hold. When not in use, the size of the silence within is awesome."

Ed saw that around the town center the buildings were higher and larger, including what looked like rather grand private residences, mansions built by people or families with more money, yet done in a harmonious fashion. Other taller buildings appeared to be shared accommodation - elegant apartments and flats in some cases built around enclosed courtyards and private gardens.

With amusement Ed commented to Michael and Agnes how his judgmental mind was getting knocked about. When he first saw the word *organic* in many of the visitor-oriented stores, he had presumed he was in some sort of ecovillage; one of those intentional communities in which long discussions about values established how its residents are supposed to live. The ecovillages he read about tended toward values that disapproved of rich people, or building homes that displayed substantial wealth. "Strike that thought", he said with a laugh. The district with the larger buildings had that formal smell of well-spent money: hand-forged black wrought iron fences surrounding private rose gardens in front of architectural masterpieces of grand homes. It was clear Villageton looked for harmony among buildings, but not conformity among people. Here, it seemed it was OK to be rich or not-rich. This was the district for mansions, mixed in with three and four upscale apartment buildings, clustered around the tallest buildings in the town: the town hall, cathedral and clock tower on the square.

The model showed Villageton surrounded by the high, attractive wall Ed had seen on arrival. In some places it was adobe type masonry as they had seen walking in, but in other places it appeared to be a living hedgerow with its walls made of a thicket of woody shrubs and vines, impenetrable by cats and dogs, but home to many birds and small animals. The model maker even painted on blooming flowers and chipmunks peering out. The wall formed a boundary condition that clearly established a fixed and permanent line between urban and rural. On the outside of the wall, almost all, except the Motorpool, Industrial Park and Freight Depot near the front gate, was designated as a Greenbelt.

Ed understood the implication of such a wall – to mark the boundary. He explained to Michael and Agnes that the word *urb*, the root of *urban* comes from Latin, meaning a walled city or town. Remembering a line drilled into him by Mr. Hooper, his 5th grade Latin teacher back in the dark ages when he wore short pants, Ed recited Virgil. *Interea Aeneas urbem designate aratro...*" Agnes eyes lit up and she translated for Michael "*Meanwhile Aeneas designates the city-state-walled-boundary with a plough...*" then she giggled, "I can't believe I had to wait this long in my life to find a use for my school-girl Latin."

Ed smiled with his eyes and continued, speculating how it appeared that unlike medieval walled cities, this wall around Villageton was not for defense, not for protection of those within, but to protect that which lay outside – the domain of Nature in the Greenbelt and the very different life of the surrounding host region... what in the jargon of his profession was called a buffer zone to prevent cross-boundary conflicts. It was clear to him that at its inception this town declared by its wall that the town would be a fixed size, that it would have no further expansion. It set out an absolute boundary, with no plan, intention or place to grow. Amazing!

Ed explained, "Most developments grow in stages because home sales depend on people moving into the region, and for the most part they move because the economy expands and creates more jobs. It can take a decade or more to finish a subdivision, with each stage opening after the previous stage sells. When the developable land is filled, the town then rezones the adjoining open space or farmland for development, and the next farmer cashes in. In many parts of the country, farmers now look to that as the endgame for their business, and slowly our local food sources turn into suburban lawns. Eventually one town sprawls so far so that it hits the border of the next town, and the region becomes one mass of low density suburban sprawl dependent on cheap and abundant gasoline to keep its economy going."

"What I am looking at here is an entirely different approach to urban planning. At the moment, I'm having what my daughter would call a mind-melt-moment. From what I can figure, Agnes, all the buyers came at the same time, because they were not dependent on the regional economy, but brought their own jobs or businesses with them. There must have been an intense building phase, a first-day-of-school like chaos as everyone moved in, and after that no more construction – that idea of declaring an instant historic district is brilliant. I would love to have met the planning department that had to oversee this one," Ed laughed. "Half of my department would have thought they had died and gone to heaven to be a part of such a project. The other half would have called in sick until it was over."

Agnes confirmed Ed got it right, except that the planners did not have the staff to devote full time to the intensive planning stage, so the Village Organizing Company paid the county to bring in top temporary staff. She asked Ed "you mentioned your department, and you analyzed this model like a forensic scientist. Are you a professional in the business?"

"Yes", Ed replied, "I am an architect and urban planner. My whole working career was with Blandville, or rather I was until I retired. Today, I am moving from Blandville to Heathcliff Manor, from an anonymous town to an anonymous retirement home a bit further west from here where I am not sure exactly what I will do except be pleasantly entertained by the staff and my fellow inmates." Agnes felt some energy sap out of her at this matter-of-fact description of Ed's past and future.

Ed then turned attention to the Greenbelt, where he calculated its width equaled the radius of the town. This meant there was three times as much Greenbelt as urban development. "Interesting land use", he said out loud. "Only one quarter of the land owned by Villageton is built. The rest is given over to various domains of Nature."

The Greenbelt in the model had signs to indicate their different uses. Closest to the motorpool and car parking was the festival and sports fields. Next Ed saw equestrian grounds that led into a productive forest, a place identified for timber intended to be grown, cut and used to make things. That forest had separate trails marked for riding, jogging and cycling. After the production forest came open land identified as community gardens and private leased plots. Then another forest, but this one marked Native Timber, where people could walk, jog or ride horses, but not wander or cut the trees. Other parts of this timber reserve were completely off limits to people except scientists and students– a scientific reserve for Nature's wild creatures only. Beyond the reserve the land opened up again, this time into a field of flowers and high grasses.

Agnes saw him looking quizzically at it, and she explained the field of flowers was planted and maintained purely for romance - for people to walk or run through fields of flowers, for children to play in the tall grasses. These fields adjoined the Villageton cemetery surrounded by a simple picket fence. Ed's face looked wistful as he reflected on how very few developments build cemeteries nowadays. "What a lovely way to approach a cemetery," he said. "Walking through a field of flowers shared by young lovers and children playing." He was thinking of Helen.

Finally, Ed saw the Greenbelt came full circle. Near the Industrial Park the land was marked as waste management and biofuel where it appeared sustainable systems were used to process human effluent and waste. This was technology Ed would have to ask about. He took a deep breath and turned back to Agnes. "So how was it possible for this to happen?" Ed asked. "It is so different from anything I have experienced in my 45 years of urban planning. It's awesome!"

Agnes thought for a moment, and then replied. "I'm not the most articulate person to answer that question, but this is what happens when people act as citizens instead of consumers. America was founded by people who valued citizenship. They came in groups, they founded towns. Their homes and public places reflected their values and aspirations. Their taverns were famous; much of our democracy was born in dialogue there by citizens who had other jobs and professions. About the time you and I came of age that era ended. Citizens lost those powers. Instead developers proposed tracts of homes, strips and malls of shops and blocks of offices. Freedom became the freedom to chose products on the shelf; people ceased to have their character embedded in the things of their lives. We did not do that here in Villageton. We were asked to act and think like citizens. The result is authenticity, character and a far better place. But tell me Ed, you seem interested. Do you want to learn more?"

Ed replied "You bet. I've never seen anything like this in my life."

Her eyes twinkled, and she said "There is a fellow who just popped into the Visitor Center; let me introduce you. "Morgan", she called, "do you have a minute? We have a visitor who is looking at your model with a professional eye."

# Chapter 3

# The Idea of VillageTowns Explained

"Baby Boomer" thought Ed with amusement. Levis 505 jeans, casual worsted sports jacket over a form-fitted black tee-shirt, Ed guessed the man's dress style had not changed since he left college. In Ed's generation, the young hurried to become adults, becoming grown-ups so they could take life seriously by age 20. The Baby Boom was different. Now in their 50's and 60's they still resisted becoming grown ups both in dress and in their heads. He wondered what they would do when they got to his age, too many of them and not enough money for retirement or medical care.

Morgan came over and introduced himself to Ed. "My guess is you are trying to figure out what this is all about. Am I right?" Ed allowed it was a smart guess having something to do with the slightly perplexed look on his face.

"Probably the best way to explain it is that what you are looking at here and what you will see in Villageton is what one would call 'normal'. So much of the world has become abnormal, doing things that any normal, rational person would say borders on insanity. But that insanity has become so prevalent that it passes for normal. So you find yourself puzzled." Ed raised an eyebrow in response, giving little away.

"Where's your home, Ed?" Morgan asked, shifting his approach slightly.

"Funny you should ask that, Morgan; at the moment, nowhere. You caught me in the middle of the largest transition in my life since I got married. I've coming from Blandville where I lived all my adult life until this morning. Michael here is driving me to the Heathcliff Manor retirement home where starting tonight I will live until they have burned through my life savings, provided I don't die first or end up drooling in a nursing home wheelchair."

"Sounds grim, didn't you have any better options?"

"Not really. My daughter lives a Bohemian life on an island overseas; she refuses to grow up. My son invited me to stay with his family, but his life is a train wreck waiting to happen. I fear it's only a question of when he will lose his job, then house and finally everything that defines him as a person. They have no room or role for grandpa in their suburban rancher and I would probably drive them nuts being there."

"As I see it, the economy is in trouble, not only because of the breakdown of the banking structure, the subprime mess and Wall Street putting our monetary system at risk, but because the system's very fundamentals are flawed. People like me and my son are completely dependent for our survival on those systems. We played by the rules they set out, and they broke their promise. The trouble is I don't know who 'they' are... the government, society, the business leaders, the Fed... all I know is the something has gone horribly wrong. As I drove out of Blandville today, I fear I played a little part in helping it get there."

Ed took a deep breath. "Sorry Morgan, I must be sounding dreadfully depressing; you caught me at a bad time. It's been a bad day. I'm not looking forward to moving to a place with nothing but old people. I know I look old, but I don't feel old. I'm going to a place where I will be comfortably retired out of harms way, sidelined, irrelevant and eventually a burden to society and a worry for my children when finally I can't pay my way anymore. Then as Michael drove me out of Blandville, driving past my life's work as Blandville's Senior Planner, I saw my work in a different light. What I saw for the first time made me ashamed. As Pogo said, *we have met the enemy and he is us.*"

Morgan saw the pain in Ed's face. "Given what you are saying, it's interesting you arrived here for lunch rather than at a fast-food pit stop along the freeway. I agree with your analysis, and more to the point, 10,000 people living here not only share it, but did something about it. Perhaps I can explain." Ed appeared attentive, so Morgan continued.

### WHEN MONEY BUYS FREEDOM

"When you were a kid, a millionaire needed about a million bucks to be rich. That million bought them freedom to do things you or I could not do. They could stop working to pay the bills and instead work at things that fulfilled them, at things which gave meaning to their lives. Of course some did not, but that's not the point. They had the freedom to reinvent their life because they were rich."

"Today, to get that kind of freedom, you need about $10 million, maybe a $100 million – whatever the number, very few people will get there, so the question is academic. If we go to the heart of the matter, it's not about the money, but the freedom." Ed nodded, so Morgan continued.

"As you know many people express concern about the direction our society is going. At the fringe, some see conspiracies under every rock, arm themselves to the hilt, and move to the hills where they build survivalist compounds. Others, like your daughter, leave, moving to far-away places not yet corrupted by the system you began to question this morning. Most continue their lives day to day, taking the hits as they come; worrying about money, the future and every so often about the world we leave to our children or grandchildren."

"But our system is not all bad. It is not a totalitarian state where the government prohibits private property ownership or a centralized state that devalues individual initiative. An awful lot of what is wrong came about through millions of small, short-sighted, bad decisions rather than any conspiracy to deprive citizens of their freedom. The fact is we still have a great deal of freedom, if only we know how to use it." Morgan said.

Ed turned this thought around in his mind, *cogitating* is what his father would have called it. "Would you mind expanding on that, Morgan?" Ed finally asked.

## Purchasing Power

Morgan replied. "What I mean to say is that people have far more resources at hand than they appreciate. Resources including what today is called *purchasing power*. Money talks, people listen. As individuals we do not have the clout of the millionaire, but if we combine our lesser clout by working together, we have purchasing power to secure not only freedom from those things closing in on us but more importantly the freedom to choose the life to which we aspire."

"From what you described, Ed, it sounds like you would prefer to live the remaining years of your life in a place where you live among young people, not solely people your own age. You want to be vital, involved, a participant in society, not finding ways to keep yourself busy while waiting in a halfway house to death. You have some savings, but you need them to pay your way, hoping they hold out so you need not end life on welfare, as a ward of the state. You don't see your life savings as clout but as sand in the hour glass running out in a race to death."

Ed nodded in agreement, so Morgan continued explaining. "It sounds like you seek opportunity for your son and his wife that not only enables them to secure economic wellbeing derived from their hard work, but also to spend more time with your grandchildren and to assure they get a good education so they may find a place to stand tall in their world. And it sounds like you wish your daughter could find a wonderful place to live in her own country."

"Yes, that is all true. Please go on, I'm still with you."

"On your own," Morgan continued, "you lack that choice. There is no place for you. You get to chose one retirement home or another, which is a fairly limited definition of freedom. Your children have the choice of getting sucked into a system built on debt or dropping out. Your grandchildren have the freedom to switch channels on the TV or to choose which computer game to play."

"Yup," Ed observed sadly. "That accurately describes my grandson's life."

"However, what would happen," Morgan asked, "if you combine your savings, your purchasing power with other people to plan and build a place for your retirement, a place for working families like your son, and for creative free spirits like your daughter?"

Ed thought and replied. "Sounds good in theory, but how do you do it?"

"Let's first look at money and what we call critical mass. As it turns out the two work together. Critical mass means the number of people a community needs to be financially robust and socially and culturally diverse to keep life interesting. In our research we found four thousand families – about 10,000 population in total is the right number. If four thousand families buy homes at an average sale price of $250,000, that works out to a billion dollars in purchasing power. A millionaire gets clout with $100 million, so how much clout do we have with a billion?" Morgan asked Ed.

"A lot of clout, I would say." Ed answered.

Morgan agreed with Ed's assessment and continued. "If you were the County Manager, and a corporation announced it was seeking a location for a new business campus worth a billion dollars residential plus more for commercial and industrial space, that would bring in about six thousand new jobs earning say $250 million a year and it had no adverse environmental or social effects, how would that be received by you and the elected officials?"

Ed replied. "We would do whatever was required to convince them to move in, especially in today's economic climate. We would probably get the state involved and offer substantial tax concessions, rezone the land they needed to build the campus and do whatever else was needed to win the bid."

"In other words," Morgan said, "your billion dollars in purchasing power buys you the freedom to dictate terms. You get to design your life in a way your $250,000 on its own can never buy."

"That's a convincing argument, Morgan, please go on," Ed said.

"The next question moves into practicalities: Now that you have the freedom that purchasing power can buy, what will you do with it?" Morgan asked. "The challenge comes because the billion dollars is not yours personally, but the collective purchasing power of 4,000 families. Do they share sufficient interests and discipline so they can agree on a plan and then turn it into reality? Can it work, or is it like herding cats?"

"Excellent question, Morgan." Ed replied. "I look forward to your answer."

## People or Citizens?

Morgan smiled, enjoying Ed's dry but insightful manner, so he continued explaining. "The answer to that question goes to the heart of what it is to be human, both as individuals, and as we live in society. Most human beings are social animals. We like being around other people. We live in society. We cooperate. We enjoy each others company. But before I go further with this, I may need to get agreement with you on the meaning of some key words. Do you remember by any chance the 1960's when John Lennon did the song *Power to the People*?" Morgan asked.

Ed replied. "I did not remember it was one of the Beetles, but I do recall a poster my daughter Liz had on her bedroom wall with that as a slogan along with a clenched fist on a red background, if I remember correctly. Why do you ask?"

"Because in order to explain Villageton, I probably need to introduce some old and slightly out-of-date words, one of which is *citizen*." Morgan answered. "While *people* is a perfectly good word, it sometimes is used in an *us versus them* context, such as the people versus the establishment, which is why your daughter put the poster on her wall. In contrast, the word *citizen* has a clear sense of belonging, of entitlement to full civil rights, and of equality. Citizen implies a relationship between person and place, but it only makes sense in a social context – our relationship to our land; us as an organized group. Am I making sense?"

"Yes," Ed replied. "I can accept your distinction and find it helpful."

"So while people like to be with each other in a social context, when we speak about citizens getting together, we speak about more than that." Morgan said. "For example, as social beings, we find that people cluster into different groups; they share what we would call different tastes and different values. Some people join a club, others a church, and others still a political party or all three. Others take up sports where they play in teams and in groups. In stroke-play golf you compete against your own handicap, but few stroke-play golfers play alone; it's a social game. Some people work to live, and others live to work. A few people, like your daughter chooses a life surrounded by beauty in an exotic community – I am presuming the island she selected overseas is beautiful." Ed nodded yes.

"But", continued Morgan, "it is unlikely your daughter would be considered a citizen on that island. By that I not only mean that she would get a passport and the right to vote, but that she would become fully integrated and accepted by its citizens who deeply and longly live there."

Ed thought about that for a moment and then nodded his head. "In Liz's case, you are right. She loves her life there, but she is living day-to-day and does not feel that she is part of that society, if I may put it that way. Her roots are not there; she has not grown new roots there, and I think it unlikely she will."

"Nicely stated!" Morgan said, impressed how poetically Ed had captured the point. "So in understanding how we enable four thousand families to build their villages, it adds clarity to describe them as *citizens*, rather than *people,* or perhaps describe them as the founding citizens of a future common locality. Already most will share national citizenship, but this is not enough. The intent is to not only organize their purchasing power, but for them to take on the role of citizen."

"Now the first fact about citizens is that they do not come with one view about what is important, what they value, what fulfills them. If we organize the purchasing power of four thousand families as a single group, we are doomed to failure. But what happens if instead of trying to get four thousand families to agree, we were to ask them to divide them up into twenty groups of approximately two hundred families clustered around what they deem important in life?" Morgan asked.

Ed replied, "I'm glad you introduced that, because frankly I too would find it hard to imagine organizing four thousand families. But Agnes explained how you divided the town up into twenty discrete villages, which makes more sense to me."

"Yes, it does make more sense," Morgan replied. "We found it gets a whole lot easier, especially since the ideal size of a face-to-face community where people know each other is about five hundred people, which works out to two hundred families."

"Not all of those two hundred families will participate at an equal level," Morgan explained. Some will be happy picking where they want their home to be, and let others work on the look and feel of the plaza – what is called the *village design code*. Some will be too busy. It's no different than in politics where some people volunteer, serve on committees and work their tail off, while others are happy just to vote."

In a nutshell," Morgan said, "that's what you will find if you take a tour of Villageton today, and you will see and hear how well it works. We have twenty different villages plus the town center, each with its own look, feel and character each of which was decided by its founding citizens in a formal, structured process."

"If you take that tour of Villageton, I'll venture to predict you will hear yourself saying *I remember that* to sights, sounds, feelings, even to tastes and smells. This is because what you remember was normal back when this country was populated by citizens. Somehow that normal life slipped away while we were distracted with this new consumer world we all invented. And if you are not clear on what I mean by this, consider how somewhere over the last forty years, we stopped calling people *citizens* and began calling them *consumers*."

## Consumers or Citizens?

Ed considered this last comment of Morgan's. He was amused how elegantly Morgan had returned to his theme about *normal*. Ed also sensed there was more to learn from Morgan about Villageton, so instead of allowing the conversation to end on what he felt was the punch line, Ed said: "This morning as we were driving out of Blandville I told Michael of a meeting I had with the Blandville Mall developer whose business plan was based on turning citizens into consumers. I find it interesting that you use almost the same words here. Would you say more on that?"

Morgan answered. "Let me reply in this way. It's no accident that the rise of the credit card parallels the rise of the shopping mall. In the old days, people carried a purse with cash money made of metal – gold, silver, nickel and copper. Spending was limited by the cash they had on hand, and there was very little real inflation. Sure they could go to the bank or the pawn shop to borrow money, but it was difficult, thus by necessity, most people had to live within their means. Some stores offered monthly store credit, but since they were taking the risk, they did not press it too hard."

"All of this changed with the introduction of the credit card. People began to spend today money they did not earn until next month or year. In prior times, shops competed to get into your purse or your next paycheck. When the credit card came along, shops began to compete for your credit line; how much you would borrow at usurious rates of interest. New business models emerged to maximize your debt. They did not do it to stress you out; they did it to sell more goods and services to you."

Ed found himself thinking about his son – maxed out on credit card debt, stressed to the point of desperation, and Morgan's contrasting view that from the shopping system's perspective, it was nothing more than a way to increase business.

Morgan continued on this line of thought. "With this massive new source of retail buying power, a new social science emerged to study how to extract the maximum amount from people, and a new name was needed to refer to this new type of human being – *the consumer*. That name came about because another new angle was added to this new economy. In the past goods were made to last; they were called durable. It would not be unusual for a tool to be passed from parent to child, or solidly made furniture to be passed down for generations. In this new economy, it became important to make things that broke, wore out or were deemed no longer fashionable – we became a disposable society. In doing so, the concept of consumption became a central tenet of the new economy. Ironically, consumption used to be the word for a fatal disease."

Ed smiled at this last crack, and then asked Morgan, "I wonder if the growth of consumerism would have been possible without the simultaneous invention of television? I'm not only thinking of the advertising, but also of what passes for news. I remember when I was visiting my son, I sat down and actually listened to the news... not the stories themselves, but how they were reporting it, and the words they chose to use. An awful lot of the stories used the word *consumer*, but I cannot recall a single time when they used the word *citizen*."

"Television is a very powerful, almost hypnotic medium," Morgan replied. "Some of our best and brightest minds conduct study after study to determine how TV may most effectively manipulate human behavior to serve the agenda of the company that pays for the show. In its infancy, there was a barrier between the show and the advertiser, but that now has been removed. Thus we have created a whole society that revolves around buying and selling. While this has given us an unprecedented level of personal comfort and abundance, it has come at a cost."

"I can think of many costs," Ed commented, "but you were talking about citizens versus consumers, so how would you see the costs in those terms?"

"It probably has to do with arrested maturity," Morgan responded. "Take a child into a store, and it wants all the shiny things. It wants sugar that tastes good in the mouth, and when told no, it will raise a howl, especially in today's society. Take a mature citizen into a store and that person will buy things they need or if they have some discretionary cash, something they love. What the store needs are overgrown children – adults in form and earnings power, but immature in their desire to buy everything they see; to create a *culture of want.*"

"This culture of want reshapes more than the buying habits of such people. As an unintended side effect, it changes how people interact with each other, what they talk about, how they treat each other. Gradually, people become more isolated, less of a sense of *we* and more about *me*." Morgan concluded.

"I hear your words, but I don't quite follow. Can you give me an example?" Ed asked.

"Sure," Morgan replied. "I will give you two. First consider the trend in houses. They are getting bigger. Do you know why?

Ed replied, "in fact I do. People are buying more things. They now have a video room instead of going to the movies. They build their own gym and stock it with workout gear that rarely gets used. So what you are saying is they are becoming more self-centered, in both meanings – isolation and becoming more selfish."

"Yes," Morgan answered. "Second, consider in architecture the outside face of a commercial building. Today, as you drive down any conventional commercial strip in any major suburban sprawl, such as your Blandville Boulevard, you will see many large buildings that are nothing more than massive boxes plastered with signs and brands. They are not beautiful; they add nothing to the streetscape. They exist solely to attract as many consumers as possible."

"Yes," Ed said. "That was what sparked my crisis of confidence today as Michael drove me out of Blandville. I oversaw the approval of all of those buildings, and until recently never gave it much of a thought. They were clean, sanitary, met the fire, traffic and safety requirements, and our elected officials supported their construction because their owners made campaign contributions, the businesses provided jobs and they made Blandville look like it was a prosperous town."

Morgan acknowledged Ed's comments and he continued. "So, let's travel back in time, Ed. Think of the American cities built in the 19th century and look at the remaining commercial buildings. Except where the ground floor has been redecorated to remove all architectural beauty in favor of plate glassed windows, the buildings are beautiful with carved stone or wood details of the era. Go to older European cities and many centuries-old buildings are even more beautiful, and the names of some of their architects such as Wren or Palladio still are known today. Why?"

Even though Ed heard this as a rhetorical question, he chose to answer it because it was his area of expertise. "Speaking as a trained architect – for that is what I am – it is because the people who hired them were proud of their city, and had the money to commission works that would be appreciated by all. Commissioning a lovely building boosted their stature within their society and this was important to them because they, and all others in that society, lived with the results not only day-to-day, but for future generations."

"Precisely! Those people, who I suggest are best described as citizens were connected to their cities" replied Morgan. "Citizens view themselves as part of their city. They do not view their city as a place to exploit because it is their permanent home. They built within a social context; they were connected."

"Now," Morgan continued, "when we examine the people who build those big-box stores, franchises and branded consumer businesses, they have no connection to their city or town because there is nothing there to which to be connected. It is nothing more than a multi-lane road with bland, meaningless buildings surrounded by acres of paved parking. In many cases, they do not even live there. It's just an investment."

"So," Morgan concluded, "we come to the core question. *Why do we build communities?* Or perhaps I should ask *why would citizens build communities* and how would they be different than communities built for consumers?"

## Why We Build Communities - For the Good Life

"Interesting distinction" Ed commented, finding this line of thinking energizing, as Morgan was discussing Ed's area of professional expertise – asking the sort of questions Ed's team never asked. "Citizens *build* communities whereas consumers are passive – suburban sprawl *gets built* for them. So what answers did you find?"

"We found citizens build communities for *the Good Life*," Morgan replied.

At this answer, Michael the driver interrupted. "Morgan, I am beginning to get one of those déjà vu moments, except I can tell you when it last happened. When we were driving out of Blandville, Ed talked about Aristotle's *good life*, and he explained that it was best understood as having four or five parts."

"Yes, that's true, Morgan." Ed added. "I quoted a book by Victor Papanek that my daughter gave me; a book that triggered my questioning my life's work. He said something had gone terribly wrong with our communities, and he then rather accurately placed those failings at my doorstep – that over the past half century or so my planning department and those of my peers around the country failed to ask the right questions." Ed saw that Morgan was listening carefully, so he continued:

"Papanek said the timeless reasons to build communities is to enable *conviviality, religion, artistic & intellectual growth* and *politics*. I had difficulty with his translation of two of the social desires he listed, *politics* and *religion* because these words have taken on different meanings since Aristotle wrote them. Politics has an unsavory side to it, whereas citizenship means to belong fully to a community. Religion has taken on an aspect of conflict and division, whereas spiritual development and fulfillment captures that part of religion that is its core before institutional men began to claim they had divine knowledge and understanding that caused violence, suffering and even wars. But other than that, I think that Aristotle and Papanek set out a better reason to build communities than any reasons that guided my planning department in Blandville for over forty years – and having to face that is not an easy thing for me."

Morgan's face showed his surprise. "This definitely fits into the small-world department. Victor Papanek died in 1998, and while he is known and admired among a small circle of professionals, I must say I am surprised to hear he and *citizenship* came up in conversation. Ed, do tell me if I am preaching to the choir."

Ed grinned sheepishly. "Actually, more like a novice. My daughter gave me the book probably a decade ago, and I took one look at the title *A Green Imperative* and shelved it, unread. It was only when I was packing up the books to sell that it fell open in my hand to the very page that precipitated, shall I call it, a crisis of confidence. So please, do tell me what I stumbled upon. I'm all ears."

Morgan saw Ed's note pad and said, "Would you mind if I drew it out for you as if it was a house?" Ed handed Morgan the sketchbook and a drawing pen.

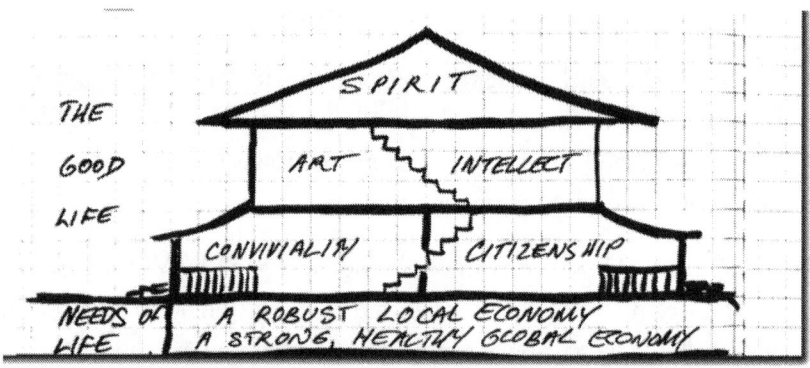

"In this view, the economy forms the foundation. It needs to be strong, durable and able to support the life built on top of it. Unlike our present day society, in this drawing, the economy knows its place. Money-making exists not to foster more money-making at the expense of the good life, money-making exists to support the good life." Morgan explained.

Ed summarized what he had heard. "So you began by asking the people who wanted to live in Villageton to take on the role of founding citizens. You first made sure they were able to contribute to a diverse, self-supporting local economy, and then you got them to frame their purpose, creating the good life, as in the drawing?"

"That's not a bad way to put it." Morgan replied, enjoying Ed's clarity of thought.

"I'm still trying to work through your difference between citizens and consumers. Both use money, both buy things, but somehow they handle money differently. Would you expand on that?" Ed asked, fascinated at how many turns this was taking.

Morgan was quiet for a moment and then he reached into his pocket and took out a silver coin which he handed to Ed. "I have carried this silver dollar around with me since my dad gave it to me in 1967 for Christmas back when I was a kid. It's called the Peace Dollar because they were first struck to mark and commemorate the end of World War One. Unlike the previous Morgan dollar – no relation of mine, sorry – this coin had two additional words on it: on the front, *Liberty*, and on the back *Peace*." Ed looked at the coin, turned it over and read the words. He had never thought much about what words the government put on money, and he asked Morgan about it.

# Money

"Words can be token words or they can covey symbolism." Morgan explained. "I believe the words they decided to put on this silver dollar were heartfelt by a nation emerging from the trauma of World War I. Take out a paper dollar from your wallet and you will not find the words Liberty or Peace. Whether intentional or not, I think this is symbolic in the change in relationship between citizens and their government in regards to the foundation which is our national economy." Morgan explained.

"How so?" Ed asked.

"Money has a relationship to Liberty," Morgan replied. "Money represents the fruits of your labor. When coins were invented, they represented real value because silver and gold are rare. When this coin was minted, they also printed paper dollars called silver certificates but these could be redeemed for silver, so the paper was merely a convenience since carrying silver money was heavy. In buying and selling with real money, my purchasing habits were my own business and all of the money in the transaction went to the buying and selling. No computer tracked what or where I bought or sold. No bank or credit card company took a percentage of my purchase, and no one was logging my buying habits to develop a profile on me. In that way, money had a stability and freedom now lost. Sure, we can still use cash for small transactions, but more and more we are moving to a computerized world where my business is subject to computer profiling, and where private institutions charge a fee to process the transaction. That clipping of the ticket gets added to the cost of the things I buy. But these things are tangential to your question. The core of your question has to do with integrity of government and money."

"When the government detached silver from the dollar, it introduced a new tax called inflation. When the silver dollar I handed you was minted in 1935, it was worth a dollar in metal and in purchasing power. It was still worth about a dollar in the 1960's. When they removed silver from the dollar, the worth of a paper dollar dropped. Today the metal content of that one dollar coin you are holding is about $14, or put the other way, today's paper dollar is worth about seven cents of that silver dollar. That's a huge drop in the value of paper money, and it means that citizens no longer can count on dollars to give a stable representation of the fruits of their labor. If you save money, it will be worth less when you need to spend it." Morgan said.

"So what you are saying" Ed said, "is that we need to be spenders, not savers, because if we save our cash, it will lose value – that as long as we are consumers, spending and borrowing to spend more, it does not matter; but if we save our money, we lose."

"Sadly, yes." Morgan answered. "Governments began coin money to enable fluidity in the economy. It's easier than barter. When money is based on a stable medium, ordinary citizens can count on their economy; they can trust its basis. When government replaces a stable medium with paper backed by faith in the economy, they have an obligation to assure it will not lose value. As a matter of fact, the US Treasury on their web site explains that *Federal Reserve notes are not redeemable in gold, silver or any other commodity, and receive no backing by anything. The notes have no value for themselves, but for what they will buy.* When the notes keep dropping in value, so they buy less than 10% of what they did prior, then the fundamentals of the national economy change."

"What are the implications of this fundamental change?" Ed asked.

"Essentially," Morgan replied, "money ceases to represent long-term wealth. Putting your savings into money, even earning bank interest, becomes a bad investment. In theory, bank interest should pay more than inflation, but in reality the official measure of inflation no longer reflects my actual experience when I buy goods and services that I need. The money I leave in the bank to earn interest buys less when I take it out."

"I've noticed that as well," Ed observed. "As I have always been on a fixed public sector income pegged to the Consumer Price Index, I find it seems to be misaligned with real costs. Even though my generation placed a high value on saving money, you are suggesting that's a chump's game; that for whatever reason, holding on to cash is not smart. So what is the smart money doing?"

"In times of real inflation," Morgan said, "you will find smart money invests in tangibles. This works for the rich, who can invest in oil futures, pork bellies or gold mines, but it's hard for ordinary citizens. For ordinary folk, the big tangible investment they make is in their home. However, the value of their home is then determined by what happens to their neighborhood and the economy. If the schools fail, the real value of their home fails. Likewise, when the national or global financial systems fail, the ordinary homeowner loses. Today, we are not only facing a deteriorating currency, but an unstable economy. For normal folk to find a tangible investment that allows them to save the fruits of their labor, they need to combine their purchasing power."

Ed looked at the scale model and said "So Villageton is the ultimate tangible investment because it is all around you, every day. You and every citizen of Villageton invest in your life. That's brilliant!"

"Yes", Morgan answered. "It is simple, elegant and comprehensive. It weaves together almost all the tangibles people need in a way that works with the national and global systems to achieve a better outcome. However, it is an unusual investment since most investments realize their value when they are sold. In the case of Villageton, while there always is a resale value, the true value comes in living here, not moving away. The key difference is the comprehensive nature of the life experience. It offers security, opportunity, stimulation, and a good life for all ages and stages in life."

## The 80/20 Local Economy

Ed thought about this idea for a moment, probing it for weaknesses, and then asked, "The fact remains however, that you are a part of the national and global economy. Let's take a worse case scenario and say the national systems collapse, like they did in the 1930's. How much is Villageton dependent on the national economy?"

"To put that answer in context, it may be useful to look at the difference between France and Australia in the Great Depression." Morgan explained. "France hardly noticed, Australia's economy was devastated and its people suffered greatly. The difference came in the way France ran a more local economy. French country food was famous for its flavor, much of which was locally grown and processed. They made their clothing, tools, furniture, and many other essentials for day-to-day life. In those days people did not drive much, as their lives were local. In contrast Australia's economy depended on global trade; when it dried up, no one had money to buy the things they needed. Today, our world operates more on the more risky Australian model."

"So are you saying you have nothing to do with the global economy?" Ed asked.

Morgan replied. "No, I'm saying we have a smarter and safer relationship with the global economy. Unlike the city-states back in Aristotle's time, we are part of a global economy, and we no longer need a local army to defend our village-town from invasion. However, we do need to defend the local economy from the predations of the global economy – not with an army, but by assuring that when global systems fail to deliver, such as we saw with the huge price rise in gasoline or the more recent failure of the banking systems, Villageton is protected."

Ed thought about this for a moment, and his mind clicked, as he made the connection between the ancient city-state and Morgan's term village-town. When ancient Troy was rediscovered, it was found to be about the same size and population as Villageton. However, its walls were to repel invading Greeks, whereas Villageton's walls were to keep pets within and to protect old people and babies from wandering off. There were more layers to this place than he imagined. "So how do you establish a smarter relationship to the global economy?" he asked.

Morgan replied. "To participate in the global economy, we saw the importance of Telepresence. While some businesses still need to be near their customers, suppliers or even competitors, increasingly the convergence of technology means I can physically be here, but have a meeting with you a thousand miles away. It means teams can collaborate or operate sophisticated remote machinery using computer terminals linked by broadband. Many people can now move their businesses anywhere they have good telepresence links, provided there is reasonable access to a major airport, mostly to provide for timely overnight delivery, but also to catch a flight when a face-to-face meeting is necessary. One unique value of telepresence is the fact that our people can have a presence anywhere in the world, so if one region is suffering, they may find business opportunities in another region without having to move their office."

"Our studies suggested at least 20% of the businesses need to be local to global business, *money-importers* as we call them; so we made sure to support these businesses with the best telepresence technology available." Morgan explained. "We also made sure our industrial park and small producer businesses have excellent shipping facilities and that we have good access to global transport when people need to meet face-to-face. Our Villageton bank has correspondent relations internationally, so our local to global businesses can effectively operate in the global economy."

"However," Morgan continued, "it was equally important that for all our basic needs and some of the luxuries that we enjoy, that we establish local businesses that will continue to operate and thrive no matter what happens globally. These local-to-local businesses are driven by *money-turn*, which is based on enlightened self-interest – the simple economic principle of *It's My Money*. What I mean by that is no one tells our citizens how to spend their money, but at each shop an electronic display linked to our intranet tells the local content of any goods or services on offer. Our citizens understand that the more they buy local, the stronger their local economy, and the less vulnerable they are to the ups and downs, and sometimes predatory practices of the global economy. Informed citizens make smart decisions, and they have every right to do so, because it's their money."

"When you go to lunch, you will be supporting a local business... actually quite a few local businesses including the restaurant, the farmers, the cheese-maker, the miller and bakers, the brewer, the fuel plant, the community bank, and so on. As part of the planning for a local economy, Villageton made a concerted effort to weave together essential local industries so it is large enough to be self-sufficing." Morgan explained.

"How did you make a concerted effort, as you call it?" Ed asked.

"Some of the folks attracted to the idea of living in Villageton were very successful business people with strong strategic backgrounds in finance, marketing and business culture. They agreed to form several groups that would focus on identifying realistic industries and businesses that could be supported by 10,000 people, and they then set out to identify people with such businesses, or a passion to start such businesses. They also sourced investment capital based on solid business plans, and put the investors and the plans together. In some cases they would take a capital interest in these emerging businesses to make their involvement more that just words."

## Conviviality and Citizenship

Ed found his head spinning at the level of economic sophistication being described for what in national terms was a very small town. Blandville was far larger, yet it had no such coherent sense of self-preservation, and it was suffering badly for this omission. However, conscious of the time he was taking from Morgan, and yet the desire to learn more, he moved the conversation on. He then said, "I think I now understand the basics of your local economy – what you drew as the foundation in the picture showing the good life. Would you next tell me how you built on this local economy in the planning for Villageton? But first let me check in with Michael as I don't want to be abusing the kindness of my driver. Michael, are you OK with me talking with Morgan at this length? I realize we are supposed to just be stopping for lunch."

Michael smiled and said "Perfectly OK, Ed. In view of how you were feeling this morning as we drove out of Blandville, I would say this is the best thing we could be doing right now. Please, Morgan, go on and do not feel pressured on my behalf."

Morgan thanked him warmly and replied to Ed's question. "We have already talked at some length about citizenship, but in summary it is about being a part of both society and a common locality. People here belong as citizens, and most of them moved here not as a temporary investment but as their permanent home. This is it."

"The next part of the good life is conviviality which comes from the Latin words for *to come together* and *to live*. It is associated with feasting, celebration, enjoying others company. Today we would include the café lifestyle, the travellers' inns, parties, friendly sports events, or a pleasant stroll through the village streets, stopping to greet others and lightly chat. Go into almost any community designed before our present age, and you will find the tavern, the pub, the coffee house or the inn that welcomes members of the public. Thus any design the founding citizens would set out should include an open plaza around which there were places of conviviality. When you go to lunch you will find this a very different experience than say the food court of a shopping mall."

## Artistic and Intellectual Growth

Ed commented. "I can see how that part would not be that difficult, provided you encouraged owner-operator establishments with character and authenticity rather than branded clone-franchises. But how do you foster artistic and intellectual growth?"

"Intentionally." Morgan answered with a smile. "We decided early on that cultural and social enrichment was essential to making Villageton interesting, and the way we did this was to put money behind it. What we created can best be understood as a kernel around which a broader base of artistic and intellectual activity will develop and thrive. The core is found in each plaza, in almost every village, and it is called *The Artist Guild Hall*. Each group of founding citizens for each village was given a generous budget to call for an artist guild hall. We borrowed from Richard Florida's books on the Creative Class in broadly defining *artist*, so it included not only the painters, musicians or actors, but also inventors, designers, engineers, film-makers, and so on. The artists came together to form their guild, to specify what they needed in terms of their hall, and how they would add to the enrichment of the community. In dialogue with the founding citizens of their village, they wrote their own ticket. In order to assure they would never get priced out of Villageton, each member of the guild is given what we call free-base housing for as long as they are an active member of their guild."

"The effect of this approach has exceeded our wildest dreams," Morgan went on. "While not everyone is of the creative class, it became a major stimulant within Villageton. People who never viewed themselves as creative are exposed to creativity every day, and some began to take classes at the guild halls. In addition, once the village themes were established and the guilds were determined, we found that universities and research institutes approached us to see if they could establish branch facilities in Villageton. People saw they could start local businesses that normally would need a much larger city to thrive, but by virtue of the enriched cultural environment would attract the customers they need to remain profitable. Our festivals have become increasingly popular, further stimulating creativity. We have become known as a hothouse for invention, innovation and entrepreneurship, all because of the cross-fertilization that comes from the kernel of intellectual and creative hosting we invited from the onset. It also is proving hugely beneficial to our local economy as Richard Florida predicted in his books on the Creative Class."

"So every village has its own artist guild hall?" Ed asked.

"No, not quite" Morgan answered. "What we call the industrial village, because most of its citizens work in blue-collar jobs in the industrial park, asked if they could have a Sports Club instead. But the other 19 villages do have guild halls."

### Spiritual Development and Fulfillment

Having absorbed these parts of the good-life details, Ed then asked, "I have already asked Agnes about the churches, cathedrals, temples and other religious buildings, so you don't need to explain the details, but tell me how you approached spirituality in a nation that not only does not share a common religion, but has many people who are agnostic or atheistic - sometimes aggressively so."

"We took from Thomas Jefferson." Morgan replied. "He wrote *Religion is a subject on which I have ever been most scrupulously reserved. I have considered it as a matter between every man and his Maker in which no other, and far less the public, had a right to intermeddle.*"

"Religion is personal and a shared experience." Morgan continued. "Thus if a village is formed by founding citizens who wish to share (as opposed to intermeddle) their private religious experience, it is their private money, their homes and their private choice to design their village around their religion. In fact, if you tour Villageton, you will find one village that employs a full-time Catholic priest, yet less than 20% of its citizens consider themselves religious, much less Catholic. What Villageton did was to make a distinction between *religion* and *sacred spaces*. Religion implies a belief system, often a dogma and sometimes a hostility toward other religions that supposedly worship the same Supreme Being. Following Jefferson's lead, Villageton considers religion a domain where Villageton as a semi-public institution shall not meddle."

"However, Villageton considers sacred architecture to be important to many, if not all people, regardless of what they believe. Architecture shapes the environment. In your profession as an architect, buildings or interior spaces can be described as uplifting, inspiring, peaceful, tranquil or hallowed, and we believe for a community to be whole, it needs to have such spaces. For this reason, each village was encouraged to design and set out a sacred space. In the case of villages that formed around their shared religion, that became their consecrated church or temple. In villages that did not, it might be a place that one may visit to experience the sacred on ones own terms. I have to say, that this approach has been consistently well received, even among those who call themselves atheists – to the point where we no longer have any *aggressive* ones as you described them." Morgan observed.

## Green Architecture

"If I may, Morgan, I would like to shift topic, and if I am monopolizing your time, please tell me. You have spoken almost exclusively about the social desires of the Good Life. Today, in my profession, both as planner and architect, green architecture is the hot topic. The professionals getting the attention are those who design carbon-neutral – the green buildings and communities. The young planners are pressing for TOCs – transit oriented communities so we will get out of our cars and into trains and busses. I note you have no cars, but no one seems to brag about car-free in terms of greenhouse gasses. What is the story with green architecture here?" Ed asked.

Morgan laughed and then said. "If tomorrow I invented a machine that swept all the excess greenhouse gasses from the air, and kept the skies clean so we could burn all the rest of the coal, oil and gas remaining in the Earth's crust, would we have solved the many challenges facing humanity? I realize that is a rhetorical question, but a serious one. So I need to answer your question in two parts."

"The first part is to say that as much as possible, we selected designs that do not subject Nature to concentrations of substances we extracted from the Earth's crust, or substances produced by society, nor do we seek to degrade Nature by physical means. Those standards came from an international body known as *The Natural Step*. What that means is we seek truly green architecture, rather than what is today called greenwash. For example, we designed these buildings to provide shelter for centuries, and we designed Villageton so people do not need transport. Commuter trains and busses are not green; they are just less polluting than cars. What your planners call TOCs, we call tweaking a failing system."

Morgan continued. "The second part of the answer is to cite the problem that comes when one tries to design communities in response to a negative. Let me ask you a question. Do you recall the pivotal Congressional Act that changed America to a transport-based society?"

"Funny you should ask that Morgan," Ed replied, "as I presume you are speaking about the Interstate Highway Act of 1956. Indeed I do, and as Michael was driving me from Blandville this morning, I spoke of it. My whole career has been in suburban planning that was originally developed as a way to keep America from relapsing into a Depression after the war. It was crucial to America's growth and in large measure is why this country went from a weak country to the pre-eminent super power – the only one running under a democratic system of government. I was telling Michael of the irony that the pivotal law that changed America – the Act that funded our system of interconnected freeways – was sponsored by Senator Al Gore Senior, father of Vice President Al Gore Junior, who is now reinventing himself as the spokesman for the dire peril of human induced climate change. I've often asked myself how is it possible that such smart men like Senator Gore Senior manage to come up with such bad answers?"

Morgan smiled, delighted with Ed's depth. It was apparent that Ed was well read and formed his own views. He then said, "I often give this lecture when people want to learn about VillageTowns, but rarely do I have an audience that knows the subject better than I do. In answer to your question, a couple of years ago a Congressman who voted for the Interstate Highway Act of 1956 wrote a public letter to his grandchildren. Now in his late 80's, former Congressman Stewart Udall, later Secretary of the Interior, described that vote as a colossal error. He wrote *As a freshman congressman in 1955, I regrettably voted with my unanimous colleagues for the Interstate Highway Program. All of us acted on the shortsighted assumption that cheap oil was superabundant and would always be available. This illusion began to unravel in the 1970s, and it haunts Americans today.*"

"That's the problem, Ed. We see something that threatens our way of life, such as the risk of a relapse into the Great Depression or today's threat of Climate Change caused by human activity, we focus on it, and we come up with a plan that solves it. It then takes on a life of its own, as vested interests discover how much money is to be made, until it becomes a beast of a problem. What we don't do is look at the whole picture, to ask all the questions and make sure we are not glossing over inopportune facts that may spawn new and different threats to our children's way of life. To be frank, I am becoming worried today how the issue of greenhouse gasses and climate change seem to be following that same pattern. For sure, we need to change how we live; but if we focus *all* our attention on reducing the amount of $CO_2$ back to some percentage of 1990 levels, we may find we trigger new threats to life because we approached the challenge linearly rather than holistically," Morgan concluded.

## Alarmists vs Skeptics - Who's right about Climate Change?

"I am curious Morgan," Ed asked, "to know your personal view on the Climate Change. Are you an *alarmist* or a *skeptic*, if I may quote terms used in a book by McCrystal and Morgan called *Poles Apart, who's right about climate change?*"

Morgan sighed and answered the question. "Neither. If it is important to classify me, consider me a Hobbit. I am a small fellow in a very large world where lots of big, important experts clash and two opposing sides try to persuade me of their truth. I operate on what I experience and on common sense. So I ask, do cars pollute? Yes. Will they melt the ice caps? I don't know. But I don't need to know because polluting is enough to say No. My reality is local. Villageton takes 6,000 commuter cars off the road, increasing quality of life and lowering our daily cost of living. We try to avoid polluting the farm lands, the rivers and the air. We use less energy and most of it comes from the sun, either directly or indirectly. My reality is Villageton. When we built it, we sought to tread lightly on earth, so no matter what the final verdict on climate change, future generations will judge us part of the solution, not the problem."

Ed smiled at the Hobbit description, and said, "That is a humble answer, but as long as I am on a roll, let me ask you another question relating to your politics. Where do I place you on the political spectrum? Usually, the right wing uses words like freedom and citizenship, but then they follow it up by extolling the free market as the answer to everything. In your explanation, you seem to base a considerable amount of Villageton's design on those principles, except you tend to view the global free market as potentially predatory and dangerous. On the other hand, you also seem to be talking about caring for people and the environment, and these are typically political platforms of the left wing and the greens. So what are you; *red, blue* or *green?*"

## Left and Right Wing Politics

Morgan laughed. "I grew up when TV, newspapers and my box camera photos all were black & white. In those days, you were either a good guy in a white hat, or a bad guy in a black hat. I try to be one of the good guys, and I reckon the news business sold their soul when they shifted to color. I have little use for the left and right the media loves to shove in our face nowadays. The media seems to love setting up conflict, or trivializing people into *us* versus *them* groups like red states versus blue. They can always count on someone looking for their 15 minutes of fame to fill their airtime."

"If by left wing you mean Socialism, with centralized control, then no, Villageton is not there. All property in Villageton is privately owned. Personal property, such as homes or workplaces, is owned by the individual. Shared property is owned by the Villageton Council which is a corporation 100% owned by the citizens of Villageton as stockholders. Shared property such as the streets and plazas are open to the public, including visitors as long as they are law-abiding. The means of production are privately owned by private businesses run by the citizens of Villageton. Services better run for the common good, such as the Villageton car rental company in the motorpool, are run by the Villageton Council as a tax-paying, for-profit enterprise. Any corporation who wants to set up competition to the VT Car Rental, for example, is free to do so, but given that the profits from the VT business return to the stockholders, it's unlikely the VT stockholders – also known as our citizens would rent from a competitor. Think of it as enlightened self-interest." Morgan explained.

"However," Morgan went on, "if you then seek to presume that Villageton subscribes to a right wing ethos that calls itself Capitalism you would also be off the mark, but not for the reasons you might think. The problem is that while the pundits, media and politicians use noble words like the free market to extol the value of what they call capitalism, the reality in front of our face is different."

Ed was looking forward to what Morgan would say next. He was feeling more alert than he had in years, and he saw Morgan was about to challenge presumed beliefs.

## Corporatism

"While boffins, bloggers and talk-back radio hosts keep ranting on about socialism, communism and capitalism, in fact we have seen the emergence of a new "ism" called *Corporatism*. Emerging out of capitalism, the corporations become stronger than individuals and often stronger than nations or states. *United We Stand* took on a new meaning under corporatism as one corporation uses its united power to advance its own interests at the expense of the public and individuals."

Morgan continued. "The world today is run under the principles of corporatism. Rather than fight it, we joined it. Villageton is a corporation owned by about 4,000 families and individuals so we can stand tall in this new world of corporate dominance. Like every corporation, ours serves the interests of its stockholders, and it has sufficient clout to fight off attacks from hostile corporations. Unlike the old days, where such fights involved soldiers and battlefields, now we use lawyers and courtrooms to defend our people and way of life. We use wholesale buying groups to lower our citizens' cost of living and limit non-recyclable packaging. We use corporate law to structure our governance, so we are not vulnerable to manipulation by the legislature. While we call our CEO *the mayor* and we call our Board of Directors, *the Villageton Council*, we operate under the same rules as any corporation. We have both a for-profit arm that pays taxes, and a tax-exempt non-profit arm."

"I'm not quite following you, Morgan" Ed interrupted. "How did Villageton go from being a developer project to a citizen-owned corporation?"

"Good question," Morgan said. "What they did was form a *shifting control company*. We began with a group of investors that we call The Company because the word *company* used to mean *a group who shares bread* and we felt that was appropriate to what the investors bring to the table. They provide the investment capital for the Village Organizing Company or VOC as we call it. The VOC is funded with a mandate to build one VillageTown – in our case Villageton. At that point it is not a democracy but a profit-making business. However, it enrolls future property owners, the citizens who will own the village-town when built. They have control over their own future through the Dynamic Engagement design process, but do not have control over the VOC, except indirectly. This is not unreasonable, because at that point, it is the investors and its VillageTown company that has put up the money and invested the hard work."

"So what you are saying is the citizens become more influential as they become more vested?" Ed said. "How are their interests protected before they fully vest?"

"Yes, you've got it." Morgan said. "Obviously, it would be chaos trying to run a development project with 4,000 bosses, and it would be inappropriate in-so-far as they do not make the final payment on their home until the deed or title passes to them when everything is built. But in order to assure checks and balances, the Village Forum work at arms-length to the VOC. People sign up with the Village Forum, and when they hit a critical mass when it looks like a village-town will happen, the forum sets up a kind of *buyers group*. The investor's company is required to fund the forum's buyers group that retains lawyers and negotiators to assure the citizens' interests are paramount during development."

"Then the VOC works similar to a hi-tech company or a college seeking to build a new campus that includes residences. As a corporation it negotiates with local governments to find land and get proper rezoning and other concessions. It is run as a business that represents the interests of 10,000 people."

Ed broke in, "It sounds a bit complicated, but I can see the sense of it. I can see how it would look from the local government's perspective, where it is like winning the billion dollar corporation decision to select their jurisdiction to build the campus. I can see where *campus* is a good word for it."

Morgan nodded and continued. "I described it as a shifting control company, and by this I mean that at one point the VOC morphs into the citizen-owned corporation. During development, when the VOC works as a developer, the citizens have control of their *future*, but not of the VOC. When all is built, the VOC pays the investors for their risk and allocates a portion of profits to build future VillageTowns. The VOC then morphs into the VillageTown corporation, what we call the Villageton Council, with an asset base, a constitution, an agreement with the County on who pays for what, and stockholders' agreement based on checks and balances. The VOC owned the streets, the greenbelt, public buildings like the guildhalls and motorpool, and it leaves these assets, plus millions in the bank, in the asset base, so when the private citizens takes title to their homes and workplaces, they also get a stock certificate of considerable value. However, they cannot sell that certificate unless they sell the house. In this way, the stock is not liquid, but has real-life value." Morgan concluded.

Ed took in a deep breath. "I'm not a businessman, and I confess some of what you just covered about stock and assets will need a few repetitions before I would get it, but it sounds like it works which is always a good test. But tell me a bit more about corporatism, as this is not something I have thought much about."

"Corporatism is neutral," Morgan went on. "Good corporations are a brilliant way to organize people to get things done; indeed the wealth of the world would not have been possible without such organizations. Bad ones may be the death of the world; toxic to humanity, powerful, large enough to sway governments to let them do bad things. Some corporations are run like dictatorships, where employees must do as they are told or face the boot. Others are run brilliantly where everyone working there loves it, and give it their all."

"Over the past half century, the powers under corporate law have grown, while at the same time, the ability of government to govern has diminished. I should qualify that because it is not universal." Morgan noted. "I remember once meeting a high ranking Chinese official touring Villageton who said: *In America business runs government while in China government runs business.* In my view, both are a problem, government should regulate business to protect the common wealth and public interest, and business should mind its own business and keep its nose out of government where vested interest defeats public interest. The interesting part is that America calls itself a capitalist democracy and China calls itself a communist state, yet in terms of corporatism, both are playing the same game."

Ed thought about what Morgan just said, and began to appreciate the complexity of the global economy. While America fought a Cold War against Communism for over fifty years, most products for sale in American stores are either made in a communist country or contain components from there. He summarized this by saying to Morgan, "It's not the same world that it was in the 1950's, is it?"

Morgan replied, "Eisenhower warned us back in the 1950's but since then corporations have gotten bigger and smarter, each vying to take a larger portion of the consumer's income. But interestingly, in contrast, corporate buyers get better prices from the same vendors, often substantially better because they have purchasing power. They can buy wholesale or if volumes are great enough they can go directly to the source and purchase to their own specifications. So we took a close look at this, and saw that it was smarter to set ourselves up as a corporation as well as a community. In one sense, we pay our corporation to run our town, but we also buy through the corporation so the profits that otherwise would leak out, stay within our local economy and reduce what we need to pay to run the town. Because we own the corporation, and no one can buy stock unless they buy a building in Villageton, we realize the financial benefits."

"Can you give me some examples?" Ed asked.

"Yes, I can. Morgan replied. "Health care, for one. One benefit of working for a corporation is medical benefits, including insurance against catastrophic medical costs and ongoing health checkups. Many of the citizens of Villageton are either self-employed or working in very small businesses of less than a dozen employees. Usually such people must pay more or get fewer benefits. But a corporation with 4,000 families can negotiate for better terms and services. We do the same with home and life insurance. Any Villageton citizen is free to buy insurance from anyone, but with our corporate buying power, our plans are the cheapest and best. In home insurance we also negotiated lower prices because our buildings are class-two noncombustible, built to the strongest earthquake standards, and our crime rate is considerably lower."

"Good idea," Ed commented. "Another example?

"Litigation." Morgan said. "Villageton retains a team of courtroom and patent lawyers both to protect the business interests of our citizens and the collective interest of our community. For example, we decided that the inventions and patents that come out of Villageton are valuable to the whole community, even if they are owned by individuals who profit by them. Scientists, engineers and inventors often get exploited by predatory industry vultures, so we decided it was important to protect them and take an agreed percentage of their long-term capital gain. As a result, we attract some really bright, inventive people, and our local economy thrives by their presence. It's a voluntary program, but almost everyone who needs it, uses it."

As a retired civil servant, Ed found these concepts mind-blowing as his daughter would say. He said to Morgan. "Amazing! What you describe would be impossible to be provided by a local government, yet these would be standard benefits or functions within a corporation. The difference is that this corporation is not providing those services for employees or the corporate body, but for the stockholders who run independent businesses and who also want local governance. You're right, the 20th century models of capitalism, socialism, communism and fascism don't fit at all."

Morgan laughed, delighted at how Ed was trying to make it fit. "Let me try to summarize centuries of political thought on *isms* in a few lines...

- Communism is *us versus them, using violence* to take and hold ideological power
- Socialism is *us versus them, using bureaucracy* to take and hold ideological power
- Capitalism is *me using them to gain power* through capital investment and ownership
- Fascism is a *national form of cult using violence* to take and hold egotistical power
- Corporatism is *us organizing them to further our pecuniary interest*
- Consumerism is *them using me to further their pecuniary interest*
- Reality is *me among us surrounded by them, all on one planet*, where each of us may choose to create, maintain, degrade or destroy"

"I realize this is an over-simplification," Morgan laughed again, "but I find it useful to explain where we are coming from. Most of the 20th century isms are about who gets to hold power. Villageton is too small to have a need for ideology about power. We have citizens who hold the full range of political views, from far left to far right, but on a day-to-day basis, most decision-making and action is pragmatic.

Ed found this to be more than his mind could hold all at once. He was unsure how to respond, so he asked Morgan to continue with his theme on corporatism.

"It's really very simple, Ed. It's our money; it's our lives. Remember, it's a lot cheaper to save a dollar than to earn one, so we begin by lowering our cost of living with an intent of improving the quality of our lives. We did not make the rules that benefit corporations, we simply decided to use them to protect and advance our interests."

"And your interests are more than just profits, they include the good life." Ed said.

"Yes" Morgan replied. "As you can see the idea of VillageTowns is not driven by isms, but by looking at what works. Corporate law is stronger than local government law, so we see that it makes sense to use it."

"Can you give me an example of what you mean?" Ed asked.

"I can," Morgan answered. "If the voters put a slate of politicians in power and they sign a contract with a corporation, that contract remains binding no matter who comes to power. But if the same politicians agree to do something for their constituents, the next election it can all be overturned. If our 8,000 registered voters gain a concession from the county council or the state, it can be overturned after the next election. But if that same government signs a contract with Villageton as a corporation it remains binding until both parties agree to change it, or a court overturns it on legal grounds. Because our Villageton corporation is run by professionals, the governments actually prefer working with us because there are no surprises."

### We Hold These Truths to be Self-evident

Ed then chose to move the subject slightly. "We may be getting very far afield from what was supposed to be an explanation about how Villageton came to be, but I am finding this discussion to be challenging in a good way. When Michael was driving me out of Blandville I made the connection between Aristotle's Good Life, and Jefferson's famous words in the Declaration of Independence where he wrote *We hold these truths to be self-evident, that all men are created equal, that they are endowed by their Creator with certain unalienable rights, that among these are life, liberty and the pursuit of happiness.* We all know those words, especially *life, liberty* and *happiness*, but we rarely seem to figure out how to apply them to our day-to-day life. I am beginning to get the sense that in Villageton, you have done so. I would like hear how."

## The Meaning of Liberty and Freedom

"It's helpful to begin by making a distinction between liberty and freedom," Morgan replied. In my view, liberty is the sum total of all freedoms and rights within the framework of citizenship – in other words, the freedoms that come with being a citizen of a free and just land. You cannot speak of liberty outside of citizenship."

Ed broke in. "Can you expand on that? I don't completely follow you."

"Sure", Morgan replied. "Politicians in this country use the word *liberty* a lot, but I'm not sure how many of them actually think about its meaning. I hear it used more as a slogan or a word on a bumper sticker. In fact liberty is a word that has meaning within a social order – when people live together in close proximity. What I mean by that is that it's both about people and place. If we live in a village or town, the place is fixed; sociologists call it the common locality. But in the days when people were nomadic, the place was the campground they set up, or the caravan when they were moving. They had a social agreement that kept them together and safe, and the concept of liberty emerges out of that social order."

Ed found once again, Morgan was shedding new light on concepts he thought he understood. He asked Morgan "How did liberty emerge from the social order?"

Morgan gave his view. "To oversimplify it, the first social unit was the extended family. As food production required more cooperation and family size grew, the social order expanded, becoming a tribe, often run by the elders. But then, as conflict or war arose with other tribes, the best commander, the strongest warrior emerged to become the chief. Once he solidified his rule, that chief or his descendents began to control his *subjects* for reasons other than to serve the best interest of the tribe. The lust for power kicked in, that heady feeling that comes from controlling others. It's a curious thing that in our language, we don't have a word for this drive."

"I don't follow you on that last comment; would you explain it?" Ed asked.

At this question, Morgan smiled, aware that with Ed's sharp mind and curiosity, this line of conversation could open up all sorts of new directions and Michael may never get to lunch. "If you had bible classes when you were young, one of the things they taught about was the seven deadly sins or vices. Each of them were short, mostly four or five letter words."

Ed did remember and recited: "Lust, greed, gluttony, sloth, wrath, envy and pride."

"Right," Morgan said. "Each of those vices is considered a vice or a sin, because it possesses the individual in a sort of crazy-making way, making the person unpleasant but also disrupting the social order and often making other peoples lives miserable. But, here's the curious part. When we look at hierarchies, organizations such as government, corporations and institutions, we find certain people vie for leadership driven by a similar sort of vice. They crave power like a drug, and will do anything to get it, including destroying other people, and then use force or make rules to hold on to power. They allocate perks, privileges and pay to concentrate their power; they control who gets to talk to whom about what. They shape what people come to accept as reality, but they do so not for the social good, but to keep themselves in power."

"Having worked in local government for over forty years, I certainly have seen that craving kick in many times, both in our appointed and elected leaders." Ed observed.

Morgan acknowledged Ed's comment and continued. "What I find interesting is the absence of a vice-word like *lust* or *greed* to describe that head space. Power can be an addiction. Of course, when the Church promoted its list of seven deadly vices, it was a hierarchy where to get to the top the unnamed vice would be useful, which probably explains why it remained unnamed. Never-the-less, it is this eighth deadly vice that creates the need to articulate liberty."

Ed saw how Morgan had brought the conversation back to his original question about the origins of liberty. "You were speaking about lust for power taking over."

"Yes," Morgan said. "At one point the people doing the work get annoyed as the chief overly meddles in their lives, over-taxing the fruits of their labor or telling them how they must live. Those people demand limits on such interference and controls. Eventually those limits become codified into a list of freedoms. Collectively those freedoms are liberty. In securing them, these subjects become citizens."

"So what do you mean by freedom?" Ed asked.

"Freedom is an ancient principle. The concept of freedom has a noble lineage. Freedom comes from the same Indo-European root as the words *friend, dear* and *peace*. True friendship is the one social relationship that must be entirely free. There is no contract made between friends in order to have a friendship. Freedom is a social word; it is meaningless outside of society. Even the individual who crosses the frontier into the wilderness to be free, does so in the context of escaping the bonds of the society left behind. When I use the word freedom, I use it closer to the meaning of friend than *buy one, get two free*."

"Noble words" Morgan continued, "like freedom, are constantly being hijacked by people who want to put spin on ignoble desires – for example those who extol the freedom of choice when what they mean is the right to choose between Pepsi and Coke. Freedom is the ability of an individual and a group to live their lives as they choose, not in a way that is destructive but in a way that allows them to become who they are without others improperly seeking to control them. The way I see it, as I said earlier, there is a continuum with freedom on one end and slavery on the other. By slavery, I include wage slaves such as your son who is afraid if he loses his job, the debt he has taken on will come crashing down on him and may put his family out on the street. He is not a slave at the deep end of the continuum scale, but he is not entirely free either; he is desperate."

Ed blanched slightly. "That is a very harsh term, wage-slave and an even harsher one when you give the example of my son, Jared, but I fear you make a valid point. I am reminded of Thoreau writing *lives of quiet desperation*".

"I am sorry, Ed if I sounded callous just then," Morgan said apologetically, "that was not my intent. But to answer your question, I see Life, Liberty and Happiness as three qualities of a way of living, rather than three different principles. Let me explain:"

"Life is the miracle of our planet. Its richness is beyond the capacity of any human to know. Human life can and should be the most wonderful of journeys as we are born, grow, learn, love, create, become wise and when our time has come, to pass on."

"Yet this wonder can only come with Liberty. We cannot enjoy the miracle of life if other people or institutions interfere in our lives, interfering in what is not their business. The perpetual tension between liberty and governance is defining that line between minding ones own business and meddling in the affairs of others.

"Finally," Morgan said, "when Jefferson wrote of happiness, he encompassed both enjoyment and joy. Conviviality brings *enjoyment*, whereas the higher artistic, intellectual and spiritual pursuits can bring *joy* as one grows as a human being. We can be miserable in those pursuits, but like being in an unhappy marriage or career, we must then ask *what's the point?* If we create an environment that fosters conviviality and the higher pursuits, we may then pursue happiness. No guarantees, but it sure beats the reality of being stuck in traffic, in an awful job or substituting television for the real experience of our heart, mind and soul. So, we considered these things when Villageton was being established. We sought to design buildings and open space in a way that provides the physical environment that facilitates life, liberty and pursuit of happiness."

Ed found he needed to write down what Morgan had just explained. *Life is the miracle of our planet. It is the most wonderful of journeys. But for it to be wonderful, it must be lived with liberty – the sum total of all freedoms, and the purpose of human life within a free society is to pursue the good life, those four elements that enable people to realize happiness.* It made sense; it was based on ancient wisdom both western and eastern, but especially on the founding principles of America; and Morgan explained it as the basis for their planning and design. He then asked, "This all sounds perfect. Is Villageton a utopia?"

### VillageTowns Are Not Utopia

Morgan was surprised by the question, but then he laughed. "Definitely not. Not in theory, nor in practice. I should be clear that Villageton is not some ideal place where all live free and happy lives. It is not a Camelot where snow is forbidden until winter, it only rains after dark and by morning fog must disappear. Villageton has all sorts of people, bringing all sorts of views, politics, damage and agendas – in short a fairly representative cross section of society. It has no ideology, and it has no grand vision set out by some great leader. It is a culture, not a cult. In fact each village-town around the world has a very different culture because each one is the sum total of the people who live there, reflecting who they are and what they create."

"What makes Villageton different is careful attention to checks and balances within a corporate structure, balancing public and private space, with design details that reduce the aggravation that otherwise makes it harder for people to get along."

Ed broke in, "Can you give me some examples?"

### How Design can Protect Liberty

"Yes, I can," Morgan replied. "In corporate structure the governance system in Villageton is based on checks and balances. Someone once said that Utopias always fail because they do not plan for human corruption. Here we presume human corruption is inherent in any gathering of people, so we make sure that corruption cannot easily be hidden from public scrutiny. The founding documents spread power out in a way that assures no one can take over in a way that does not serve the public interest. Things do get out of whack from time to time, but they always come right."

In designing space we found different cultures need different balances of private and public space, and the biggest complaint of people who grew up in small towns was gossip – the lack of privacy. So you will find private spaces throughout Villageton, including space in homes and in the Greenbelt, places where you will look around and realize you are the only one there. Then we also design for vibrant public space, most notably the plazas, where each one is remarkably different, with its own look and feel. Each plaza has its own culture, which also tends to defeat boredom."

"Finally," Morgan explained, "we have design details such as walls between homes made thick so no noise can be heard from next door. Also, in studying attached housing we found narrow buildings had two outside flash points for neighbor conflict... the back fence and the front yard, so we used a different design with no flash points. While the streets and plazas are the place for public life, both homes and the Greenbelt are designed with private space. Wider connecting streets are public space, but if someone wants to walk to the Greenbelt, for example, and not meet a lot of people, the very narrow footpaths provide that private space outdoors."

By this time, Morgan figured Ed would have just about as many words as could be said, and it would be time now for him to see it in real life. The theory is helpful in understanding what one is looking at, but there is no replacement for a non-derivative experience. He began to wrap up the conversation by saying:

"Ed, we began this part of our conversation talking about freedom and liberty. Here in Villageton people are more free in very practical terms because its local economy intentionally lowers the cost of living and therefore lowers unhealthy pressures on everyone. It maintains more diverse opportunities to earn a living, so people like your son have more choice of occupation. Further, the community is structured so its citizens own and control most of the resources that affect their lives. If the world economy tanks, for sure they will suffer. But they will get through because what they need is under their own control. Unlike the survivalist who establishes an armed compound on the side of a wilderness mountain, and who therefore thinks himself free, Villageton is a contract among citizens who unite to stand tall."

"If the citizens of Villageton are happier, and in my experience they are, it is because it is a more supportive place and a more culturally and socially enriched society. The stresses placed on people and families in what we call *the outside world*, break people and break families. Here in Villageton the inherent design causes less stress. It's safer to raise children here. Parents get relief by sharing the load. Old people have a role; they are needed and feel wanted. Young people have role models and when it is time for them to stand on their own, there are jobs and homes they can afford to buy. The creative people are not only appreciated here, but are supported in their calling in life – they can make a living here pursuing their art and afford to remain here. And what is most amazing about this is the price of admission. For the founding citizens of Villageton, the average cost of all this was about the same as the average home in the suburbs... and they save money because they don't need to drive." Morgan concluded.

Ed saw it was time for Morgan to go, and he was also looking forward to seeing Villageton with very different eyes than when he had walked to the Visitor Center with Michael less than an hour earlier. He returned Morgan's silver dollar to him and thanked him for a most enlightening and challenging briefing session. "Not only have I shaken off the gloom I was feeling this morning, you have introduced an optimism I have not felt for years – perhaps not since the early 1960's. Thank you so much for taking the time."

"The pleasure was mine," Morgan said. "I do brief visitors on Villageton from time to time, but rarely do I meet someone who subjects my briefings to such clear and evaluative an eye. I enjoyed it, and hope you enjoy seeing Villageton. If I may recommend it, rather than just eating lunch here, have a guided tour. There is a lot to see." With that, Morgan shook hands with Ed and Michael and thanked Agnes for calling him over.

Agnes stepped forward and asked Ed if he would like to tour Villageton. "I would", Ed replied, "but I have a driver here who is halfway through a four hour drive to our destination, and while we are stopping for lunch, I would not want to impose any further on his time." At this, Michael spoke up and indicated that would not be a problem. "Except for this one job, I have nothing on for the day, and would be delighted to accompany you on a tour. Let's have lunch and see the town". Agnes smiled, picked up the phone and made a call.

While waiting, Ed looked at wall displays that contained magnetic cards featuring what were called Pattern Cards. According to the signs, these were used in a planning process called Dynamic Engagement. Ed was familiar with Christopher Alexander's 1977 book *A Pattern Language* and he saw that each card was a pattern from the book. Then some others with a different color code looked like they must have been patterns developed by the citizens of Villageton during their planning process. Looking more carefully, he saw that each card had a person's name printed on it and a telephone number. The explanatory notes said that one participant who was particularly passionate about a particular pattern would take ownership of it, to make sure it was not overlooked during the planning process.

He smiled and thought to himself, 'a lot more to learn'.

# Chapter 4

## Sophia – The Tour

Within a few minutes, an attractive young woman with long dark hair, apparently a university student arrived, and introduced herself as Ed's guide. In a lovely European accent he could not quite place, she said, "My name is Sophia, and I am a third year student doing my year-abroad here in Villageton," she said. "I have been here about six months, and still find so many new things to discover. Let's begin with finding you a place to eat. Do you have any preferences?"

"I've always loved Italian food," Ed replied, "and I saw that one of the plazas looked very much like the architecture of Tuscany." I too did a year abroad when I was a student. I studied architecture in Florence, living in a restored medieval castle in the nearby town of Fiesole where I had the time of my life."

"Great choice," replied Sophia. "The Italian village – that's what it is called – has both first and second generation Italian chefs, including some trained in Slow Food in Italy. I am confident you will find some flavors that are new to you."

The walk over to the Italian village was short. While there were side streets that could have taken hours to stroll, in Villageton almost every destination was within a ten-minute walk. Sophia explained that for the most part the layout includes:

- One central square large enough to hold all ten-thousand population so they could see and hear speakers on the Town Hall balcony.
- Twenty village plazas, considerably smaller, where the public life of each plaza played out, surrounded by the businesses that have the highest foot traffic.
- Primary market streets where people who operated businesses with moderate customer foot traffic would have their workplaces on the ground floor, and then live above or behind.
- Secondary streets exclusively residential, although home offices that did not attract foot traffic are permitted
- Foot paths suitable for walking only.

Sophia pointed to small side streets, and explained. "While there are direct routes to get to places rapidly, these are another set of streets that one can walk in labyrinth fashion. You can walk for two hours or more without backtracking. Many people use the labyrinth routes for taking walks after work, visiting different plazas for a change of scenery. With 20 villages, each with its own character, it can be a bit like traveling from one country to another all within an evening stroll."

## New Urbanism

As Ed looked, he was reminded of an architectural movement called the New Urbanism, and while he appreciated that Sophia was not an architectural student, he thought he would give it a try and ask her. "This walkable design and mixed use reminds me of the principles of New Urbanism and their sustainable communities," he said. "Are you familiar with New Urbanism, and if so, how is this different?"

Sophia responded brightly, as she wrote a paper on the new urbanism and Villageton as part of her studies. "Yes, I am familiar with the ten principles of urbanism, and I would say that in many ways, Villageton is aligned with them. However, they come from a different perspective, I would say."

"How so?" Ed asked.

"Well, first of all – and I don't wish to offend you in saying this Ed – the promoters of new urbanism are people in your profession... planners, architects and designers. The sad fact is that they are relatively powerless in bringing about the changes they seek. They want to see changes in things like transportation policy, lending policy, safety policy and regulations that favor suburban sprawl. Policy is driven by money not planners. Planners would like to be in charge, but in fact the politicians who make the laws do so in response to pressure and incentives. So if the real estate development industry as well as the automobile, petroleum, retailing and franchising industries pressure for rules that favor their money-making, the planners have difficulty speaking louder to get the rules changed. The industry drives policy not the technicians."

"So what you are saying," Ed broke in "explains why Morgan focused his briefing not on sustainable development but purchasing power and the good life."

"Yes," Sophia replied, amused at how differently Americans conversed, finishing other people's sentences for them. "The new urbanism movement has done a wonderful technical job setting out both principles and then processes to get there, but because they are mostly in the technical professions, they fail to get what you might call *traction*. Money is traction. Purchasing power is traction. If one wants to align the principles of urbanism with purchasing power, it must come from the people who will live there, because the developers in the industry make enough money – or did until recently – by not changing the suburban sprawl formula. Developers know the rules, they know who to pay to get it done, and until recently what they built sells so they make their profits. Why should they change that to satisfy the new urbanists?"

"You make a very good point there, Sophia." Ed said. "While the ideas may be good, they may take longer to put in effect because there is no incentive to change. But other than that, is Villageton new urbanism with traction?"

"Yes and no", Sophia answered, pleased that she was able to use information she had studied for a school paper in a real conversation. "New Urbanism seeks to change the industry, therefore it must try to address many different situations. A VillageTown has the luxury of *focus* - one project at a time. In this way, it acts more like a developer; it is the industry changing itself. In doing so it first asks *Why do we build communities?* Its development brief focuses on the social pursuits asking how capital investment, design, the local economy and governance can foster the good life, because that is what its stakeholders, its future citizens seek. In contrast, when I read the ten principles of new urbanism, the tenth said that if the nine first technical principles of sustainable development are followed, quality of life will follow."

"In planning Villageton, its organizing company saw the need to go much further than presuming that the technical design matters will result in a long-term durable local economy that can then foster the social pursuits they call the good life. So instead of a single principle that talks about quality of life, Villageton went deeper to understand how money and investment can work toward the timeless purpose of the good life. It invested in very specific public buildings and adopted a governance system that uses checks and balances to enable its citizens to protect their community from the scourges destroying our cities and suburbs. It looked at our failing national and global systems with eyes wide open and then asked how to implement local systems not so vulnerable when those large systems fail to deliver on their promises. These are luxuries we can afford because Villageton sought not to change the national rules on habitat, but only to gain approval for its citizens to build one real development."

"That is a clear distinction." Ed observed. "Are there more differences?"

"Another point of difference is how Villageton pursued *character and authenticity* in streetscape design and feel." Sophia replied. "Villageton looked at wonderful historical towns and found each building reflected the character of its first owner, not a same-schooled architect. It's a subtle difference, but somehow the early showcases for new urbanism looked and felt too perfect. It was no accident that Jim Carrey made *The Truman Show* in the new urbanism showcase of Seaside Florida. Character comes from individual personality, sufficient funds, local artisans, local resources, and time. Here we asked if one could compress time but keep the others and still get character and authenticity. The answer is yes, but only if each building's shape and facade reflects the personality of the first owner and each village reflect the values of its community, not the vision of a master planner. To compress time, one has to start not with architects but with a community of citizens defining their own vision of their place. Then within the framework of a design code, and with architect and design assistance, they set out the design brief for their own homes and workplaces. So Villageton started with its future citizens rather than build an new urbanist design that is then sold to consumers."

"That's a difference in process, what about in results?" Ed asked.

Sophia found herself enjoying Ed's challenging questions. He was a good listener and a clear thinker, she thought. "One difference relates to *transport*. New Urbanism tries to tame the automobile, to slow cars down, to make cars fit in the common locality. Villageton said you can have machine-scale or human-scale but if you put them together, human-scale loses. They concluded cars are too big, too fast and too dangerous especially for children playing in the streets. So they adopted what Christopher Alexander called a *Local Transport Area*, keeping cars in the motorpool for outside use, but not driving inside the villages. In this, we are like a big shopping mall," Sophia laughed. "You drive your car to the outside, then walk in the pedestrian mall streets. The difference is that our mall has residences, work places, schools – everything our citizens need day-to-day. Locally, we commute without cars or busses."

"I'm impressed. Thank you, Sophia." Ed said. "So... where are we walking to?"

Sophia smiled to herself, pleased she had passed a real-life test in explaining New Urbanism and Villageton to Ed. "Our first destination is the Italian village. It was founded by about 200 families, some of them first generation from Italy, others of Italian extraction, and others with no Italian ancestry, who simply love the Tuscan way of life, its architecture, food and its sense of design. As it happened, the first three village coordinators all proposed ethnic villages... Italian, Greek and Celtic."

### The Role of the Village Coordinator

Hearing a new word, Ed asked "What is a village coordinator?"

"The person who calls together a village." Sophia replied. "I should explain that the way a village-town gets started is someone volunteers with the Village Forum to become a Town Coordinator. Such a person does not need to have a specific skill base, such as your skills in Town Planning, but they do need to be passionate about the idea, work well with people and be well enough organized to make it happen. The Town Coordinator then begins to seek out twenty Village Coordinators, one for each of the twenty villages and each village coordinator defines their village's core theme."

"A village should have about 500 people, give or take 250, and if you figure the average household has about two and a half people, that works out to about 200 homes. So each Village Coordinator needs to recruit about 200 families, some of which may be large, and some may be a single person, all of whom collectively become the founders of that Village. The Village Coordinator proposes the general theme of their village. In fact in our village-town, in addition to the Italian, Greek and Celtic villages, we have a Chinatown, an Indian village, a German village and a Hispanic village. The other villages are quite a mix of themes and if you have time, I will try to show you all of them," she offered. Ed looked interested so she looked down and said:

"I'm glad to see you have sturdy walking shoes, because otherwise we need to rent an NEV - a neighborhood electric vehicle, which is like a golf cart with a stylish weatherproof body. If you look over there, up the street you will see an NEV and an electric motor scooter at that charging station. Hop in, swipe a registered bank card, and drive off. They don't move above a brisk walking pace, but for people with bags or who can't walk well, they are great. They also make them in truck and bus sizes which I will point out if we pass one. The Villageton Council owns the public use ones, and the billing system is automated. The Villageton Council, which the citizens collectively own, also runs its own bank that it established when the initial billion dollars in mortgages were packaged. In this way, community generated profits stay within the community and keep turning. But I digress," Sophia said.

### The Village Mortgage and Savings Bank

Ed broke in and asked. "Would you mind holding with that digression for a moment? Tell me about the bank while I sketch that electric cart. I'm fascinated"

Sophia flushed slightly and answered. "I'm probably not the best person to ask, and technically, I am not sure it is an official bank or something more like a credit union, but it works like a local bank. As I said, it was started to provide a way to secure wholesale mortgage funding from pension funds and then market those as retail mortgages to village buyers. With a billion dollar portfolio, it got a jump start in the money business. It offers standard bank services, like checking, savings and electronic banking, and it operates its own advanced debit card system that includes smart software that calculates the local content of goods so buyers know how much of their purchase stays within the local economy. It also has a large vault for people who wish to hold or trade in tangible assets, and the electronic banking enables people to have the instant exchange rate if they want to pay using tangibles instead of dollars. As I understand it, the primary purpose of having the local bank is to keep profits within the community."

Ed thanked her for that digression, and encouraged her to continue telling them about the different villages. "Tell me about more villages, about your village, Sophia."

## About some of the Villages

Sophia grinned proudly. "My village is great. Our village coordinator had an academic interest, which is why our university third year program is based there. It probably has the best library and book store in Villageton and some of the most interesting intellectual debates especially since they built it near the village where many of the people who work in the Industrial Park live. When those two different views of reality meet up – the academic and the industrial worker, the discussions can get hot. I love it. I grew up in what we call a peasant family and am the first ever to go to university. I get frustrated sometimes by the views of my professors and love to see their well-crafted arguments challenged. I have to say though, as they talk both sides moderate their views as these debates expose them to different views of reality."

She continued to explain. "On the other side of the industrial village, is the youth zone, a village where youth housing has a special subsidy. When it was first sold, the homes were built for single people and priced affordably for someone under age 25 who had to prove they earned the money, and did not get it from parents. You can live there 'til you're a hundred, but when you go to sell, it has to be to a buyer under 25, which assures a stock of affordable housing for first time buyers. In so many nice places in the world, housing has become unaffordable for young people who find they are forced to move away from family and friends – not so in Villageton."

"By setting aside housing for under 25's, it creates a parallel market. Originally, they had thought such homes would be interspersed throughout the town, but the youth said they preferred their own zone. They wanted to be loud without disturbing others, with dancing in the streets and impromptu parties. So they ended up on the loud end of the noise overlay, not far from the Industrial Park. Even though we don't have cars within the village, some of the guys have rented a space in the industrial park to work on and customize the love of their life. I suppose car-tinkering is a guy thing; I don't relate. I enjoy going over to the youth zone in the evenings after class, because there are more people my age, and I enjoy getting to know American boys." Sophia said.

"We will now walk through one of the most interesting villages, in my opinion. I may not have mentioned that when each village is designed, the development sets aside some of the profits to subsidize construction of what is called an Artist Guild Hall. The definition of artist is broad... not only musicians, actors or painters for example, but also scientists, inventors, designers... you, as an architect might want to establish an architect's guildhall, for example."

Ed was about to protest this last suggestion based on his jaded view of his egocentric architectural profession, but a bicycle bell interrupted his thoughts.

---

### Pets, Bikes and Rules

Ed turned his head, just as a man on a bicycle rode by. It was a most unusual bicycle; instead of a large front wheel, it had a small platform upon which a golden retriever was happily sitting. The man greeted Ed as he pedalled past, obviously used to the pleasure it gave people to see his dog's mode of transport. "Sophia, I've been meaning to ask about dogs. Are there any rules about pets?"

"Not any more than in a typical community." Sophia answered. "They need to be safe, under control and not a nuisance. Keeping a pet indoors barking all day is frowned upon, although the houses are so soundproof we may not notice. Part of the reason for building the wall around the town was to keep pets within. Some probably do get out, but far fewer than if it was easy to run into the Greenbelt. Pets are required to be on leashes in the Greenbelt to protect the wildlife."

"And, as long as I am asking about rules, tell me about pedestrians, bicycles, these golf-cart sized cars and the motor scooters. Any rules about them?

"Yes," she replied. "As I mentioned earlier, the speed limit inside Villageton is a fast walk. So bicycles are single speed, and NEVs, what you call the golf-cart sized cars, have a speed governor on them, as do the electric motor scooters."

"Anyway, as I was saying before the dog bike diverted us, this next village is most interesting because it is based on the film industry. Not only does it have a film-maker's Guild Hall, but the owners of the buildings on the plaza and one of its primary streets decided to keep the anchor bolts in the exterior walls facing the street when they poured the walls. Usually these are filled afterwards, but they wanted the ability to bolt on what they call "facings" for the buildings. These are like masks, and it's amazing to walk into the village that last week was an elegant Victorian London Street, yet when we walk through it today will look like medieval Barcelona," Sophia reported.

"What in tarnation is that?" Ed asked with surprise, pointing ahead.

### The Prancing Pony or Having Fun Building Your Life

Sophia followed his pointing finger, and laughed. "Oh, that is our Hobbit-mad Canadian's exact replica of Tolkien's Prancing Pony, as in the *Lord of the Rings*. Or to be more precise a replica of Peter Jackson's interpretation of the tavern in the book. The fellow who built that said he has watched the movie, or all three movies, over 150 times. He even went on a working holiday to New Zealand where he got a LOTR map and visited every site location Peter Jackson filmed. When it came time for him to design his home, on the ground floor and exterior he did a replica of The Prancing Pony. He runs it as a tavern, and yes, he allows patrons to jump up on the tables to dance and sing. It's funny, because in real life he was trained as an architect, like you Ed. He says the buildings he used to design for clients were all minimalist – hard lines, lots of steel, cold green-tint glass and concrete floors with details he calls edgy and quirky. Yet when it came time to design his own place he created a warm, fun tavern where you can image Chaucer sitting at in a dark corner at a table writing the Canterbury Tales

– with his laptop of course. The beer he makes in his cellar is great, by the way. Even though it is not part of the official film plaza, it is often rented out for commercials."

## The Film Set Plaza

"But back to the film-set plaza," Sophia said. "All of the building masks are weatherproof and durable, and usually they leave the last film set up until another one is needed. It is one of the strangest experiences to walk into a real community, with a great café life to find it jumping from one century to another overnight. Now that everything is filmed in high definition, the building faces must look absolutely real and it's a real trip." Ed smiled at her use of American slang, enjoying her tour-guiding.

Sophia continued. "This plaza is proving to be a huge boon to the Villageton economy. Between the big film productions, the village secures day contracts from advertising companies and television shows that pay between $3,000 and $15,000 a day, and their producers can spend hundreds of thousands here on the local professional skills they need. The plaza rental profits go to this village's local fund which is governed by the people in this village, sort of a mini-council. They use it to support a special pension fund for retired actors and musicians."

This was new information for Ed. "So in addition to the town governance system, which I understand is corporate in structure, you have local village governance?" he asked.

"Sort of," Sophia replied. "It's not a legal body; more like a department of a company, but in real life the local village has its own bank account and gets to decide how to spend the money after the town accountants sort the income."

Sophia continued. "When this village was proposed, it resulted in a strong contingent of artists associated with the film industry choosing to establish related Guild Halls. The actors' guild consists of outstanding professional actors whose first love is theater, but who earn their bread and butter in the film productions that have become a regular part of the local economy. We also have a computer animation guild that divides its time between global contracting and village film work. The writers guild includes screen writers as well as poets, novelists and non-fiction writers."

Ed found Sophia to be a delightful tour guide, extremely well informed, and he asked her how she knew so much.

"I am in my third year of studies. I am writing my thesis on Villageton. So I ask everyone about their lives, their businesses and their passions. Sometimes I am not sure if I am a scholar or the town's leading gossip," she said, laughing with a crystal clear laugh that Ed found utterly charming.

"But now, to be serious and continue telling you far more than you want to know; this is the only village that has traffic lights in it, except here it is not to regulate cars, but to signal pedestrian traffic when filming is on. When that happens there are special rules about silence and not walking in front of the cameras. No one seems to mind however, since everyone who lives in the film village loves the business – that's why they chose to live here. During filming this is the one plaza where driving cars is allowed – the Villageton motorpool includes classic cars that anyone may rent, but which also serve as film props."

Ed was fascinated. He had never seen anything like it. Just as Sophia had promised, he felt he was in a medieval Spanish city. The walls looked as if they had not been cleaned in centuries, the gothic arches lit with a dark golden glow. Looking carefully, Ed could see where the heavy bolts held these wall masks in place, and examining one he saw that on top of the modern bolt, a blacksmith had welded a hand wrought cover, so it looked perfectly authentic and aged.

The signs were in Medieval Spanish installed by the set designers, but inside they were normal shops and offices. Well, not all that normal, he thought, one store was selling styles of clothing that he last saw when visiting a museum.

Sophia commented. "Yes, the products they make here are real. In fact, I bought a beautiful pair of 14th century Poulaine shoes from the cobbler over there. These shops supply the film industry, historic reenactors and the costume industry, selling mostly over the internet. They also do a surprisingly large business from visitors delighted to find products that you'll never find in Blandville Mall."

"The people who live in this village have an awful lot of fun with it. Many of them have a closet full of costumes at home, and when a period piece film set goes up, they will go to work in their normal jobs dressed to match. This morning, Scott, an IT professor who is an expert in virtual worlds invited me for coffee dressed in full battle medieval armor. He called to me... *Hail Mistress Sophia, Good Morrow, I see thee well, for it is day. Whilst thou join me for a bagel and a double flat white to break thy fast*? At least he did it in medieval English rather than ancient Spanish." Sophia laughed. "While they do it entirely for fun, the filmmakers love it because they have instant, properly dressed extras who go about their business in the background needing no choreography."

As they walked Ed saw an armorer's smithy that he first presumed was a stage set, but then saw in fact it was fully operational with a blacksmith hard at work. Dressed in a leather apron, the fire from the forge lit his face orange as he heated a long iron rod thrust into the coals that flared with each pump of the bellows. Ed began to sketch the workshop so she told his story. "Hamish the blacksmith used to be the managing director of a factory that made high-end

office furniture. Ever since he was a child, he really wanted to be a blacksmith, so after he had a major illness, died on the operating table and had a near-death experience, he decided to pursue his passion. He closed the business, learned the art of smithing, and the rest is history. And, he is a hale and hearty 83 year old!" Sophia said with affection.

As they were passing by the guildhall, a commanding black man with a shaved head wearing a long black and white robe came dancing out, singing *"I'm going to play Othello! I'm going to play Othello!"* Spying Sophia, he ran over, picked her up, gave her a huge hug, and said, *"Sophia, darling, I did it! I got the part. I'm going to be Othello!"* He then put her down, and declaiming at the top of his lungs, *My parts, my title and my perfect soul shall manifest me rightly!* he danced out of the plaza.

"What was that?" Ed asked Sophia, not sure if he was amused or alarmed.

"Oh, that was Jonathan," she replied, slightly flustered. "He is a professional actor who moved here from New York. He is a member of the actor's guild, and ever since I met him, his ambition has been to get the part of Othello in the Shakespeare Festival. It sounds like he got the part. I would have introduced you, but he might have lifted you off the ground in a bear hug as well. Normally, he is not quite so exuberant, but he does have the best laugh in the village."

### SALLY'S VILLAGE - FRIENDS & RELATIONS TAKE CARE OF THEIR OWN

"Next let's go to a more normal village." Sophia proposed. "No one knows quite what to call it, so it took on the name Sally's Village after its village coordinator. It was a group of friends who went to high school together, and while they were scattered all over the country, they kept up with each other. When they heard about the village-town idea, Sally passed around the idea of building their own village. The core group was about 20 families, but those families had their own friends, relations and by the time they finished making all the contacts, they had enough people to form their own village. Some were easily able to shift their businesses, and others managed to convince the companies they worked for that if they put in what is called telepresence systems, they could do their job effectively without needing to be in the office."

"The architecture here is nowhere near as imaginative as in the film village, but that was not a priority for these people. They wanted a nice homey atmosphere where no one locks their doors, where the children travel in packs and everyone looks after everyone else," Sophia explained.

Ed's experienced eye saw kindness in the architecture. Windows had flower boxes, cared for by their people to bring beauty to the streets. Many of the homes were set back slightly to allow more plantings in front, even a few picket fences draped in roses. The homes were simple, with pastel finishes that looked like tinted whitewash. Many of the front doors were open and young preschool children ran in and out. The workplaces had large windows some with a step on the outside so a child could stand and look in.

As they walked into the plaza, Ed noticed a large number of school-aged children, perhaps twenty or so seated around an older man with cherry-red cheeks and a magnificent white beard. "That's Barry," explained Sophia. "Barry is one of the best storytellers in the town. He's 72 years old and used to be a university lecturer in anthropology. His knowledge of lore is deep, and his ability to pass that lore on to the younger generation is wonderful. I can sit and listen to him for hours. Those children are officially in school, and you can see their teacher sitting over there on the side. The teacher makes the Board of Education happy since she is certified, but the real teacher today is Barry. Those children will remember Barry's stories seventy years from now, and if they are sufficiently impressed, one day they will have white hair and sit telling the same stories to future generations. If Barry stands up, you will see he is short. The children all say he is an elf, and in some ways he is; the children love his stories and he makes learning a magical experience for them."

## Medical Care

Ed next saw a building with a sign reading *Medical Center*, and it occurred to him that except for Morgan's briefing on medical insurance, he had not asked about health care. He asked Sophia about it.

"Every citizen," she began, "including students like myself, is a beneficiary of the corporation that we call the Villageton Council. We comprise a 10,000 person institution for the purpose of medical care. This means we buy medical insurance on the wholesale market just like any other billion dollar corporation, and we then make it available to our members at cost. The same holds true for prescription drugs, where the medical council of Villageton buys them at wholesale and dispenses them on a non-profit basis."

"However, on the local level, Villageton finds it makes more sense to keep people healthy than pay for illness, so they set up medical clinics that work to keep people well and catch illness early. When it comes to injury, the clinic is like the emergency room. Seeing a doctor or nurse is free, but the clinics can charge a hypochondriac fee for those folks who burn up staff time unnecessarily."

"The decisions on how to provide and fund medical care were made by the founding citizens shortly after the VOC turned over governance to them. They voted to go with catastrophic medical insurance for the major operations and treatment that requires going to a hospital, but for all day-to-day medical attention to be provided on a local basis. In essence, the 10,000 people formed their own self-insuring group, paid out of their annual fees. When it comes to salary compensation, each medical staff member earns a bonus to keep our citizens healthier than national statistics."

"Keeping people healthier is not only done in traditional medical terms, but also in other aspects of Villageton life. For example, the Greenbelt provides exercise stations in the woods, and the whole design of our streets encourage people to walk. And, of course, our focus on local, healthy food plays its part." Sophia went on.

"The idea is to keep costs under control while keeping people as healthy as possible. To participate in the plan, the right to litigation for medical malpractice is waived so the stockholders - the citizens of Villageton are not paying huge insurance policies and unnecessary testing to protect themselves from themselves. Instead, we have independent oversight of our clinics to assure our medical practitioners are properly prepared, supported and not over-stressed. If a visitor needs emergency medical care while in Villageton, part of their fee is a liability insurance fee."

"In addition, the Villageton medical plan includes an anti-slow-suicide clause which says that people who wish to damage their health by clearly defined self-abusive practices such as smoking, alcohol or drug abuse are free to do so, but they must purchase their own medical insurance to provide for treatment. The Villageton plan will provide palliative care, but no expensive medical treatment for any conditions that could have been caused by specific, named self-abuse."

"How does that work in practice?" Ed asked.

"It's a local community," Sophia answered. "If someone is determined to sneak smokes, for example, perhaps they can fool neighbors, but that's not a game easy to play here because people have low tolerance for that kind of fraud. Why should you pay hundreds of thousands of dollars to treat me for something I do that is known to cause illness? Everyone knows the rules of the game, and if they don't like them, they buy traditional insurance and pay a whole lot more."

"In addition to this fairly conventional medicine, Villageton pays especial interest to medical breakthroughs, including those not necessarily the domain of the mainstream industry. We have biologists and ethnologists who bring a far wider knowledge base than solely the pharmacological industry, and because we collectively pay for the cost of keeping us healthy, some of our citizens will volunteer to test new or rediscovered medical breakthroughs." Sophia said.

"So what happens if someone needs instant medical attention" Ed asked.

"Every building has wired intranet, which means calling for help is pressing a panic button." She explained. "We have an emergency services team that is based in the middle of Villageton that have electric vehicles without speed governors that can get to every building in town in less than two minutes. They are outfitted with the usual emergency services equipment and can function as an ambulance. The same station also has fire fighting equipment, although it rarely is used as all the buildings are fireproof and sprinklered. If someone needs to be flown by medivac to a major hospital, we have a helicopter pad just outside the village gate and we contract for high priority services. However, for 90% of the emergency services, the Medical Clinic you just saw is staffed to deal with them. In addition, again because of the intranet and how we work here, all medical staff can be paged anywhere, instantly, if needed."

How sensible, Ed thought, as it sounded so simple. Focus on keeping people healthy, treat illness early, don't waste money on litigation, hold people accountable for their own health.

## Care for the Elderly and Infirm

When they walked through the plaza, Ed saw infirm elders being wheeled from what appeared to be a residential care facility on the plaza to the outdoor café. Sophia explained. "Almost all the plazas have a nursing bed facility for our old people who become ill or disabled. Actually, there is no age criterion, but most happen to be old. Sally's Village was one of the first to fill their elder haven as they call it. Some families moved in with four generations including old folks nearing the end of their days. Their children desperately wanted to have them die normally, in their community among their loved ones. The results were fantastic, and in some cases, surprising."

"Tell me more," Ed said, "as this seems to be an area where society has failed."

Sophia was happy to comply. "Some of these old people moved into the nursing facility looking like death warmed over. But a few weeks later, they started brightening up. Previously most lived in nursing homes, and in addition to their ailments, they were suffering from depression in response to their physical environment. It took some of them a while to shake it off, but wheeling them into the plaza on nice days, with family members walking from their nearby offices to share a cup of tea during a break at work brought some of those old people back."

"One great grandmother connected with a six-year-old girl whose beloved blanket – *Blankie* she calls it, was coming undone. The grandmother was wheelchair-bound but her hands were still good. She crocheted the holes for the young girl. You can see the two of them over there now sitting in the sun. The girl is learning how to knit and a special relationship has developed. The girl's father is grateful because before they moved here, his children seemed to be spending most of their time in front of the television, and as a solo parent, he lacked the time to offer them any alternative. As an added bonus, with the pressures off him, I hear he's no longer a solo parent."

Ed heard this story with a mix of emotions. It reminded him of his destination after lunch – Heathcliff Manor Retirement Village. Here he was a normal person, feeling in good health and enjoying the tour, not walking slowly like an old person. Yet he was booked in to a retirement village. He began to wonder if he could afford to move into a place in Villageton. He asked Sophia and she explained.

"Villageton has purpose-built elder-housing. These are small apartments on the ground floor, that are never more than 50 paces from the plaza. They are simple, providing for the settled life. They have special features, such as stoves that shut off when granny falls asleep and the dinner in the pan starts to smoke. They provide panic button sensors in case an old person falls down and cannot get up. These homes received special subsidies when they were first sold to make them affordable. As a perpetual condition on the title, they can be resold for any price, but only to an elder. This tends to keep the market price affordable. However, I have to say they are in short supply. Villageton could probably have built rooms for 10,000 elders alone and found they all sell out. There is a waiting list, and in many cases, they are locked up in pre-sale contracts with older people now living in larger village homes."

Ed took this news stoically. He was not a man to make rash decisions, and he was surprised that he had even asked the question. "I'm a bit like the QE-II," he used to say to his staff, referring to the huge Cunard cruise liner. "You need to give me a week to change direction." He remembered this 'Ed' with a smile. Things were certainly happening a lot faster today.

Sophie broke into his reverie by saying, "Ed, we're almost there. This gate marks the boundary into the Italian Village. It looks like carved stone, but in fact it is a replica of a two thousand year old Roman arch. The original probably took years to carve, but thanks to technology, this replica was completed in weeks. I don't fully understand the process, but as it was explained to me all of Villageton was built using a bulk material called Variable Density Concrete or VDC."

## Bulk Building Material - Variable Density Concrete

Ed asked her if she would not mind stopping for a moment so he could draw a sketch of the gate. Its detail was most impressive. While he drew, he asked Sophia to explain VDC, as it was not a building method with which he was familiar.

Sophia was happy to explain. "Apparently concrete is a very 'plastic' material, meaning that when it is wet, it will fill almost any mold shape. The problem is that regular concrete is very heavy and dense, more than it needs to be for walls. Back in the 1920's the Germans invented a way to mix air bubbles in the wet concrete, making it less dense. The system had its problems, mostly in keeping the bubbles where they belong until it hardened, but now in its second generation, they seem to have found additives that enable them to precisely specify the balance of air-to-concrete. The engineers calculate the strength and insulation needed and prescribe a certain density. It feels fantastic to live in, and the soundproofing is incredible. It's a great insulator and I understand the fire safety people love it because it has a five hour rating. But that's only half of the magic."

"The other half comes in the making of the molds. Because the concrete can be poured so it becomes the insulator, you don't need to cover it with insulation and siding. This means that the poured VDC becomes the finished product. If you poured it in conventional forms, it would look as ugly as 1980's Soviet state housing or a prison. So the VOC – that's what they call the developer – brought in a mould-making system. They take a large, thick slab of soft carving plastic and put it on what is called a CNC router. I'm not sure what CNC stands for, but it works like a huge computer printer that prints in 3D. Whatever three dimensional drawing the computer operator programs in, the router knives and blades cut in reverse in the soft plastic."

Ed asked "When you speak about forms and molds, do you mean they pour the walls standing up rather than pour them somewhere else and move them?

"Yes," Sophia replied. "A huge machine that looks like a container port crane rolls down the street setting up the forms *in situ* as they call it. The molds are set inside and then they install the reinforcing, conduit, pipes, doors and windows and everything else get locked into the walls. Then they put on the inner form and pour the wall. They have a similar system for the floors and roof."

"Forgive me for constantly interrupting you Sophia," Ed said, "but I am fascinated by some of the technical aspects of what you describe. How do they use forms to pour the roof and floors?"

"No problem at all, Ed" she replied. "As I understand it, they use a set of hydraulic lifts that they install on the ground inside the building. They raise it to the top level install a platform on the lifts and pour. Then they lower the platform and pour the next lower floor and inner walls, and so on. When all the floors and walls are poured, they dismantle the lifts and take them out the front door to do the next house. I am not sure exactly how they do the roof structure; it may be the same, or they may pour the roof on the ground and have the crane lift it into place.

"Thank you," said Ed. "You were speaking of molds when I interrupted you."

"Yes but I do not mind, Ed." Sophia continued, "I was saying the magic is in the molds. In some cases, artists and designers do new designs using the computer, but in the case of the Italian village gate they took precision photographs of the original using a three dimensional camera. All of the painstakingly carved detail that probably took years to chisel in marble was replicated in hours in the plastic. Then the molds were set into the form and they poured the whole gate in place, standing where you see it now. They used steam heat, so two hours later, they removed the moulds, and the gate was complete. All they had to do was detail finishing. For the gateway, they used white cement with white oxide which is why it has such a brilliant, almost marble look to it. Because this was to be a one-off, they took the mold back to the industrial park where they made it originally. After water blasting, they put the plastic and its shavings into a low heat oven that melted it back into a new block ready for re-carving."

"While they used a 3d camera to program a cutter, other molds are hand-made by professional sculptors. They carve moulds using hot knives and grinders. I'll try to remember to point out some buildings signed by the sculptor as a work of art. Later a number of these sculptors formed one of the guild halls."

Ed listened to Sophia as he sketched the Italian gate and some of its details. His staff had always marvelled at his ability to sit in a meeting, completely focused on the discussion, and at the end show them a sketch he was doing while being fully engaged with the subject. He showed Sophia his rendition of the gate.

"I am so jealous of that talent, Ed. I would have sat there half the day and gone through a whole pad of paper, and not captured what you did in minute or two."

Ed found himself blushing. "It's part of the training to be an architect, or at least it was in my day, before architecture went to computers. I always had a knack for drawing, and that's why my parents encouraged me to take up architecture. It is one of the few artistic professions where one can earn a decent living, although as you heard, I ended up not drawing houses but instead zoning districts."

The three of them walked up the Italianate promenade with its profusion of potted plants, delicate iron work and the warm colored plasters in golden tones of ocher, red and brown. The smell of fresh-baked bread wafted out of a busy bakery on the street near the plaza. Villagers walked down the street with paper-wrapped loafs under arm, while others loaves poked out of baskets on bicycles.

As they arrived in the plaza, Sophia declared to Ed and Michael, "This is it, the Italian plaza. You get a choice of where to eat, but given it is such a lovely day, I would suggest we eat at *Spice,* a wonderful cafe, and sit outside in the plaza. We can sit at a round table where the three of us can talk, or at the long tables where, as a visitor on tour with me, you can count on meeting some locals."

Before they walked to the tables, Ed asked if they would mind if he did another sketch. Michael and Sophia watched as he drew, pad on the low wall.

"The design of this plaza is brilliant." Ed told them as he drew. "It makes references to their culture, but not slavishly so. Without a doubt the colors are Italian in spirit, but it appears they have used clay slurries which suggest they used local materials. Also, I can see the importance of alfresco dining and the emphasis on conviviality."

Ed pointed his pencil at the center of the plaza and said, "Note how they have placed the seating in relation to the sun and the wind. In the center where they have the fountain, they placed broad concrete or stone seats so in the summer people can sit and talk or read, being cooled by the water spray of the fountain. Yet over there, facing the sun by that dark wall, they have created a micro-climate for sitting when it is cooler. The wall will absorb the lower sun rays making it comfortable to sit outside even when the air is chilly." Ed then pointed to a low wall. "I will bet that is for young children to play with balls. Just low enough to allow adults to keep an eye on them, but high enough so the balls stay inside and not disturb others." With that comment, Ed finished the sketch and showed Michael and Sophia what he had drawn; she cooed with delight. They then walked over to the outdoor café.

Ed chose the long table and Sophia explained that while they would be served by café workers, the tables and chairs actually belonged to the village, not the café, so people were welcome to sit as long as they wanted, and not feel they had to buy food or drink to stay there. Sophia said, "This has the added benefit of lowering the cost of business, as the cafés do not pay rent for the tables or their space. You will find food here substantially cheaper than in other places. Not only do they save on the rent, but the wholesale price of food here cuts out the middleman, so the cafés and restaurants can make a profit with lower prices."

Ed looked over to the chalk board featuring the day's specials, and also noted that at a nearby table two young people were playing chess with an appreciative audience making comments. 'They have time here,' he thought to himself.

After looking at the menu, Ed confessed to a quirk he had learned from his grandfather. Seeing apple pie on the specials board, he told Sophia and Michael that whenever he visited his grandfather, they started with a fruit pie and then afterwards ate lunch. The waiter was happy to oblige and brought out three slices still warm from the oven. Ed was in rapture. "I think I must have died and gone to heaven," he said. "I have not tasted apple pie like this since I was a child."

Michael chuckled, reminding Ed of Morgan's prediction: *"I remember that."*

Sophia explained that when Villageton was in its development stage, they had a food specialist who traveled around the region seeking out heritage trees, plants and flowers. "These particular apples came from a tree planted by a pioneer over a hundred and fifty years ago. It had been in the back yard of an old farmhouse, and the elderly lady was delighted someone showed an interest in it. She told the story of her great grandmother bringing the seedling with her, and how it was a wonderful apple for making pies. She provided this café with the recipe, taught to her by her grandmother. This apple pie is only served for one month out of the year. The tree now has been used to graft new apple trees as part of Villageton's farm contracting program."

## Slow Food

Sophia continued. "Apple pie is considered American; in fact I think you have a saying *As American as apple pie*. So you might ask, why is this featured in the Italian plaza? To answer my own question, the Italian connection to the pie came from what is called the *Slow Food* movement, which began in 1986 in Italy. As the story is told, a McDonalds fast-food restaurant opened near the Spanish Steps in Rome. An Italian by the name of Carlo Petrini was sufficiently offended by this fast food approach to food that he started what became known as the Slow Food movement. Eventually Slow Food became a world-wide organization of communities with chapters in over 130 countries. Communities that join the slow food movement are called *convivia* from the word *convivial*."

"As I said, the fundamental premise of fast food offended Carlo. He saw this standardization of food, where food is same, filling and fast – like filling up your car at the gas station – as demeaning what it is to be human, especially human within community. Instead of protesting, which is essentially a reactive approach, he founded the Slow Food Movement to offer people a very different choice about how they wish to live; a choice that connects people to the land in a way no industrial-based global franchise can ever do."

As Ed listened to Sophia's story on slow food, he found himself experiencing his apple pie with the same pleasure she was describing 'Sublime bliss', he thought.

"Slow food is not about Italian food, which is why they are OK about serving an American icon here. Slow food is about preserving and serving the rich heritage of flavorful and healthy foods that Nature offers to humans in abundance; foods man ignores in favor of a few monoculture foods that can endure the treatment of long-distance storage and distribution. The apples in this pie do not travel well. They must be picked, delivered and cooked within days, and unlike some other varieties, they do not store well in a cool-room. You only get this apple pie this time of year, and you only get it near the tree that grew them. The recipe is local and uses local ingredients because in those days all food was local."

Ed was amused, getting used to the fact that in Villageton it seemed even the simplest of things came with a story.

After the pie, the meal continued backwards, as Sophia proposed ordering a plate of fresh cheese made by Italians living in the Italian village. She explained:

"While the cheese-makers are from Italy, the cheeses are not *Italian*. The cheese is local because our water is different, the food the cows, sheep and goats eat is different and the soil and climate is different. The cheeses have become local; they are Villageton cheeses. The Italian connection is the fact that Italian cheese-makers were invited by Victoria Rossi, the Village Coordinator, to move here. She was a second generation child of Italian immigrants and she sought out a village that honored her ancestry. The privilege – and fun – of being a Village Coordinator is getting to set the theme, although you then have to negotiate with the 200 other families to agree on the details. Victoria traveled to her grandparents' village in Italy to see if any cheese-makers wanted to move here and bring their skills with them. Several of them were delighted to accept the invitation, and Victoria was able to arrange for immigration visas. The cheese-makers brought their tools and knowledge with them, and now are running a very successful business… demand for their products are now spreading throughout the region, and even to the boutique food stores in the big cities."

"When they came here, some of the farms were already in dairy, but the cheese-makers deemed the farming methods unacceptable… cows injected with hormones to increase production, and with various antibiotics used to keep cows healthy due to the intensity of the farming methods used. The farmers did this because increasingly, the food buying monopoly pressured them to increase yield. They achieved this by using chemicals both on the land and in the animals – all to squeeze out more production per acre. The farmers' costs increased, especially using petroleum based fertilizers and chemicals, while the farmer's portion of the retail price of food kept going down. Even so some of our farmers were close to going broke."

"So the Village Organizing Company's food specialist met with the cheese-makers, and identified what they would need both in terms of quantity and quality from the farmers. Their farming came with the high cost of the middle-man, due to the complexity of the supply

chain and the middle-man's profit expectations. By cutting that part out in selling to a local market, the dairy farmers could meet the higher quality expectations of the cheese-makers and earn a better and more stable living with lower-yield and less toxic farming."

As Sophia ended this cheese story, she looked up and saw Victoria Rossi crossing the plaza. Fashionably dressed, she looked very much like she was coming over to have lunch at the café. Sophia hailed her and made introductions.

Victoria gave Sophia a big hug, kissed Michael on the cheek and greeted Ed affectionately. With a bubbly chuckle that warmed his heart, she confirmed it was lunchtime, and she would be happy to join them at the long table. Folks shifted to make room, and Victoria looked at the specials board.

"Ed, the wild mushroom risotto and braised bison with poached San Giovanni pear is sublime. The chef stirs the risotto creamy to perfection yet still al dente, the free range bison – is there any other kind of bison, Sophia?" she interrupted herself with another of her effusive laughs "Sorry Ed," she said, putting her hand on his arm, "the bison is braised to perfection and the pear is so indulgent, it's... oh my god listen to me, I sound like I am in love, not describing lunch. Anyway, Ed, as you have probably worked out, I recommend it. The bison, also called American buffalo, is local from a former cattle rancher now building a herd on his land. It's now large enough to supply Villageton with free range game."

"With an endorsement like that, who can resist?" Ed replied, signalling the waiter. "Victoria, I'd love to hear your story and how you came to be coordinator of this Italian village; and would you mind if I do a portrait of you walking over while I listen?"

Sophia told her "Ed has a talent for doing sketches, but even more impressive for a man, he can pay complete attention to what is being said to him at the same time."

Ed said to Victoria with a smile, "Well, I promise not to interrupt your story, anyway, as Sophia disapproves of my constant interruptions." As he listened, he began to do a sketch of the image captured in his mind when she was crossing the plaza coming in their direction.

# Chapter 5

# A Village Coordinator's Story

"My grandparents came from Italy, from a small country village, shortly after they were married. They sought a better life and believed the American dream offered it. Italy was poor and backwards in those days. They did not come alone; many of my relatives made the same move at the same time on the same ship."

"I grew up in a row-house in an Italian-American community in Brooklyn New York. I remember when I decided to study at the University of California in Berkeley. The furthest I had ever traveled was to Pennsylvania, so when I went to the airport not only did my parents, little brother and grandparents come to see me off, there must have been twenty aunts, uncles, cousins, nephews and nieces as well. It was that kind of family and community."

"My trip to California gave me the travel bug, and my boyfriend and I bought a motorcycle to tour Europe and Asia for what turned out to be seven years. In the first few years we would return to the States to earn enough money to keep traveling, but eventually we found we could work anywhere by setting up shop to teach English as a second language. It seemed the whole world wanted to learn English so they could move to America and become rich."

"During my travel years, my family's community in Brooklyn began to break down. Drugs and guns started appearing, and the police seemed to have no interest except to contain it. My father died unexpectedly of a heart attack. My brother, who had been a sweet kid, hit puberty bad and lost it. My mother remarried and moved away. The same thing happened to most of my friends' families. Some got out, some lost it, some died young."

"The streets and buildings reflected the chaos. Stolen and abandoned cars appeared on the streets, some burned out hulks. The city would leave them for months. Graffiti and tagging hit the neighborhood, first the walls, then windows, trash cans and almost every surface within reach. They stopped cleaning the streets; as litter became the norm, our community fell into squalor. Illegal drugs destroyed many. With drugs came guns. It got so bad the police ring-fenced city blocks – in effect saying, let them kill each other, we'll just keep them inside until they finish each other off."

## Grandmother's Insight

"While this devastation was happening to my childhood home in the New World, I visited my grandparent's old village back in Italy. It was still poor, but everything was neat, in its place. Drop a wrapper on the ground and someone would give you the evil eye or even make a sharp comment. Do it when no one was around and invariably someone picked it up and tossed it in the bin. I asked my grandmother, *What's the difference?* Her reply was insightful." Victoria said.

"In the old country, in their village they were the people of the land. Not tenants, but people whose ancestors built that simple village. Their roots grew deep, and the stories of that land were the stories of their people. They were not the first peoples; they knew the lore of the others who lived there before them – confirmed later by archaeologists doing digs – but her people were the people of the land. By that, she did not mean they owned the land, more like the land owned them. When new people came to their village, usually through marriage, they developed that same relationship to the land and its buildings."

"When they crossed the ocean by ship and came to Brooklyn, they found a place where land was not respected. Land was a commodity. The buildings represented passive income for landlords, not the walls that shelter a community. For a time the elders were able to maintain order within their families, based on the strength they brought from the old country, but as they aged and the younger generation took over, the rootlessness of the Brooklyn streets eroded the family and its respect. The parents detached from their own children – too busy – and peer pressure became dominant. Hollywood did not help as it began glorifying punk and thug lifestyles. The switchblade featured in *West Side Story* gave way to the 9 mm pistol."

"To avoid that dispossession, she said we must create permanent places to live. Places where the people who live there form a permanent bond with both their community and the surrounding land. Most need not only to own their homes, but to have an emotional attachment to it and the surrounding community and open land. She felt it was most important the community have a cemetery, not only to honor the dead, but to enable the living to connect with their land."

"My grandmother was a wise woman." Victoria concluded.

"What a remarkable story, Victoria." Sophia said. "With such a person in your life, I think I understand how you were able to accomplish so much here as a Village Coordinator calling your village into being."

Victoria looked down, slightly embarrassed by the compliment, so Ed asked her "How did you go from travelling on a motorcycle to building your village?"

Victoria smiled appreciatively at Ed and answered. "A long time later, motorcycle sold, travel over, boyfriend gone, it seemed it was time to get a real job. I came back to New York and got a job at one of the universities. It was good work, but I was not happy. I felt I was doing nothing but walking a treadmill whose destination was death. I had a job, I had an apartment, but in my heart I felt hollow."

### Building Our Village

"One day, someone sent me a link to a web site in Australia called *Nourish*. It was a book review of a book called *How to Build a Village*, written by an American living in New Zealand. It was a great book review. It struck a chord deep within me. I ordered a copy of the book through the campus book store, read it, and went to the web site listed on the back cover of the book. Talk about a milestone marking a change in my life. It spoke to me, giving words to the yearning within. It reminded me of my grandmother's words – create permanent places to live, not places where we are tenants, not homes we buy with an eye to resale value."

"The book and website were not selling anything; they set out an idea, inviting me to become involved. But it wasn't trying to enlist me in their idea, so much as to provide me a framework where I could build a village, my village – not alone but with others – my idea of a great way to live, not someone else's. It was about freedom, the citizen freedom to create, not consumer-freedom to buy."

"By this I mean that we live now in a manufactured world, where professional experts do surveys and studies to figure out what people will buy. Then other experts design the products, and we, the consumers, get to decide which product we will select. In this world, freedom of choice means *to buy or not to buy*."

Michael chose to interrupt Victoria at this moment by commenting, "Yes, when we were driving here this morning, Ed made a rather subtle play on words in Latin, taking Descartes' *Cogito ergo sum* – 'I think therefore I am', and saying today it is more like *Pēnsō ergo sum.* 'I shop, therefore I am'; although *Pēnsō* can also mean a kind of thinking – more like weighing up the worth of something."

Victoria took out a piece of paper and pen, and asked Michael to repeat the phrase so she could write it down. *"Pēnsō ergo sum. I shop therefore I am.* Cool!" she said. While she was writing, Ed was looking at Michael with some surprise. 'There is more to Michael than I had reckoned,' he thought to himself, sensing he had underestimated the depth of his driver. But before he could find a tactful way to explore this, Sophia asked Victoria to continue with her story.

"The book and web site proposed a different type of freedom, to examine both what we need in life and what we love, and then to make it happen – to create a place that serves and fulfills us, with design support by experts to assure we get it right."

"This was both empowering and terrifying. It's a strange experience to come face to face with freedom, and I almost ran back into my own prison cell. I had always dreamed of the idea of creating my own world, but until then I had put that in my fantasy box… a nice place to think about, but not a part of my real world. If I may butcher Hamlet, it was more like *to do or not to do.*"

"This freedom was offered to everyone who participates in the design of their building, but to get it going, they created a job called the Village Coordinator, the person who champions a specific village, names its essential character and calls together the others who want to live there."

"The "job description" for a Village Coordinator surprised me. It did not look for professional qualifications, but rather for clarity, passion, leadership and discipline. I was not sure I had those qualifications, except for discipline… teaching English overseas meant I had to create my own jobs. I was excited about the idea, loved it, so maybe that qualifies as passionate, and I am a good communicator."

"Anyway, I finally worked up enough courage to send them an e-mail, and after a few messages forward and back, we made arrangements to talk on an internet conference call."

"What I expected would be a job interview turned out to be nothing of the sort. First, there was no pay, not yet at least. If I was successful, compensation would come, since it would be a billion dollar project, but those contracts would only come as the project took shape. The people involved were delightful. They were having fun with this project, and only wanted to play with others who would share that fun. Even if it fell apart, they wanted to work with people who would become friends. If that spark did not happen in the conference call meeting... well, I suppose that would have been the end of it, but in my case the spark was there, and we got right into talking about my dream village."

"My first choice was *where?* There were projects around the world, including a few unlisted ones in the USA. While the ones in New Zealand and Australia were appealing, my travel days were over and I liked being in a place where I did not have an accent – although my bubbly Brooklyn accent still sticks out here. Besides, my mother, now widowed a second time, expressed interest, and moving overseas was not likely given her health."

"While I lived on the East Coast, I had no attachment to it anymore. My childhood home in Brooklyn went from a solid Italian community to a crime ridden drug zone and more recently is becoming an upscale yuppie haven. I chose a location that had not yet been listed. I selected it because it had four seasons, nearby hills, with fast running streams, yet on the other side had rich farmland. While Villageton would offer its own enriched experience within, the surrounding environment was almost park-like. I wanted to do an Italian Village, so I found I was now both a Village Steward and the Italian Village Coordinator for Villageton."

"So, now I had a blank canvas and the invitation to paint the community of my dreams. That is probably the best part of being a Village Coordinator, the freedom to set out your dream. Being pure Italian, the first thing I did was call four of my cousins and have them over for a jug of wine, loaf of bread and a bottle of peppery green olive oil from my grandparents region in Italy."

"What began as a single meeting ended up becoming weekly gatherings that kept growing as my cousins invited friends, who then brought their younger brothers and sisters, aunts, uncles. It even included the couple that ran the bakery down the street where I bought the bread for those first meetings... they now own the village bakery, right over there on the street that enters the plaza."

"I loved the way the enrollment process works. If you think you might like to live in the village, we start out conditionally and proceed toward commitment only as people become comfortable with the process and the expected outcome. It's a bit like asking *would you marry me if I asked you?*" Victoria explained with a chuckle.

Ed worked out the question first, and said "That's got to be a first for a trail close question for real estate sales!"

As the question sank in, the others at the table laughed and Sophia said, "I can see that working in progressing toward a major purchase decision, but it sure would put a damper in the romance department... sorry, Victoria, do continue."

Victoria eyes answered mischievously, "Well, I can think of one or two boyfriends where I probably should have asked that question before getting into a relationship that went nowhere, but we probably should not go there. Back to the enrollment process, there were only three questions I needed to ask:

- Do you want to live there?
- Can you afford to buy in?
- Can you move your job with you, or find work there to pay your way?"

"Affordability was easier than expected. Pricing offered a range of options, so almost everyone could buy in at one level or another. One of the most interesting concepts was that of the Parallel Market for real estate. Let me explain, but stop me if you find I am getting too deep into details," Victoria requested.

Ed replied, "If it's similar to what Sophia explained about special housing for old people, please do tell. I find the concept of tailoring market-forces instead of state subsidy housing to be fascinating. I want to hear more, Victoria."

## Gentrification v Parallel Real Estate

Victoria was glad someone shared her excitement about what could be regarded as a dull topic. "In almost every successful real estate project, affordable housing disappears when the place becomes desirable. The first families who bought affordable housing make a killing when they sell up, but after that the market is only for the affluent. This has some undesirable effects because whole communities need a wide range of people, not only the upper income ones who bid up the prices."

"When I was a teenager, my friends and I used to take the subway to Greenwich Village in New York City. Rent was cheap, and the place was teeming with poets, writers, jazz and folk musicians, avant-garde photographers, painters and brilliant eccentrics of all colors and sizes. The coffee house scene was amazing; so much creativity the walls kept glowing with it after everyone finally went off to sleep at 5 a.m. Then the hip, young advertising executives from Madison Avenue started moving in. Rents started going up. Buying a loft or apartment required more money, and slowly the creativity began to drain away as money outbid them. The art galleries shifted, more up-market. When the Wall Street brokers started buying buildings, we knew it was over. They call it gentrification, where a wonderful place gets loved-to-death by too much money."

"It's not only the artists who need their own market. Many people work in salary or wage jobs that have fixed pay grades. Society needs teachers to assure the next generation has the skills to keep and evolve civilization, but we pay them on a fixed scale. In a place like Villageton, the first teachers are able to buy in at subsidized prices, but over the years the price of those houses shoots up. The same holds true for other sectors of the community... youth, elders, essential workers especially in what used to be called blue collar jobs. Someone has to collect the garbage and sweep the streets."

"The 20th century answer for this was socialistic, where the state buys or rents a certain number of state houses, and then provides them to low income or fixed income tenants. This has several drawbacks. The cost of managing state housing creates its own bureaucracy. Like all bureaucracies, getting work done becomes tedious at best, and maddening when its people stop caring. Someone has to pay for all those managers and their repair contractors, and knowing it is the state, some contractors rip them off. The tenants always know it is not their home. If on a whim they decide they want to paint the living room bright red, they can't; it's not their house. Or if it is a slumlord, there is no incentive to make wonderful homes. Owning your own home implies a stronger form of citizenship; you belong rather than if you are state-supported because of your circumstances."

"In Villageton, we use a different structure. Developing it was harder because of anti-discrimination laws designed to protect the very sectors of society we were trying to help. We identified each target sector, such as teachers or youth, as a distinct parallel market, and when the Village Organizing Company or VOC built the homes, they built a fixed number as Parallel Market homes. They designed youth homes in collaboration with youth with interesting ideas like the recycling and trash bins outside, under the kitchen counter, so no one had to take the trash out. Elder housing offers compact, ground floor living within 50 paces of the plaza. Teacher and public servant housing looks and functions no different than the house next door, because their parallel market homes are about affordability. With artist housing they did it differently, providing a free base that can be rented out where the artist keeps the rent if they want a bigger, open-market home."

At this point Ed spoke. "I promised not to interrupt, but I wonder, Victoria, if you would not mind explaining to me the business basis of that. I can understand why it is good for the community, but how does the developer justify it?" He also showed her the sketch he did of her walking over.

Victoria burbled with delight at the sketch, then answered his question. "As I said, when a member of the target market first buys such a home, the VOC prices it affordably. In business-speak they call this *opportunity cost*, which means VOC sells it for less money than if they sold it on the open market. Think of it as a concession the investors must give in order to get the right to subdivide and build. It becomes one of the major concessions proposed when the local government which must approve rezoning considers the application. Remember that the land was previously zoned as rural, perhaps allowing ten homes on this amount of acreage. The VOC asked to build over 4,000 homes on the land, so it offers a concession of the parallel markets."

"The new idea in parallel market homes kicks in when the home comes up for resale. In an open market, the seller does not pass on the first time affordability, but keeps a windfall capital gain – nice for them, but bad for the community. In a parallel market, the VOC passed on the opportunity cost to the successor Villageton Council owned by all the owners living in the villages. This means the Villageton Council holds a permanent, restricted interest in the home. This interest is either on the title, or in a successor contract, and to sum up the lawyer language, it says the home can only be sold to a buyer within the target market. So a teacher can sell to another teacher, or possibly to a public servant whose pay scale is similar to that of teachers. If someone cheats, and the buyer is really a yuppie who declares he teaches sales teams how to be more effective, the Villageton Council invokes its rights, and can force the home to go for public auction where bidders must prove in advance they are qualified to buy."

"Of course there will be grey areas such as the teacher who decides to quit and go into profitable business, but these are sorted out as they arise. It does not happen enough to cause gentrification – we still keep most of our essential population, and if it is a genuine career shift, people leave it alone. In most cases, we find the homeowners act responsibly since they see the need for parallel homes, and feel the disapproval of neighbors if they hog one. So far, when it has happened, when their new business or job gives them the means to afford a mainstream home, they sell the parallel home so they can enjoy the benefit of capital gain."

"How about welfare?" Ed asked. "Do you offer welfare housing?"

"We approach it differently," she replied. "Villageton set aside what we call *bounce back homes* so when someone suffers a crisis that means they can't pay their way, they don't end up on the street. Along with that comes a community effort to help them get back on their feet. If it involves alcoholism, mental illness or other disrupters we deal with it medically and emotionally. We do not support chronic welfare, however.

Victoria sipped from her cup and smiled, "Ed, I hope I did not bore you with that tale. They say I'm poured from my grandfather's mold, telling the whole story when a few brush-strokes would have done just as well."

Ed replied, "Not at all, Victoria. You are a lovely storyteller, and I am delighted to sit here and listen to you, while slowly enjoying one of the finest meals of my life. Besides, I promised not to keep interrupting, a promise I broke only a couple times. I'm fascinated with your solution; low-income housing was a problem we never fully solved in Blandville. It always ended up segregating society, and it produced problematic and sometimes nasty side effects. But, if I may shift the topic now, tell me about how you designed the Italian plaza and village. It has a distinct Italian feel to it, but it does not look like a Disney replica of old Italy. How did you do it?"

### Dynamic Engagement Design Process

"Fun, exhilarating, mind-bending and creativity on rocket boosters... how's that for short?" Victoria answered. "What an experience! Having become used to freedom meaning the choice between product A and product B, the idea that we get to choose a way of life took some rewiring of everyone's brains. I swear there were days when I could feel the synapses growing inside my head."

"Because ours was one of the first, we used the real scale model primarily with the internet virtual model copying it. I understand other villages went almost entirely on-line with the 3D model being built after-the-fact. Italians use their hands a lot, so shaping and moving model buildings around – as well as lots of hand waving as we argued what should go where and why – is part of our culture. It also was a great way to get to know each other; now that we are neighbors, we have a closer bond because we co-designed our neighborhood."

"It took far less time than I expected. Before the workshops, each of us ordered a scale-model home. For the most part, our budgets drove this. Height, depth and street frontage are the key factors. We negotiated the roofs during the design phase. So when we arrived, 100:1 scale models of each of our homes and our workplaces awaited us on tables. They were foam-white, and we were given a box of paints to color the walls, paint in doors and windows and decorate our building. Some villagers really got into it, taking their "home" with them at night to turn their basic building shape into their dream house. Some painted potted plants with climbing vines flower boxes, cat in the window. One family changed the exterior wall color seven times until they found the perfect color. In doing this first exercise, we got to know our future neighbors."

"First we discussed the design code. Professional architects and designers ran this workshop, asking about the general theme and the detailed implications of parts of the theme. We knew we wanted "Italian", but the designers challenged us to articulate what that meant. Does it mean the row houses of Brooklyn, built to serve the interest of factory owners needing to cram as many workers in as small a space as possible? Or does it mean the tight housing in Italian hill-top towns built for defense? They showed us photographs of Italian villages and towns, including ones like Pienza, built by a Pope and used for making Zeffirelli's film *Romeo and Juliet*. We discussed columns, arches, covered walkways, exterior steps, big windows, small windows, plate glass, divided light, carved doors, statues and water fountains, nooks for teenagers to kiss and benches for the *poltrone* – the old men who bask in the sun and argue politics."

"They put up a big white board with business card sized fridge magnets on which *patterns* were written. Some came from an amazing book written by Christopher Alexander in 1977, called *A Pattern Language*, and then they taught us how to write our own patterns. From this we developed an Italian village pattern language, in part based on our culture and in part based on us. We discovered that *Italian* meant something very different depending on our personal history and geography. My Italy was second generation, mostly from the South. Others brought their Tuscan heritage. The most interesting revelation came from the fresh-off-the-plane Italian immigrants. Their 21st century Italy was very different than the time capsule of mine."

"So that's how the pattern cards were used," Ed said. "I saw it in the Visitor Center."

"Yes," Victoria replied. "From all of this raw data, the professionals pushed and prodded us to shape a design code. In the end, we were both happy and exhausted because it all happened in at once. Because we were in charge, we pushed hard. We slept, we ate and we worked, and some hardly slept. On Saturday night, I was tossing at 2 a.m., so I got up and went to look at the scale model. Surprise, there were six people there, two like me in dressing gowns, and the rest having never gone to bed. And I should say, because we are Italian, we decided to dispense with the catering. My mother got together with the other mothers, and some fathers, and they did the cooking. We sat outdoors on saw-horses with checked table cloths, and kept talking through the meals. In fact, some of the best planning occurred with fork in one hand

and bread in the other."

"What was the purpose of the Design Code?" Ed asked.

"It sets out what our village will look like so the architects and designers who help draft individual building size, shape, street-face, windows, doors, lampposts, pavers, roofs and other details have a harmonious look and feel while encouraging founding villagers to implant their character on their own buildings.

While Victoria had been telling the story, Ed had continued to sketch. She noticed how Ed was fully concentrating on what she was saying, but at the same time was doing a series of drawings of people. She asked him about it.

"Ever since we sat down," Ed said, "there has been a rolling dialogue over there. See that group standing with the lady on the bicycle? It has been an ongoing conversation with new people joining and others then going on with their day." He showed Victoria the sketch he had been doing.

"Ed, you are amazingly talented." Victoria exclaimed. She then looked over at the talkers, and laughed "Yes, I suppose that is the glory of our kind of commuting. It still takes half an hour, but that is two minutes for walking and 28 minutes for conversation.

If you do more sketches, Ed, watch the hands, people in this plaza speak with their hands as much as with their mouths."

"I will do that." Ed promised. "But don't let me break your story, I am fascinated about the planning process you used to design your village. It's completely outside the scope of anything I have ever considered, yet I find it compelling. And while I am listening, I will draw the hands of those two gentlemen over there. They look like they are conducting an orchestra!"

"Yes, that's Vinny and Frank." Victoria said, then turning back to continue her story of the Dynamic Engagement planning process. "When the workshop began, all they set out were the village boundary, the plaza and the access streets. We designed the rest. We wrote the design code, although by writing, I mean on whiteboards with pattern cards and notes all over them. Afterwards an urban planner cleaned it up into proper language which we tweaked and finally signed off. The scale model became the master plan, reduced to paper by another draughter. Weird to set your own home down, realizing the person putting his home next to you is your new next door neighbor. This actually worked out well, because people who hit it off decided they had to be neighbors, and those who did not get along moved their home to another street. Designing for sunlight exposure was a fascinating exercise, as some people like morning sun; others want shade to protect the furniture."

"Probably the hardest part was designing the plaza. This was our public stage, and we all agreed it was important to get right. We knew that our Artist Guild Hall would be about music, especially singing, and even though many of us are no longer church going, we deemed it important to have a church. Both these buildings are paid for by the development. With advice from the architects, especially one trained in classical and sacred architecture – he was a walking encyclopedia who could not only draw, but tell a story – we created a harmony of classical and vernacular architecture that is the setting you see around you."

"Oh, I almost forgot... your role, Ed – the town planner's role," Victoria said, putting her hand on his arm. "They called it Dynamic Engagement, which defined the role of the planners in a way they found both exhilarating and a learning experience."

"As you know, usually developers go to the planners with an application to rezoning. It then goes through a complex process where the planner identifies adverse impact and externalized costs... impact like noise, lights, increased traffic, pressure on schools, social disruption, demand on utilities, bad land use, and so on. With Villageton this whole process was turned on its head."

"Instead, the County Council and the Village Organizing Company reached an agreement in principle that there would be a village-town with the location, urban site and greenbelt identified - all subject to the planners approving the details. The County agreed to participate in Dynamic Engagement where all plans, details and issues would be reviewed by the planners as they are developed. It's a bit like what happens when a county versus developer dispute goes to court and the judge orders the parties to talk. After years of wrangling, the issues get resolved in weeks under the gun of the court. In Dynamic Engagement, they front-end it. This saves lots of time and grief."

"Unlike a developer, a Village Organizing Company's brief includes *effects based design* which means their job must assess and avoid or mitigate any aspect of the development that would produce significant adverse impact on people or the environment. Because the people involved in the design are those who must live with the impact, the whole process becomes collaborative rather than adversarial. This is what made it such a learning experience for the town planners."

"The greenbelt eliminated cross boundary conflicts – planner-speak for upsetting the neighbors. The trees block noise and lights. Access roads have no commuters and no cars with a *Mom's Taxi* bumper sticker – Villageton is inwardly focused. Further, because it's a blank canvas, Villageton gets to do its own advanced and sustainable handling of its utilities… it does its own water, sewage, solid waste and road maintenance. In this county, law enforcement and education are locally funded, so the agreement allows us to run our own police and school departments that we pay for. In the end, the planners loved the process," Victoria explained.

"It would be a head-shift for them, but I can see it working." Ed opined.

Victoria continued. "When the workshops began, we had three parties:

- The citizens or what we called the villagers who will live and work there,
- The professional support staff – architects, engineers, designers, etc,
- The town planners working at arms-length

The planners were not there to develop the plan, or tell us what to do, but to assure our evolving plan met the rules. By watching it come together, they were able to make judgment calls immediately, and where it would be struck off as non-complying, they were obligated to say so immediately. In most cases, we discussed the problem they raised, and we moved things around until they agreed it was resolved."

"As each piece was put in place, the planner pulled out a sticker, signed and affixed it, signifying provisional approval. I say provisional, because the planners got two more hits. When the final work was done, at the end of the workshop, the planners get to look at the overall plan to assure that items approved in isolation do not generate unacceptable adverse impact when combined. Their final review came when the 100:1 scale model was reduced to conventional paper."

"The agreement with the County specified the same planners would stay with the project from beginning to end and the development paid the County for the extra staff costs. So while the planners have the right to change specifications after the workshop, they are held accountable to explain why they did not get it right during Dynamic Engagement. In our village, and most of the other villages that I know of, the formal approval was no more than carefully examining the paperwork to make sure it was faithful to the workshop plan and contained no errors. In the end, the whole process from start to all paperwork approval took three months."

Ed shook his head with disbelief. "As you explain each step, it makes sense. I cannot find weakness in any of it. But three months for approval of a 4,000 unit development is awesome. From a planner's perspective, it sounds like the conversations we had as students wanting to help improve the world – before we entered the real world of greedy investors, dishonest developers, slick lawyers and crony politicians."

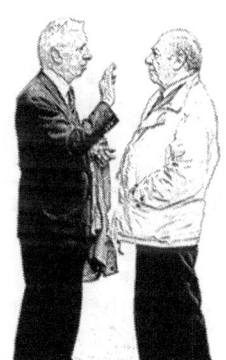  

Lunch was over.; The very reasonable bill paid. Ed showed Victoria his sketch of the hand talkers, and she laughed delightedly. "You have captured Vinny perfectly! He's always putting his fingers up to make another point." She said. "I hope you enjoyed the lunch and my story, and Ed, I wish you the most wonderful of lives."

"Victoria, I would have to say it has been the finest lunch of my life, and not just the food. Thank you so much." Ed said to her.

With a kiss and hug, Victoria bade them all goodbye and walked back across the plaza to her work. "What a loving and lovely woman." Ed said softly to himself, feeling a kind of glow inside himself. He saw Michael smiling as well.

# Chapter 6

## Suvies - *Single Unencumbered Villagers*

As they approached the next village gate, Ed was surprised to see a round road sign, white background surrounded with a green circle and the letters SUV. "I thought cars were not allowed in the villages," he said. "Is this a sport-utility vehicle zone?" Sophia laughed and explained. "I'm afraid it displays a warped sense of humor on the part of the village coordinator for this village... it stands for *Single, Unencumbered Villager*, although I think originally the *U* stood for unattached."

"As you can imagine, Nicole, the person who stepped forward to call this village into being was unmarried, not in a relationship and felt pressured by a society that was constantly trying to hook her up with a man. She enjoyed dating and the company of men, loved parties and the café scene but not as a courtship ritual whose intended outcome is to marry her off. If you recall Morgan's picture of the house showing the good life, Nicole lived for conviviality. When she heard about the village-town idea, she wondered if there were more people like her out there... enough people to form their own village. Her own address book was huge, but people live their own lives, and while most her friends loved the idea, not enough of them were ready to make the move, mostly because their jobs tied them to the city."

"Being the resourceful woman she is, Nicole put her idea on the web and sent out a message on the social and business networks where she already had amazing connections. Within a week, her in-box was maxed out to the point where she had to ask the Village Forum to redirect emails to an administrator. She thought about going through all the applications like a kid at Christmas picking the best chocolates out of the box after tasting them all. Finally she decided to sort them into a pile that was seriously qualified, then divided it equally between male and female and had a party where they randomly picked the applications out of two jars. At the party, they had a big screen TV hooked up and using Skype contacted the winners live – lot's of screams of excitement, I heard it was quite an event."

"The SUV or Suvie village has about 500 people but more than 200 homes since many singles wanted their own place – although a few elected to build roommate homes either for the company or to save money. Some homes are very small, not unlike living on a boat in the harbor. Some Suvies never eat at home, but in the cafés and restaurants both on their own plaza, and on others within Villageton. Others love home cooked food, and in one building twenty of them built twenty apartments they owned individually around a massive central kitchen with a long wooden table that seats forty people. They run it not as a business, but as a happening. Four or five of them will make a feast, everyone pays for the food, and they doubled the number of seats because so many friends join in the event. They rotate who cooks, and when no one feels like it, they hire a professional chef team from one of the restaurants. Their wine cellar is the best."

"Since almost everyone living here is single, people from the outside immediately assume that Suvieville is a hotbed of debauchery; enough so that a university sociology student chose to do her third-year thesis on the question. After surveying all 500 Suvies, she reported to the contrary, their sexual activity was less than the national average. The Suvies explained in the survey that they sought a single life without the pressure to couple. She also found the demographics reflected the national averages in terms of sexual orientation and attitudes. One of her more interesting findings was the extent to which Suvies lived in the present. Most Suvies were not anti-marriage or resistant to entering into a relationship; instead they focused on their present life; live and let live."

"One of the other unique residences in Suvicville is a place called Salvage. More warped humor in naming it, I'm afraid, but it is a combination hostel, apartment house and refuge specifically designed for the losers in a separation or divorce – a place for the partner who found his or her bags on the street and the lock to the front door changed. It's a reality in today's life, and in fact part of the boom in urban apartment life generating recovery in large cities comes from the high breakup of marriages and relationships. Where do you go when you're biffed out? Here you wash up at Salvage. When rooms are not occupied, the village rents them out as normal hotel rooms."

Sophia, Ed and Michael walked along the main pedestrian street that was busy with people coming and going, some on elegant street bicycles, frequently stopping to chat with each other, with lots of laughter. Ed noted more shops selling fashionable clothing, and saw that most Suvies took an interest in how they looked. Smart, casual, with great variety; it made sense to him as unencumbered also meant earning an income in the prime of their careers without the expenses of children. It felt youthful even if the age range covered the full gamut of adulthood.

As they walked into the plaza Ed was surprised to see a small but attractive church near where they stood and a young priest or minister wearing the collar standing outside. Sophia noted the quizzical look on Ed's face and asked if an introduction was in order. Ed was amazed how many people Sophia knew, given that she was a visiting student who had only lived here for half a year. Sophia introduced him to Andy, and asked if Andy had the time to conduct a brief tour of the Suvie plaza.

## The Priest

"Your probably wondering what a priest is doing living in a village that seems to worship conviviality above all", Andy said. Ed allowed that the thought had crossed his mind, unless of course Andy's job was evangelical recruitment. "Actually, in our business, we use the term *headhunting*, but no, that's not why I am here. For a start, I am Catholic, and I took vows of celibacy, so this is one of the few communities where my avowed way of living is normal. I live alone in a community where almost everyone lives alone. The villagers pay to support me being here, and to maintain this church, that was built and paid for at their request by the development when the village was founded."

"I would say about 20% of the people who live here came from a Catholic background, which is slightly less than the national average and most describe themselves as lapsed. Surprisingly however, almost everyone who owns a home or flat in this village voted the optional church assessment fee that is part of the Villageton equivalent of a local property tax. While part of the annual fee is town-wide, each village also gets to vote for assessments only paid by their village for their own purposes. One village pays a small stipend to the village jester, for example, a singular fellow who is part gadfly and part actor with a rapier wit– dresses outlandishly, will write you a poem for five dollars, and who keeps the village on its toes especially at village and town meetings."

"In this village, instead of a jester, they support me, and I suppose if there are a number of different brands of Church message... hell & damnation, seasonal ritual, headhunting... the message here is about love. All people need love, living in a loving community is normal, but as you probably heard from Morgan if you got his briefing at the visitor center, we live in an abnormal world where love is hard to find. Love is sharing a beer at the tavern with friends, laughing, telling stories, taking a kid from the next village to a ball game when his parents are too busy. It's bringing flowers every

Tuesday to the same old person in the nursing facility – the one who has no family and whose best friends have all died... and then listening to the same words they say each week without looking or feeling bored. They hired me to focus attention on those kinds of things."

## YOUTH

"About 20 percent of the population of Villageton is school-aged children, about two thousand kids from age six to eighteen. When they hit puberty, they enter a vulnerable time. Peer pressure can turn them to activities of danger to themselves and which offend their parents, as they try to define themselves as autonomous human beings. When children begin to transform into adults, their bodies and minds seem to go haywire. That confident, articulate 12 year-old becomes a moody, confused 14 year old that drives parents up the wall and it can take another five to ten years to come right again."

"As our society becomes more distracted and offers less structure to children that age, peer pressure results in binge drinking, drug abuse, heartless sexuality, addictions and extreme behaviors that can kill a child such as street racing or daredevil stunts. Some of these peer pressure activities can be permanently damaging, others they survive, but having missed some wonderful experiences that early generations took for granted."

"So as a community, we looked at these issues, and in talking with the older youth from the youth zone, they made it clear that at that age anything resembling a parent was instant persona non grata... an unwelcome person. In contrast, they had great admiration for what we call the Suvies because they were cool... or was it hot? Suvies dressed well, listened to great music, had elegant taste in just about everything, all of which translated to Suvies not being like their parents. Of course they fail to consider their parents gave up the material comforts and free time that comes from not having children, but instead chose to have these wonderful babies who then turned into ungrateful, pimply-faced brats they can't wait to see grown up and on their own... Well, never-mind, this is the theater that comes from being human."

"In any case, part of my job included organizing youth groups in many of the villages, and then recruiting Suvies to help run them. "Run" is probably the wrong word, since the youth elect their own leaders, decide their own agendas and pretty much manage the group themselves. The adults attend the meetings, ask the right questions, and I suppose give the parents of the youth members comfort that what goes on is safe and legal."

"The focus of these various youth groups is as varied as the personalities of young people, and each village has its own group or two. Membership is open, so a youth from one village may chose not to belong to the group in their village, but another – and some will belong to more than one. We even have young people from outside Villageton become members in some of the groups."

"Some youth groups are sports-oriented, others service-directed, and a few focus on big issues of the day where youth are especially passionate, such as saving the environment or eliminating world poverty. Most focus on human relationships however; a big issue for that age group... simple things like how to touch a member of the opposite sex without it having to be overtly sexual."

"Yeah", Ed commented, "In my day we called that slow dancing, and big bands came every Saturday to the dance hall... before Elvis killed off that form of music."

"Actually", Andy replied, "big band is not dead, at least not here. Some of the kids have rediscovered the dances of your era, and have taken up both the music and the dances. There is a young Canadian singer who seems to have hit the charts with Sinatra-era songs, and this inspired young people to begin digging through their grandparents' record albums for old gold.

"So, that's why my albums sold for so much on Ebay," Ed exclaimed. "I was expecting I would have to toss them in the trash when I cleared the house, but the auction prices were mind-boggling."

Andy agreed and then continued explaining. "At first the teens here held dances using the old shellac records, then they used technology to transfer and clean them up digitally, but more recently some of the teens in a high school band began to learn the songs and play at dances on weekends. They've become quite good, and have cut several CD's which you can buy on your way out of town near the main gate."

"Funny, isn't it? Here I am supposed to be giving you a tour of the Suvie's village yet I'm talking more about the Suvies that work with teenagers who don't live here but in other villages. So, let me point out some of the architectural masterpieces and describe what people actually do here to earn a living."

"As you can see, the architecture is premium, elegant and somewhat cutting edge; not cold but certainly polished... a lot of warm Carrera marble, bright brass that never seems to tarnish, fantastic lighting. Being single means more discretionary income and more time to hone ones tastes for the finer things in life. If I were to identify a design influence, I would say it is international, with perhaps the flair of the fashion quarter of Florence or Milan, although here they simply call it Eurotrash. Singles travel a lot more, and to more trendy places, and they bring back those experiences and patterns."

As Andy pointed out a tasteful example of the architecture, Ed asked if he would not mind waiting while he did a sketch. Sophia explained to Andy that Ed was multitasking and able to listen well while drawing.

Andy continued to tell the Suvie story. "When Nicole, the village coordinator proposed Suvieville, she gave those singles a place to blend all those patterns into the plaza here. Her rolodex was amazing. I heard one story from a mutual friend where she decided winter was getting glum, so she decided to invite 300 of her closest friends to a party. Found a loft for free, convinced a Brazilian soft drink company to sponsor it, chased up lighting, sound and put on a party that went till the wee hours of the morning. For her this was normal. She no longer lives here however, although she kept her apartment which she provides to friends and uses when she is in town. She fell in love with an investment banker whose secret dream in life was to become a vintner; they married, have a child and she is now winning world-class awards for their wines and running wine appreciation events on her spectacular estate. Goes to show you can't plan your life when it comes to love. But I digress," Andy said with a laugh.

"In Suvieville, almost everyone is a money importer, meaning they depend on telepresence to make a living; they sell local to global. We have a higher proportion of what they call "Lone Eagles", meaning professionals in the financial worlds who used to work for a large firm, developed a client following loyal to them, not the company. When they went independent, the clients went with them. These people, traders mostly, use the massive digital pipeline that was a prerequisite of Villageton to maintain a Star Trek-like communications system with their clients and markets."

With that, Andy signaled to a fellow inside an office, and was waved in. Alejandro got up out of his high-tech chair, walked to the door and introduced himself. Originally from Mexico, he won a scholarship to one of the top American business schools which then secured him a job with a major investment bank in New York. After a decade he decided to go out on his own. Most of his clients dropped their institutional accounts and came with him, as he had a knack for Latin American investments that came from his background and skills.

## The Lone Eagle

His office looked more like one of those Hollywood film sets where the CIA or NASA is portrayed with banks of computers and video displays. One whole wall of Alejandro's office consisted of stacked video displays showing live prices in world markets. Commodities, stocks, forex, precious metals and other markets ran continual updates, and above them round clocks displayed the current time in trading cities around the world. At eye level a large bank of Telepresence displays were set up where Alejandro could hold a life-sized board meeting with a dozen directors sitting in their own offices around the world.

Alejandro commented that he had more information at his fingertips here than he did when he used to work in his corporate office in New York City. E-lance provided all his back office work, meaning he no longer employed anyone, but contracted for all the work he needed to be done to conduct business. He had a team in India he had never met in person that did brilliant work in programming his proprietary analysis software. His international tax accounting was managed by a firm in Brussels, as he managed some complex real estate based instruments... not subprime, he hastened to add.

Alejandro showed reluctance to disclose his earnings, commenting only that he did well, but he did say that he fully subscribed to the principle of money turn, and made a point of both spending and investing in Villageton and its surrounding region. He still held a soft spot for stone ground corn tortillas like his mother used to make, so he invested in a local business to make them. It now supplies the restaurants, food stores and is on the food intranet, where residents buy food for home delivery. When it turned profitable, he offered to sell it to the people working in the business, and they are slowly buying him out on reasonable terms. He is happy; he did well on the investment and gets pure tortillas just like his mother used to make them.

He also provided the funds, along with a few other like-minded capitalists in Villageton, to start the fabric factory that adapted the Provencal method of dying cloth with beautiful, multi-colored floral and decorative patterns. Alejandro saw that with 10,000 people moving into to Villageton there would be a strong demand for home fabrics. Instead of seeing that money flow out of the local economy, it made sense to invest in a business that could capture the initial market. The hardest part of any business is the start-up, securing those first sales while sorting out what works and what does not. Longer term, the business will saturate the local market, so it then needs a global transition plan. If it has done well in the beginning, established a reputation for excellent quality and brilliant design, and paid for the equipment and tooling with the local sales, then it stands a good chance of becoming a solid, long-lasting business.

"To invest in the fabric business," Alejandro said, "we established one of the Villageton Angel Funds where I and other like-minded capitalists set aside some of their funds to start up such businesses as Villageton was being built. We posted our interests on the Village Forum web site, and village coordinators then sought out people whose dream job would be to own, run, or work in those businesses in the industrial park. As Angel Investors, we would provide the funds, and then sit on the board of directors offering both mentorship and connections to assist the business during startup and growth phases. Eventually, our goal would be to spin the companies off, owner-operated, to assure Villageton maintained both a robust local economy and a diverse one. In a one-company town, when the company goes bust, the town dies. In a village-town the economy keeps going even if some of its industries fail."

As Alejandro finished explaining, one of the Telepresence screens lit up with the face of a man, and the words along the bottom flashed *Beirut 9:14 p.m.* He pressed a button and said "Good evening Jameel. I will be with you in just a moment." Andy and the others thanked him for his time, and continued on with their journey.

As they left his office, stepping onto the plaza in the bright sunlight, Ed commented that Alejandro's office would not be one with high foot traffic, which made it an unlikely candidate for a plaza location. Andy replied that while this was true, Alejandro enjoyed the high activity of the street and was prepared to pay a premium land price for the location. Working alone as he did, or connecting with people via high definition video links, he took frequent breaks on the plaza where he connected with real people to keep himself grounded.

## Divorce and Children

The ages of the people in the plaza varied widely from 20's through grey hairs not much younger than himself. Ed noticed that most were in good physical shape and appeared to be enjoying their lives. He reflected back on his Blandville years, and realized how segregated his life had been, single people, or Suvies as they called them here, did not choose to live in Blandville. If they grew up there, they moved away as soon as they could. He also recalled the tension when friends of theirs separated or divorced. It became awkward socially, as he and his wife had to decide who to invite to parties or dinners. Usually the husband moved out, to an apartment while the wife struggled to maintain a home and children on alimony. In different ways, it turned out to be tough on both of them, although the ex-husband usually came out better financially and socially. He had a sense the breakup left lasting damage on the children. He found it fascinating to see how Villageton took care of the 'tossed out' spouse. He wondered how it would take care of the parent left with the kids. He asked Andy.

"First of all," Andy explained, "we see less family break-ups in Villageton than what passes for normal in the rest of the country. Villageton life places less pressure on families. Children play outside without adult supervision. It's not unusual for a pack of them to be racing around the plaza or on the back streets, or even out in the Greenbelt without parents worrying. In winter a whole mob of them will be out playing in the snow, and then someone on the street will herd them all in, dry off the wet clothes and bake some cookies, just for the sheer pleasure of it. This gives parents more time to get on with the rest of their lives."

Ed smiled, thinking again of Morgan's comment about remembering. "Yes, that's how it was when I was a kid. My mother had a cow bell. Each family had a different sounding bell, and when it was time to come home, they would ring it. No one worried like they do nowadays, to the point where children live like prisoners, always under someone's official supervision."

Andy replied, "While it has become a cliché, it really does take the village to raise the child, and more importantly, the village takes the pressure off families."

"We do have break ups however – less of them and more release valves so they can blow off and then work it out – but some relationships cannot be salvaged and others should never have happened in the first place. It becomes a community problem when the relationship involves children."

"Usually it is the mother who ends up with the children, but sometimes she is the one to walk out, leaving dad with full time child-care responsibilities. In these cases, the face-to-face quality of the villages makes a big difference. Neighbors help each other. They offer to carry the load. One of the distinctive qualities of family homes in Villageton is the bed count – there are more beds than children. Instead of babysitters, we have sleepovers where children stay at each other's houses. When a family breaks up, other families help carry the load."

"Another aspect that makes a difference is proximity to work. Mom and Dad work nearby. So does everyone else. This means that when a child needs attention, it's easy – a short walk either by the child or the parent. This helps keep families together, and if they break up, makes it easier to manage the responsibilities. Of course, these are not new patterns; this is how any tribal society worked back when people did not suffer divorce but premature death due to childbirth, injury or illness. Everyone lives and works close by and pulls together in adversity."

"Then, there are the solo parent families that moved here when Villageton was being designed. Some wanted conventional homes, but a small number found they wanted more than their alimony and income could support. They created a concept called Quad Homes, although not all of them involve four conjoint units," Andy explained.

Ed asked Andy to say more about *quad homes* and *conjoint units*.

Andy replied. "It began when a number of divorced mothers came up with their own plan to carry the load of child rearing on low incomes. They wanted to own, but could not afford conventional housing. So they proposed a square donut type building where each side was a separate title home, but the hole in the middle was a common courtyard and play area open to all the homes. The mothers share much of their homes with each other, and the children have free roam of all four homes. It was not communal living however; the mothers made it clear that each wanted their own kitchen and their private bedroom was off limits."

"That sounds great in theory," Ed commented, "but what happens when someone wants to sell? What if a potential buyer has the kids from hell?"

"Good question," Andy answered, "and one they anticipated. They run it the same as co-op apartments where the buyer must be approved by all, and since everyone knows this from the get-go, it has never been a problem. It also does tend to mean such homes sell for less, which keeps them affordable for solo parents. Incidentally, sometimes the buyer is a solo dad, and other times a quad will invite an old person to buy in, to become a surrogate grandparent."

"Fascinating," Ed said. "I wonder why Blandville never considered such an idea?

### Human Damage

"Andy," Ed asked, "what is your view? Is Villageton some sort of utopia?"

Andy laughed and then caught himself. "Sorry, Ed. It's just if you were to walk alongside me in a day's work, you would see how un-utopian this place is. What is a utopia? It's a place in someone's mind, where everyone lives in peace and harmony, where everything works perfectly and it only rains after midnight."

"No", Andy continued, "Villageton was never intended to be a utopia. From day one it presumed, and planned for human corruption. Pick out any ten people on any plaza, invite them to tell their life story, and it will astound you the damage in their lives. Villageton heals some old damage and generates less new damage because it enables people to live more normally. When the insane pressures of modern life back off, people can begin to develop more consciously. They can care for themselves and others. No, Villageton is not a utopia. It is, as Morgan says, a normal place in an abnormal world.

"Andy, would you mind clarifying what you mean by *damage*?" Ed asked. "While I use the word, from time to time, I may not be using it in the same way as you do in talking about your business."

Andy smiled and explained. "Part of my job is to be aware of the private side of human lives, the sorts of things people do not talk about to their family, friends or people on the street. The ancient practice of confession was a place to unburden ourselves when we were carrying things we did that we know are wrong. But there are many other comparable things that affect us that are not within our consciousness.

They become part of our belief systems."

"For example," Andy went on, "a child who sits in front of a TV all day, whose parents are too busy to give the child love, will not develop normally. Or a child whose parents are angry and fight all the time will internalize that anger, and develop beliefs about themselves that inhibit their ability to become complete, loving adults. Sometimes this damage can pass from one generation to another. In my business, I find as I help some people explore their ancestry, they discover the damage can go back hundreds of years."

"In my profession, we have known about this for centuries, but it was only when I met a cell biologist by the name of Dr. Bruce Lipton, that I finally heard a plausible scientific explanation for what we see everyday. He describes our physical bodies not as an individual, but as a cooperative community of 50 trillion single-celled citizens that have evolved a cooperative strategy for their mutual survival. I'm not exactly sure what my boss would think of his view, but from a pragmatic standpoint it helps me. In essence when we suffer trauma, be it physical or emotional, our bodies develop a coping mechanism and store the determined response in the cells, so we will select the right response the next time... fright, flight or fight. We don't do this consciously because our brains are too slow and can't process all the information we take in."

"Can you give me an example?" Ed asked.

"Sure," Andy replied. "I was on vacation in Cornwall, England walking to the coast along an ancient path on a sunny day, when suddenly my foot froze in midair. A few moments later, my conscious brain caught up. My eye first went to my leg and said *freeze - snake!* Then having taken care of the preservation stuff the message then went to my brain and said *you may want to take evasive action because you are about to step on a snake and standing on one leg is a temporary measure only.* So my brain then registered that there was a big rock to my left, and I consciously but without too much thinking, hopped up on it, thus moving me to safety. Having accomplished that, I shifted into an even higher level of consciousness, grabbed my camera and took a photo of the rear two thirds of the snake as it slithered off into the grass... all in a matter of the few seconds it took the snake to get out of harms way. When I showed it to a native, he was impressed, saying I had almost trod upon an adder, England's only venous snake. So in that example, the trauma of stepping on snakes is hardwired into my cells, and my *freeze* behavior operates unconsciously. As long as the world continues to have venomous snakes in it, that coping mechanism is important, and I want to keep it stored in my cells."

"Well," Andy continued, "in the same way and for the same reason, our bodies record other reactions to life, and some of those make us miserable. If we were abused as a child, we respond to the world as abusive. Now, if we live in a truly abusive world – say a country where law has totally broken down, then our body will be properly tuned to survive. But if we live in a civilized world then those same messages are not only no longer useful, they will hold us back. And that is what I mean by *damage*."

"What Lipton did was show how to re-record the messages so we break the cycle of damage. And to bring this back to your original question. Villageton is not and was never intended to be a utopia; it does create a physical and emotional environment that is more supportive, so people can begin not only to rewire their belief systems, but live life more consciously, to pursue their aspirations."

As they walked out of the plaza Andy said it was time for him to leave them. In thanking him, Ed said, "Andy, you have got to be the most unusual priest I have ever met. I'm not a Catholic, but the impression I have of your religion is focused on issues like abortion, birth control, divorce, homosexuality, and here you are in a community that pays your support where you say that less than 20% are Catholic and most of those describe themselves as lapsed."

"That's true Ed. Andy replied. "In fact, I did an informal survey and found most of the people I serve described themselves as agnostic, secular or neo-spiritual, a few as aggressively atheistic – some of whom came from ultra religious families they rejected, and the rest is a wide range of liberal, evangelical and fundamentalists Christians, Mormons, Jews, Moslems, Buddhists, Hindu, Sikh, indigenous and neo-pagan. The common theme I found among all of them was they respond well to love, which happens to be a central message of the founder of my religion."

"Within most formal religions you have *the people* and then you have *the practitioner*, the one who gets paid to deliver the message, like me. As I mentioned when we met, the practitioner has a wide range of messages to select from, and I would say your impression of my church comes from a few stone tablets written with the words *Thou Shalt Not*. In Villageton however, people already seem to adhere to a lot of those injunctions."

"People here do not murder each other, we have few instances of theft, and these are addressed either by the family in the case of a delinquent child, or if there is a deeper problem by the police and courts. Bearing false witness against your neighbor or coveting things that belong to them does not need a *thou shalt not* commandment because our villages are face-to-face communities. Screw up and it's uncomfortable walking over to the café for a snack. This is not unique to Villageton, most close communities have very low social disruption and crime rates – people leave their doors unlocked. It's how it works when everyone feels they belong. Traditionally, this was called citizenship. In New Zealand, the indigenous people, the Maori, have a wonderful word for it, *turangawaewae* – a place to stand tall. Enable people to feel they are a part, and you don't need some sour-faced preacher storming on about *thou shalt not*".

"As for the issues of sexuality and marriage that you cited, these are part of the Church's job. Traditionally rites of passage were managed on both a social and spiritual plane. The media focuses on intimate issues because sex sells. My work isn't newsworthy. I am a single person, what they here call a Suvie. I help facilitate Suvies working with the rest of the community in ways that are both good for them and for the community. What I set in motion works on both a social and spiritual plane, although the spiritual is personal and shared, as opposed to laced with ritual. I do celebrate the sacraments of the Church, and it is surprising how many attend, although I do little more than leave the door open."

"I know who I am; I know what I believe, but here it is about doing, not talking. And with that sermon, I will take my leave. I wish you well, Ed. Sophia, thank you for giving Ed this tour, and Michael as always, it is good to see you."

They thanked Andy for his time, and Ed asked if the others would mind if he did a quick sketch of Andy's church. It reminded him of a church in Tuscany he drew as a student. As he sketched he wondered about Michael; a lot of people seemed to know him here in Villageton with real affection, but Ed was not sure it was his place to ask.

# Chapter 7

# The Creative Class

As they walked toward the next plaza, Ed heard classical music yet it sounded live. They rounded the corner to discover many chairs set out on the plaza; in every other one, a musician playing an instrument. Standing on a platform a conductor, and next to him a violinist playing. He looked European, hair slicked back, dark jacket, open-collar white shirt, polished black shoes. He glanced up, saw Sophia and while continuing to play, gestured with his head for them to take empty seats among the orchestra. After a few minutes playing he held up his bow for the orchestra to stop, and he began to speak. The orchestra understood this impromptu halt as they stopped immediately in a razor sharp cutoff.

"For those of you who have just joined us, welcome. My name is Miha Pogacnik and I am the director of Idriart, the Initiative for the Development of Intercultural Relations through the Arts. This is a rehearsal for the arts festival that Villageton shall hold next week, and if you have taken a seat among the orchestra, you will experience what we call *The Surround Orchestra*."

"Idriart is an international organization based in Hamburg but with its spiritual home in Castle Borl, an ancient castle in Slovenia, which local lore says is the ancestral home of Parzival. I am both a violinist and the Ambassador of Culture for the Republic of Slovenia. I am here for the upcoming festival."

"The Surround Orchestra offers both a wonderful experience and a metaphor for life, especially in business. Today we rehearse a work by Bach for orchestra and solo violin. However, instead of playing it straight through, we play, then stop, and I speak for about three minutes. The audience sits as you sit, among the musicians. As you will find, sitting among the instruments engenders a completely different experience than being in an audience in the typical music hall. When the music stops, you are welcome to get up and change seats, to move from the string section to the percussion for example, and note how you not only hear the sound, you feel it pulsing in your bones."

"In the festival itself, we encourage people to bring pen and a notepad with them, and as I begin to speak, they are welcome to make notes, or to not listen to me at all, but to write down thoughts that pop into their head. When the music plays, the emotional side of the brain becomes active. One person described it as being like a frozen river that breaks up with the Spring melt; ideas in image-form begin to flow. Then when the music stops, and I begin to talk, the mental side of the brain takes over. The images that emerged with the music become thoughts expressed in words. I invite you to write them down. Then we go back to the music, and again the brain shifts, and throughout the piece we go back and forth, giving our brain a real synaptic workout. Participants report many breakthroughs occur, as the ideas flow on challenges they are facing in their own lives. The musicians enjoy it too."

"For those who listen to me instead of writing their own thoughts, especially when I am running the *Art Sponsors Business* program, I talk about how people work and how they could work together better. The business leaders constantly seek models to enable them to manage people better. Some use sports examples, "it's about winning", but this can produce unexpected outcomes as it depends on which game. I ask how would it work if we use the orchestra as a model?"

"In great orchestras, each player constantly practices to improve his or her mastery of the instrument, the notes written on the sheet and harmony, both following the conductor and listening to the rest of the orchestra to stay in tune and on time. Imagine how the music would sound if the first violinists competed to see who sounded the best, or the drums beat to sound the loudest. In fact, we don't have to imagine it... Orchestra, let us start in harmony, but then at my signal, each of you try to outdo the others."

The sweet sound of Bach began again. Miha allowed it to go on longer than Ed had expected. He found himself relaxing into a delightful state, as the music swept over him in a completely different experience. He was sitting among the violins, and realized he had never sat so close to a professional musician at work. Drifting with the music, suddenly, the violinist on his right jolted Ed out of his trance, as she aggressively dug her bow into the instrument. Looking up, he saw Miha had given the signal. Within seconds, the music and mood completely shifted. They were still following the same score, but it felt like he was in the middle of a battle with clashing swords, rising dust and trampling horses. Again Miha let it go on long; sawing on his own violin as if possessed. Gradually both the audience and the players began to laugh and finally Miha held up his bow to stop. Everyone clapped, including the musicians, the people working or sitting at the outdoor cafés, and some workers who had come out of their offices and shops to listen. Ed noted that many offices had balconies on the upper floors, and they were wide enough for people to stand or sit. Some had brought papers out, apparently deciding to work and listen at the same time. Nice.

Miha began to speak again, explaining the metaphor for business and again inviting people to write their insights in their notebooks. As this was a rehearsal, they would not go through the whole festival program, but next would invite one of the Villageton choral groups to join them. Ed wondered what he was talking about, as no one seemed to join the orchestra. Miha signaled the orchestra to begin again, and this time he selected the Choral Fantasy for Piano Chorus and Orchestra. Ed lacked a musical education, and his taste tended to run to more popular works, but in the setting this piece again transported him to another plane of appreciation. The piece began with the orchestra and the concert grand piano played by a master. Then the choir began to sing and Ed looked up in surprise. Hearing singing voices, he saw the choir standing on balconies and roof tops; the people he thought were workers were in fact the chorus. The whole plaza became filled with the sound of voices singing in harmony: in front of him, to the sides, behind and above. He felt a surge in his chest, a response to music like none he had ever experienced. Sophia leaned over and whispered "This plaza is special; it was acoustically designed for sound. The Guild Hall here is for musicians."

When it ended, Ed felt both exhilarated and a bit light-headed. Sophia asked if he would like to meet Miha, and taking his hand, led him up to the stand where Miha was speaking with the conductor. When done, he turned to Sophia, kissed her on both cheeks, and greeted her like an old friend. Sophia made the introductions, and then told Ed that she was from Slovenia, and in the small world department, Miha was friends with her parents. "Yes, that's true," said Miha "but she left us for university and now is doing her third year overseas, here."

Ed asked him, "Miha, this is an interesting idea, *Art Sponsors Business*. Is it not the other way around – usually the artist needs business support to survive?"

Miha beamed and replied. "Yes, it is a sad commentary on our society that those who work to make life more beautiful or stimulating do not receive the same monetary rewards as those who make widgets and gadgets. However, business is run by people, and people need more in their lives than balance sheets, contracts and marketing campaigns. When business sponsors art, they do it for the PR. When artists sponsor business, its leaders learn."

"You may have heard how this community, Villageton, was established so people could enjoy the good life. The economy, which is the realm of business, builds the foundation of civilization. Once built and strong, life becomes bland if people think the purpose of life is the economy, and the highest goal of the individual is to become rich. So in the drawing they use here to illustrate it – the picture showing a house with the economy as foundation, the ground floor of conviviality and citizenship and an upper floor of artistic and intellectual growth – the arts become an integral part of day-to-day life."

"Art leads people up the stairs. You may have experienced it a few moments ago, listening to the surround orchestra and chorus. In fact, you may have been floated higher, into a spiritual realm as you felt yourself detach from your physical presence sitting in a chair, and begin to flow on another plane with the music." Ed nodded in agreement; that was exactly what had just happened to him.

"In sponsoring business, we the artists see how our business colleagues too often become lost in their world of competition, of winning the deal, scoring the points, and defeating the competition. In contrast, an orchestra is about everyone working to the same sheet of music, but with their own special talent. One outcome, many players, learning to work in harmony. In sponsoring them, the artists, how shall I say this, wake them up. Once awoken, the business people become both better in what they do, and better in who they are. They remember a better future; they become who they are."

"But, let me ask you. Has Sophia shown you the Musicians' Guild Hall yet? This is a magnificent example of art sponsoring everything; not only business but community. Permit me to be your ambassador; to introduce you to it."

Ed was amused at this conversation, for he had not gotten a word in edgewise, as Miha happily got answers from the ether. Correct answers of course, as Ed wanted to see the guild hall, and could not imagine a better host than a renowned musician who carried a diplomatic passport and an extraordinary violin.

## The Guild Halls

Miha led them to a magnificent building which anchored the plaza. Clearly a source of community pride, it reflected a form of classical architecture as opposed to the more vernacular and simple design of the workplaces that surrounded it around the plaza. The designer of this building knew his stuff, Ed thought. Perfectly proportioned, and he saw how it would enhance outdoor acoustics.

"This is the musicians guild hall", began Miha. "Actually, there are several guild halls in the town given over to music. This one focuses on what is generically called classical music, as opposed to jazz, rock or world music. Unlike some of the halls, solely made up of world-class professionals, this guild consists of a core of 25 professionals and wider association of what one might call talented amateurs. For example, the choir director is a professional who belongs to the guild, but almost all the singers have other jobs, and they do not earn a living singing. Never-the-less, as you heard today, the quality of their singing would hold their own in any world ranking."

"Most people who live in this village love music. You saw that in the plaza architecture where all the buildings include wide balconies on the upper floors, and even some rooftop platforms. We did one symphony where the audience sat in the middle of the plaza and the instruments were on the balconies."

"The conductor said it made him dizzy just trying to look at them all." Sophia told them all with a laugh. Miha laughed as well and then continued.

"The decision about music came in the beginning. Each village coordinator puts forth ideas that become the magnet that draws particular people. One of the major draw cards of this village was music. Thus, the coordinator first contacted musicians to see if they would like to move here, and what they would need in their guild hall. He focused on three levels of musician, if I may use that term."

Miha explained. "He began with the masters: musicians with international reputation, now in the senior years of their career; masters, but no longer touring or cranking out a new recording every year. These elders became the magnet for the younger musicians, perhaps in the prime of their career, full of energy and booked out for years in advance. Finally, the coordinator sought out young, emerging musicians to set in place the tradition of succession of artists."

"The developer, what they call the Village Organizing Company, then set out a million dollar budget to build and outfit the guild hall. What did the musicians need; how should it look? Let's have a look at what they decided," Miha said.

Miha walked them into the production part of the guild hall, explaining "most of the rooms on this floor provide practice space; completely soundproof. Look through the window in that door, and you will see, but not hear, a solo trumpeter practicing." Ed could see her cheeks puffing but heard no sound.

His voice dropped to a whisper. "See the red light blinking at the end of the hall?" Miha asked. "That is the recording studio; the light means it is in use. Let's quietly step into the tech-room and watch. As you can see, the equipment here is first rate. Ten years ago, this would have been unaffordable except for a major label in a big city, but computer technology knocked a zero off the end of the price tag. They designed this studio brilliantly. Look out that window on the other side; we are above an in-house stage with excellent acoustics. This enables live on-stage recording without moving the technicians or equipment." ...'Very clever,' Ed thought to himself.

Miha went on, "When the guild began, they requested that one of the town's proper music halls be nearby, and they would agree to look after it – profitably. In addition to this small hall on this plaza, the town built a large concert hall in the main town square. It also serves a lecture hall for the Villageton conference center."

The group, with Miha in the lead, then walked into a less active part of the building. He continued to explain, "This is private quarter of the Guild Hall facing the quieter streets behind. This first large room on your left is the library, with comfortable leather chairs for reading, talking or taking a snooze. Many of the musicians put their own personal books on the shelves here to be shared by all; there is an agreement that books may be read, but not removed from this room. Next door is the guild dining hall, a formal room both used by the guild and the village when they need a room of this size. Because of the wood panelled walls, this room is fitted with automatic fire sprinklers. Behind the dining hall, you would find the guild members' commercial kitchen that may be used for hire."

"Down this hallway, you will find rooms to provide visitor accommodations. Intended to generate income to cover the guild's operating costs, these rooms, although simple and spartan, prove remarkably popular no matter what the season. Some visitors are musicians, while others are music lovers. We will skip viewing the bathrooms, showers, laundry and storage areas. Because the free-base homes of the musicians are small, these rooms provide extra space. This guild offers two storage spaces, one for personal instruments, some of which may be worth millions such as this Guarneri violin I am carrying, and a second for bulky personal property needing less security."

As they walked through the guild hall, Ed felt the buzz of the place. Musicians were in practice rooms, and the recording studio red light was on. "How do they pay the bills?" Ed asked. "Most artists I know hold down day jobs."

Sophia answered, "Cut the cost of living, increase opportunities to work."

Miha then explained further. "The cost cutting comes with special artist subsidies and lower cost of living for all villagers. Villageton values its artistic and intellectual citizens. It regards them as an important contributor to the overall quality of life in Villageton. It puts its money where its mouth is to assure they can always afford to live here."

Miha continued. "Each Guild Hall has 25 members. The number selected means Villageton has 500 artists, or about 5% of the population. *Artist* is broadly defined to encompass what Richard Florida calls the *Creative Class*. Membership in the guild means the development provides two subsidies:

- A one-time capital investment in the building and fittings.
- Free base housing for guild members.

Each member artist, regardless of need, is provided a small home, intended to provide comfortable, if sparse accommodations. They have basic toilet facilities and a boat-sized galley with stove top & bar fridge, plus a very small bathroom. It's like a cross between a kitchenette hotel room and a monastic cell. We call them angle homes because they serve an important architectural function."

This comment caught Ed's professional ear, and he asked Miha to explain what he meant by angle home and architectural function.

"Did you notice how many of the streets curve?" Miha asked and Ed nodded yes. "Well, to do that someone's home has to have angled walls. So what you need to do when the road turns on a slight angle is to build a... Sophia, my dear, what is the English word for *trapez* or *trapezoidni?*" Miha asked her.

"Trapezoidal. Almost the same as in Slovenian", Sophia replied.

"Yes, of course. Well, Ed, they decided that when the road would turn slightly to avoid having straight streets, they would connect the two houses pointing at different angles with artist-base housing whose rooms would be trapezoidal. The artist's home makes the turn and the inner wall is shorter than the outer wall, so the room is not like a shoebox. Depending on the building width, there may be one, two or three such homes stacked on top of each other like flats, with the upper floor stairs giving access on the wide side of the homes."

Miha pointed to one of them. "The artist does not get title to the home, that is held by Villageton. All the artist pays for are ongoing costs such as maintenance and external charges, like property taxes, rates or fees. As long as the artist is a member of the guild, the home is theirs as if they owned it. This includes the right to rent out the home and keep the rental income as an artist subsidy."

"Why would they do that?" Ed asked. "And do they appreciate it if given for free? Often times I find when someone gets something for free they do not value it."

Miha answered the latter question first. "The artist understands they are of value to the community by doing their art. So in that way, it is not free. It is similar to the old tribal time when the creative members of the tribe were fed, clothed and cared for so they could pursue what they were best at doing. The artists greatly value the gift of support, and if anything, Villageton gets a bargain. To answer the first question, in the event the artist wants to live elsewhere in Villageton, perhaps they are in a relationship, have a family or want the benefit of capital gains, the artist may rent out their free-base house and keep the income to help cover the mortgage of their family home. In order to keep the free-base home, they must continue to be a productive member of the artistic community in Villageton."

Sophia then spoke up. "The purpose of these cost savings is to enrich the whole community. Perhaps it would be helpful if I added up all the cost savings, where only the first two are solely for artists." Ed thought that would be helpful, so she began.

- *Housing?* Free. Paid for by the development to subsidize artists
- *Professional Supplies?* Many of the tools of the trade come with the guildhall, thus keeping down the artists' professional costs.
- *Transportation?* None. No one commutes by car; no transport costs.
- *Energy?* All homes include energy efficiency; reduce the utility bills.
- *Food?* With the direct buy food program, food bought direct from local farmers via Villageton's intranet costs half the supermarket price.
- *Consumer goods?* The wholesale buying club is part of Villageton's recycling service, using collective buying power to specify sustainable packaging and saving up to 50% of the retail price as an extra bonus."

In responding to Sophia's last point, Ed commented how his daughter Liz would come for state-side visits where for a month prior to her arrival, the post would deliver boxes of internet-ordered products. "I told her there was no way she could get this mountain of stuff into her suitcases and still stay within her luggage allowance, but when she packed, the mountain was still there... cardboard boxes, plastic wrap, bubble popcorn, rigid foam, catalogs, advertising inserts and other completely useless stuff that ends up in the weekly trash collection. From a bulk perspective most of what she bought was packaging... used for delivery, then discarded."

Sophia laughed, "Yes, Europeans visiting the US shop here because it is consumer heaven. Villageton set up the buyers' club primarily to control incoming packaging that is environmental hell. The secondary intent is to lower the cost of living. As they say here, *it's cheaper to save a dollar than earn one.*"

She continued. "On the income side, artists get more opportunity to earn a living from their art. Anytime there is a concentration of any product, more people come. You see it in the mega-car strips that run for miles. The car dealers figured out that if they clustered in one place, more buyers would come. We cluster artists rather than cars, but it is the same principle... attract more buyers"

Miha then picked up on Sophia's point. "The Guild Halls promote the arts. The music guild hall includes a recording studio able to produce CD-quality recordings. Villageton runs a major internet server to promote all products made here, including e-commerce, so solo artists at the beginning of their career gain access to the best technology to market and sell their works. "

"Festivals form a regular part of Villageton life, both attracting a wide audience for direct sales, and creating an internet market as we become known globally. Our festival field can host a 25,000 person festival on it, with additional space for enjoying the more intimate setting of the village plazas, as you experienced a few moments ago," Miha explained.

He continued. "Then you will find cross-guild activity. The film makers' village requires a broad range of artists including musicians, actors, animators, digital artists, carvers, furniture makers, etc. Having all these talents in a single location makes Villageton an attractive option when scouting for a location."

"Finally," Sophia concluded, "the guild hall design includes school classrooms. We have no separate school campuses, the classrooms are on the plazas. Classes in the arts are held in the respective guild halls, where some artists secure teaching certificates, while others act as teachers' aides, meaning they can teach their art under the supervision of a certified teacher."

"Impressive" Ed replied. "And how do you deal with artists who go slack, or cease being active artists? What if an artist clings on to their room and perks, like a barnacle on a rock, clogging up the works, and holding on to a space that should go to another artist on the waiting list?" Sophia answered this question.

"To directly answer your question, which focused on the negative, the village uses a system of checks and balances. The guild runs its own affairs, and its charter or founding documents instruct it to keep the guild fresh and active. If it deems a member no longer adhering to the guild purposes, it deals with it as any organization would. However, there is a clause in the charter that gives the village certain rights as well. If a majority of the village votes a loss of confidence in its guild, the Villageton administration must step in, seek to mediate a solution, and if none can be found, the governing process of Villageton may be asked to dictate a resolution. It's never happened, and probably the knowledge of it, is enough to make the guilds consider as paramount the public good," Sophia said.

Miha then finished the answer "However, to answer it in a more positive fashion, Villageton has a critical mass of artists, with an emphasis on keeping the creativity fresh and thriving. It operates a strong visiting artists program. Active all the time, it forms relationships with other creative communities around the world, such as Idriart, especially in countries where the state or the traditional culture hold artistic creativity in high regard. Villageton artists move around a lot. Those who give up art generally move on to their new life, creating a vacancy in the guild. When the masters become elders, they move from the guild to elder housing, but keep an emeritus position with the guild until they die."

Back onto the plaza, immediately several people spied Miha and signaled him. "I am needed urgently for the latest crisis", he sighed. "A pleasure to meet you Ed, and I hope you found our little orchestra to be of interest. Sophia, my love to your parents, and Michael, my brother in name – in Slovenian Miha is short for Mihael, may you conduct Ed safely to his ordained destination". With a bow and kiss on the hand for Sophia, handshakes for the men, and before Ed could say anything in thanks, Miha was off, coattails flapping, Guarneri violin and bow in hand. Ed shook his head in both delight and wonder at the people he was meeting, their stories and he noted, their exits. It was not so much that they were in a hurry as they were living a fuller life.

As Sophia guided them toward the next village, Ed looked in the front windows of the workplaces. While some had a musical theme appropriate for the village, many were normal businesses unrelated to music. He commented the same to Sophia.

"That's true," she said, "but there may be a connection. For example, Craig's office, over there runs a consultancy in succession planning. While the business exists to help small and medium businesses do their tax planning, Craig's real passion in life is singing opera. He not only studies himself under one of the masters in the guild hall, he teaches young people. If I were to assess Craig's life, I would say he works to live, rather than lives for his work."

"Got it," Ed said, noting that this seemed to be a universal theme in Villageton.

# Chapter 8

# Entrepreneurs & Pioneers

While the building designs in each of the villages were distinctive and completely different than the village before, Ed felt all reflected timeless designs with many references to the best of the past. However, as they walked through the gate marking the boundary between the music village and the next, timeless architecture gave way to some of the boldest Ed had ever seen in his life. This village was a riot of shapes, colors, textures and form.

One home was set back with outdoor sofas and chairs on sandstone tiles in front. Next door a massive gleaming gold and red metal sculpture dominated the front of the wall that was concaved in a semicircle. The semicircle had no windows, and the concrete was cast so it looked like warm, weathered sandstone. It reminded Ed of the Buddha statues in Afghanistan carved out in a rock cliff; the 1500 year old ones that the Taliban demolished in 2001. The sign named the sculptor as Gidon Graetz which rang a bell in his memory, but he could not place him.

It was a sunny day, and Ed saw how buildings had been placed so that those with reflective surfaces caught the sun and brightened the street. A lot of attention was paid to layout. Some of the buildings could only be described as quirky, others he saw as masterpieces of architecture. The overall effect worked. As he looked more carefully, he discovered that every single building had a signature on it. He recognized some of the names; famous architects, some emerging ones known for their bold statements and other names he never heard of. "OK, Sophia, I'll bite. What have we walked into here?"

Sophia smiled and said "Welcome to the Entrepreneurs and Inventors Village." Having expected another answer, like *architects' village,* Ed's face showed his surprise.

She explained, "The artist guild hall on this plaza is the Inventor's guild. It is made up of utterly brilliant people who, well, they invent things. Most of the businesses run here follow the same theme, people who invent businesses – what we call entrepreneurs. They say if we could figure out a way to plug the town's electrical cables into the buzz of this plaza, we could power the whole region."

"The internet provides huge opportunity for new ways to do business, and Villageton provides the highest speed broadband available. This attracted a disproportionate interest from what is called Telepresence entrepreneurs, and one of them, Richard Hollingum, decided to run a flag up for an entrepreneur's village. Tied into several social networks, within days his village was over-subscribed. Instead of holding a lottery, he decided to hold a contest to find the most brilliant businesses to move in. Everyone who applied had to write a page on the village's web site introducing themselves and what they did. Then Richard sent each of them a password to view all the applicants and to vote for their top 200. Those with the most votes got in," Sophia said.

"Richard had no particular preference for architectural look or feel, as the focus in his life was doing. He runs a global business called the Department of Doing, with the motto, *Consider It Done*. He emailed every architect he could find on the net and asked them to submit proposals to design villagers' homes and offices. He set out non-negotiables such as height, but within that encouraged them to propose whatever they pleased. He required they include a fixed quote for their services. If they wanted to do more than one building, they had to submit a second or third proposal, so no two buildings would be the same."

"Richard posted all the proposals on the internet, and gave each architect ten days during which they could change their proposal after viewing their competition. He got almost a thousand proposals from all over the world. When word got out, during the ten day review period hundreds more new proposals came in. Then, after he closed the proposal submissions, he used a random number generator to assign each of the villagers a lottery number; the villager who got number one was the first to choose a design."

"As with all the other villages, Richard was aiming for a population of about five hundred people, and as it turned out, his villagers were close to the national average with 2.6 people per family. Some families were "his, hers and theirs" while others were single people, solo parents, or couples. Age range was across the board. Mathematically, it worked out to one hundred ninety homes, but Richard asked to place two hundred twenty-five. The Village Organizing Company signed off, as the vast majority of the villagers would be money importers, essential to supplying the local economy with global revenue. Two hundred and three of the families selected architectural plans, and the others arranged for their own. The person who drew the last lot, number two hundred twenty-five, said the design she chose would have been the same had her lot been the first. "

"Richard thanked all the architects, and he also invited those who did not win to put their designs up on a public web site that anyone could purchase. It started a whole new internet business for his company and then he established a charitable arm as one architect proposed he start an "open source" page for designs architects would give away for free. This became a hit world-wide, especially public architecture, where a first-world nation would pay for say a school design, and then it would be freely available for a third-world school that could never afford the fees."

"What a great idea," Ed commented. "I've often thought what a waste it is to put all the work into a set of plans and then file them away, never to be used again. I should look into that as a way to use my free time now that I am fully retired. But tell me, Sophia, what is that huge building at the far end of the plaza. Surely they do not have two guild halls in this village, do they?"

"No," she replied. "As word got out, a state university with an excellent business school contacted Richard and asked if they could open a branch post-graduate campus. Richard put it to the villagers. One who did a Fulbright in Oxford, proposed they say yes, but require it use an architectural model of an Oxford college – a four story building with an arched gateway, inner courtyard with hand-mowed lawn, with classrooms, offices and dorm rooms around the quad. These villagers who had just selected the most cutting edge designs on the planet loved the idea. The VOC reviewed it and suggested it be near to the town square precinct so its height would blend in with the cascading rise of buildings." Sophia concluded.

As Ed looked up at the massive college building, he had to admit it was the most extraordinary blend of modern and traditional one could imagine. It worked because the architect broke up the surface with considerable detail, the sort of detail that would have taken stone masons a lifetime to carve. By now, Ed understood how these carvings were done in soft plastic molds using computer cutting technology. 'Smart,' he said to himself.

"Would there be any chance I can meet this man Richard?" Ed asked. "We sure could have used someone like him when I worked in Blandville. I love the name, Department of Doing. Completely the opposite of the maddening bureaucracy that I used to call work.

"We can give his office a try, but no guarantee he will be there. He has too much fun to be standing still," replied Sophia. They went in. While Sophia asked for Richard, Ed read a framed sign on the wall:

# The Directives of Doing

These directives form the self-imposed code of conduct established by the founding partners of the company and rigorously enforced throughout the Department of Doing.

DIRECTIVE 1 (A).
If someone comes to the Department with a problem, solve it for them. This is what The Department of Doing does. It is why we exist. Never say "Sorry, we don't do that." Or "It's not really our thing." Just because we haven't done it before doesn't mean we can't do it. It just means we have to find out how. Anything is possible with effort and imagination.

DIRECTIVE 1 (B).
If The Department of Doing really can't solve the client's problem, find someone else who can. Even if it means giving the business to another supplier. It's more important to solve the problem than to get the business.

DIRECTIVE 2.
Be honest with yourself and with others. We want the Department of Doing to be ethical, honest and open. We have learned by experience that business is more productive, more creative and more fun, when people trust and respect each other. We have spent too many years working in big companies (and small) which run on fear, paranoia and deceit to want to do it all over again.

DIRECTIVE 3.
Never say, "That's not my job". The business world is full of organizers, planners, facilitators and managers. It doesn't need any more. At the Department of Doing we only want doers. We are about making stuff, and making stuff happen. We are about taking clients' problems and making them go away. That's our job.

DIRECTIVE 4.
If you don't know, find someone who does. Our industry is full of people who claim to know everything about everything. Without exception, they are all lying. They probably know a little about a lot. Enough to finish the crossword but not enough to finish the job. At the Department of Doing we are specialists. We know a lot about our core business, but prefer to seek out specialist help and advice in areas where we are not experts.

DIRECTIVE 5.
Not knowing is not a crime. Not caring is. The success of the smallest job is as important to the reputation of the Department as the biggest one. This success depends on each job receiving the same due care and fastidious attention to detail. We have a very tall building, and will not think twice about throwing people off the roof if they are in breach of Dept. Directive 5.

DIRECTIVE 6.
The directors and partners of The Department of Doing reserve the right to go sailing every Sunday morning, providing this activity does not cause a contravention of any of the aforementioned directives, and tides permitting.

DIRECTIVE 7(A).
Insofar as it is possible, the Department of Doing will only do business with individuals and businesses which it likes and respects. The Department will never associate nor trade with businesses or individuals who are discourteous, rude, unprofessional or who wear grey shoes, no matter how much money they offer.

DIRECTIVE 7(B).
There is no Department Directive 7(b)

1   Reprinted with permission. www.departmentofdoing.com

Ed looked down at his shoes. Brown. He liked this Richard already. He wished he had known about his company when he was in Blandville, although he was not sure how the idea of getting things done might go down with his former team and bosses.

As it happened, Richard was in and they were shown into his office. Just as he had seen in the office of Alejandro, the Mexican investment banker, Richard was talking with wall-sized Telepresence screens, holding a meeting with what looked like his whole design team. He counted five screens, all live. Reading the locations on the bottom of the screen, one person in the technology guild hall in Villageton, two people were in New York, three in London, one in Mumbai and another two in Kuala Lumpur. Someone was working late, Ed thought. Richard wrote on a pad of paper "Be with you in five minutes - feel free to watch".

Ed sat down where Richard motioned, next to one of the lead innovators who was collaborating with Richard and the team on the screens, pulling together a project that Ed surmised was for a client in Malaysia. From what he saw, it looked like a big project; the dollar figures on the data screens were impressively large.

Richard was wrapping up the telepresence call; they all agreed on final action points and set the next meeting same time, next day. "Sorry Sophia for the delay, Hi Michael," said Richard logging out of the calls and setting the system to its offline mode. Turning to Ed he said, "Hi, I'm Richard. Pleasure to meet you"

Ed replied. "So you really are the Director of Doing, the pleasure is mine, I'm impressed with your directives."

"Well, we try. As they say, 'doing something requires doing something but it sure helps being around like-minded people to make a real difference."

Ed let that one rattle around his brain for a moment, gave up and then asked "Sophia was telling me about what you are doing here. How does it work, and is it working?"

Richard explained. "Yes, it is working, and as to how, let me explain. I have always been fascinated with clusters and the energy they can create, but what also intrigues me is how sometimes we do not even realize that we are operating in and around clusters at all. Some have local focus but some have international importance and leading world market positions."

"I don't follow you? What do you mean?" Ed asked, feeling slightly lost in the jargon.

"Well, take financial clusters for an example. They are based in New York or London; media clusters are in Hollywood or Mumbai; an IT cluster is found in Silicon Valley; automotive clusters in Southern Germany and Detroit;, telecom clusters in, say, Stockholm and Finland or even the textile and fashion clusters in northern Italy. Being together has huge benefits."

"I see, so how does this benefit you?" Ed asked, unsure where this was going.

"Many industries are tied to their location by the need to be close to their customers or experts or even their competitors; other industries are tied to their location by the need to be close to natural resources. One of the beauties we have is that we are neither proximity dependent nor resource dependent."

"This allows us to operate with a higher level of efficiency, drawing on more specialized assets and suppliers with shorter reaction times than our clients could in isolation. But for us the real beauty is that by being closely positioned with other companies, educational and research facilities we can achieve higher levels of innovation. Our client companies can create more new ideas and while providing intense pressure to innovate and all along the cluster environment lowers the cost of their projects. True collaboration. Let me show you," Richard invited.

Exiting the Telepresence room Richard and his guests walked next door into a room with a sign that said *The Egg, a designated innovation guild room, specifically designed for the hatching of ideas.* Next to the sign was a set of lock boxes that said *"Please leave cell phones, sidearms and egos here, which you may retrieve on departure."*

As Ed looked around the room he noticed that there were six chairs all in a circle facing each other, each very different from the other and each with their own specific color.

Richard led Ed to the middle of The Egg and offered him a seat of his choice. Ed chose the retro blood-red leather barber's chair. The last time he had sat in one of them he had been about six years old. Richard took the appropriately named Director's chair. Sophia chose a throne and Michael a hand-carved chair of yellow oak. Richard said there were more choices of chairs in the chair closet. "But of course," Ed said with a chuckle "...what's innovation without a chair room?"

The room was egg shaped, sort of. All the way around up to hip level, it had shelves with books - paperback, hardbound and some ancient leather bound that Ed yearned to explore, videos, CD and DVD players, an ancient slide projector, numerous built-in speakers and all sorts of tools and... various widget and gadget sorts of things that Ed guessed might be useful to turn ideas into visual models. Then from hip to eye level it had magnetic white boards, electronic white boards, projection and video screens, an old fashioned school blackboard with chalk, cork boards and paper flip chart pads. But it was above the board level where it became most impressive.

Richard touched a few sensor switches on a touch-screen console built into the round table that rose out of the floor in front of the chairs. Above the board level up to a rounded, egg shaped ceiling, a 360 degree projector began to display an interactive planning session that they apparently used as a demonstration. It then went from detailed motion of the plans, to a starry night, then high speed sunrise, a lightning storm with earth-shaking thunderclaps and then darkness with crickets before the lights came on again.

"What an amazing room!" said Ed, feeling the energy the space created. As an architect he was trained to sense the effects of design, but this was so far over-the-top that he felt more like the six year old boy being given his first ride in a Bristol F.2 Fighter biplane at the county fair. He was impressed.

"Yep, some pretty crazy things come out of the egg." Richard replied. "It was designed by some of our geniuses, a few eccentrics and contributions by some of our artists, such as that carved-lion chair that Michael is sitting on. All the labor to build it was volunteer, and the room is bookable by anyone on our intranet."

Richard continued… "just going back to what we were talking about, the other benefit of this village within the context of Villageton is that it also reduces the cost of failure, very important for entrepreneurs, as they can fall back on local employment and the many other companies in similar fields."

"Hmm," said Ed. "Let me see if I get that one. What you are saying is that this village supports entrepreneurs who take risks. If a risk fails, and the risk-taker goes bust, all is not lost because there are many other opportunities, and since the risk-taker is known by others in Villageton, someone else will offer that person a job or a collaborative opportunity." Ed saw Richard nodding his head yes, so he continued with another question. "You seem so passionate about this place. Where does that passion come from?"

"Great question. I was raised in a small close-knit village and I very quickly learned the power of 'All together now' as we had little money and limited resources. It was down to the ideas, attitude and adaptability that created a thriving community that made a real difference and now I have been able to bring that to the fore here." Richard explained.

"In what way?" Ed asked, trying to connect the answer with his question.

"Well, the current project we are working on is a good example. It is a project for a community by a community." Richard explained. "The project you saw us discussing on the Telepresence is with a Malaysian company who discovered a way of bonding rice husks together to create building materials."

"Our *Doing Partners*, both here and overseas, have together devised a low-cost system to construct a Rice-Husk-Kit-Set Refugee Shelter in less than two hours. Kit-set is a term they use to refer to a precut, ready to assemble packaged building. We used the internet to create an open-source global search for the smartest solution and then took it to market. Over six-hundred million tons of rice husk waste is produced annually – most burned or dumped in landfills. We created a way for the rice mill owners to offset this waste product and turn it into a viable community owned business producing the kit-set shelters. A win-win."

Ed commented. "That's impressive. As a semi-retired architect and planner, I was given the Blandville contract to come up with an emergency housing plan after Hurricane Katrina showed local communities how we could not rely on federal agencies for a timely response if something catastrophic were to happen. They brought me in to develop contingency housing. I sure could have used a product like that, especially cheap and easy to store." Ed then asked "You mentioned the Innovation Guild. Is that what they call this village's guild hall?"

"Yes, it's one name for it. It's also called the inventor's guild, the egghead's guild, geek-guild, etc.," Richard answered. "Whatever the name, it works brilliantly. But it would be a mistake to think of our guild in isolation. One of the first things our guild did was to set up the Villageton Talent-match Intranet or ViTI as we call it. This is a special piece of database software where every interested resident in Villageton enters in their particular areas of expertise and interests. Then when a project is entered, it scans the database looking for matches. It then allows the project manager to send invitations for collaboration. Sometimes these are for fun, and other times they turn into money-paying ventures."

"We call an active project group a *symposium*, which is a typically awful pun that only an egghead would come up with, as originally the word *symposium* referred to Greek drinking party, and *viti* is the Latin word for wine grape. When we combine ViTI with Telepresence, we have the whole world of creativity at our fingertips and it gives us the chance to collaborate with many wonderful individuals and groups. There is an ancient saying from the indigenous cultures of Oceania that translates something like *energy flows where attention goes*. By placing attention on innovation and creativity, as we do in this village, it generates an amazing amount of energy throughout Villageton." Richard explained.

Ed was as fascinated by how Richard thought and spoke as he was about the explanations. He felt his brain was used to jogging, and he had just been asked to join an Olympic sprinter on a warm-up run. The example given was described as a profitable business venture, yet underlying it was a way to alleviate human suffering in times of emergency, deal with a major waste product so it became an asset, not a liability, and it sounded as if Richard was more turned on by the creative ideas than the obviously good living he made from his work. Ed was not sure if he was feeling old, or just soft from living too long in the aptly named Blandville, but he did like the way his brain felt after the workout.

As they were leaving the room, where Ed remembered to collect his ego, a fellow saw Richard and asked if the Telepresence Room was available. Richard snagged him, and said to Ed, "Here's an interesting person to speak with, Ed. Let me introduce you to my friend and collaborator, Michael Henderson. Michael is a Corporate Anthropologist, and he constantly calls my attention to ordinary things in my daily life that I never notice. Michael Henderson meet Ed."

"A corporate anthropologist?" Ed queried. "That's a fascinating title. Somehow, I thought anthropologists studied tribes, not people in business."

Michael laughed and shook Ed's hand. Michael turned to Sophia and gave her a kiss on the cheek, and both Michaels shook hands as well. He then turned back to Ed and answered. "Well, the *C* in CEO stands for Chief, which is a proper tribal title, and when you take a careful look at corporations, you discover that organizational culture has eight times more influence on performance variation than strategy. The company culture has a huge influence on how the chosen strategy will be engaged with by the people who deliver strategy: staff. In short, the world's best strategy is largely redundant without an aligned and supportive culture and many organizations do not know what defines their culture and how this influences their strategy."

"That's fascinating." Ed said. "How did you come to take on this profession?"

"My father worked overseas, mostly in Africa in the mining industry, so I grew up with a very different cultural experience. Among other places, when I was a teen, we lived near the Zulu, and I became enthralled with them. For whatever reason, they opened their life to me, and I learned a lot from them. In fact, something I learned from them saved my life when I contracted the usually fatal form of malaria. So when it came time to go to the university, I majored in anthropology. The conventional jobs in that field are the ones you imagine, but because of my family experience with dad being a company man, I turned my attention to the kind of tribes we form around ourselves. Corporations operate very much like tribes, with their own values, jargon and social behavior. They wage war with other corporations, using paper instead of spears. In court, the word *plaintiff* comes from the Greek word *plēssein* which means "to strike". *Defendant* comes from the Latin meaning *to ward off* or *repel*. Some tribes use ritual warfare, some tribes like the Hopi use a tug-of-war means to resolve conflict, and our modern day corporate tribes pay for lawyers to duke it out in court.

Ed thought about this, and realized that he could spend hours pursuing this subject with Michael Henderson. Ed would have loved to have asked what the Zulu taught him that saved his life. However, noting that he was needing to make a telepresence call, Ed limited himself to one more question. "Tell me about how you find living in Villageton, and in your village in particular," Ed asked him.

"I love living in the village. I regularly catch myself describing that I live in a village, because it captures my sense of being immersed in a life. I guess before we moved to the village, I used to say I live <u>at</u> *369 Orchard Street* or more generally *over on Orchard Street*. But I now say a live <u>in</u> a village. Ironically my old suburban street was named for the orchard they cut down to build the suburb"

"It's like I used to experience Orchard Street in the suburbs as a *place* to live. In the Village it feels more like a *way* to live. Simple things like walking everywhere to visit friends, or to buy food in the market, enable us to hear, feel, smell, listen, chat, watch and move – all of which means we are using our senses. We literally are experiencing more life, whereas we used to commute everywhere by car and somehow our minds switched off as we were driving. You know what I mean. You could drive all the way from the suburbs to work – an hour drive in my case –and suddenly arrive without being able to recall the journey. I often didn't know what speed I had been driving, what I had driven past to get to work. I just zoned out. Now let me tell you, Ed, this just doesn't happen in the village. First of all you're walking so you have to pay more attention. Because you're paying more attention you experience more and feel more alive. It sounds a little silly, I know, but it makes the world of difference."

"It does not sound silly to me, Michael," Ed commented, "but I would like to hear why you find it makes a world of difference."

"I think much of our typical western lifestyle has resulted in delaying such sensual gratification. We work hard often in places we don't like, to earn enough money to eventually take the vacation or buy the dream home or getaway place that makes our lives feel richer or more complete. The village offers us the opportunity to reverse that process and begin, enjoy and end each day with a place and lifestyle that nurtures the soul. Why would we want to wait twenty years to experience that?"

"The fact that I can carry my laptop and work from home or plug it into the internet at the library or the café means I don't commute at all now. Well that's not quite true, I do have a five minute walk past cafés and musicians and artists to the Library, the Egg Room or Richard's Telepresence room if I need to use it to meet with my business clients who are scattered all around the world."

"I get a sense of contributing into the community by working. The money I earn as a Corporate Anthropologist is almost exclusively spent within the village in local business. I support my friends and neighbors in the community every time I shop or eat in a restaurant. I never felt that sense of belonging and contributing when we were in the suburbs. At times it felt as if business had taken over the world. Everything in our lives seemed to have been converted into a commercial activity: health & medicine, food, education, entertainment, transport, even communication."

"In the village we still have some of that but it's locally owned and so much of it is available free, such as the entertainment and communication. I can stop and talk to people in a village lane, for free. No text or mobile phone bill for the privilege. I still use phones to call people and family outside the village of course and I'm delighted I can, but not to have as much of my communication and entertainment dependent on me buying a service or product is wonderful. I save money and have a better, more fulfilling experience. When I want to see a movie I go to the local movie theater knowing I'm supporting a local business enterprise when I buy my ticket."

"The village seems to constantly offer the opportunity to feel connected and involved in the community in an effortless manner. I love it because I get to live in the presence of others; I get to watch, share with, learn from and support people. So many people I used to live with in the subdivision would regularly talk about trying to create a sense of work life balance, and most seemed to come up considerably short. Here in the village it happens naturally."

"In the suburbs, typically I finished work and ducked for cover at home and with TV. Living in the village feels like I have changed from being an introvert to an extravert just through the opportunity and invitation of having a colorful and gently bustling life at my doorstep. Living with like minded people who enjoy the vibrancy of village life just adds to the feeling of belonging. In the suburbs I could count my son's friends on one hand. Now... well they literally fill a plaza!"

"There definitely is something special about living in a village all year round. We have visitors from all over the country and overseas visiting the village, just like in places like Santorini or an English or Italian village. I've never seen tourists in numbers visit a suburb. Why would they? We go on holiday to get away from the suburbs. So living in a village is like living on holiday."

With that, Ed saw Michael needed to leave, so he thanked him "Thanks Michael, let me know how the call went," Richard said. "Ed, I'm going over to the pub for a break, let's see if there is not someone there who can give you more perspectives on Villageton." Richard walked them across the plaza to the pub.

Sitting at a table he saw an older gentleman enjoying a cup of tea and scones. "Ed, here is someone I think you may enjoy meeting. John Bremer was one of the Stewards who helped us formulate the educational program for Villageton."

# Chapter 9

## Education - The Teachers' Story

"Ed, may I introduce you to John Bremer who developed the educational framework for public education in Villageton?"

Ed greeted John and said. "It's a pleasure to meet you. Forgive me if I sound fuzzy here, but your name rings a bell. Did Time Magazine do a story on you back in the 1970's?"

John's face brightened, laughing with delight, "you must be the only person in Villageton who remembers that. Do you have a photographic memory?"

"I wish," Ed replied. "No, my daughter was in Blandville High School at the time, and when she read the article, she shoved it in my face and demanded to know why she was stuck in such a boring school and not a place like the Parkway Program – *the School without Walls*. She was constantly railing on about how wrong everything was in Blandville, and I have to say she did her homework in finding examples of how to do it better. As I recall, the Philadelphia Public School Board needed a fifth high school, lacked the money to build one, so you started a public school program where the students and teachers used board rooms and other public and corporate spaces for their classes. It had an auto mechanics course in an auto repair shop, a journalism course taught at one of Philadelphia's major newspapers and a statistics class taught by one of the insurance companies in their boardroom by their top actuaries. My daughter kept up with your work and when your students, that I gathered were admitted into Parkway by lottery rather than on merit, got accepted to the universities and colleges of their choice, she made a point of comparing it to the less impressive results of Blandville's public schools. So, it is not so much a photographic memory as the daily floggings my daughter gave me about the failings of the establishment, and her belief that I was responsible. Anyway, enough of memory lane, what on earth are you doing here, long after you have earned the right to retire?"

Again, John laughed with mock astonishment. "I'm not old enough to retire, and I won't be until young people stop asking me questions. I was up in Vermont working on a lifetime backlog of research when a former graduate student of mine from too long ago contacted me to see if I would like to help draft a charter for Villageton's education system. They hoped to work within the public school system rather than start private schools, but they did not want a separate school campus. It was different than the Parkway Program, because the development intended to build classrooms on the plazas, in the guild halls, and on locations such as the industrial park, the equestrian grounds and the market gardens."

"So my first question when I began, was to ask *why do we educate the young?* They were already asking the question *why do we build communities?* so it was not a new-paradigm question for them. In fact, the two questions go hand-in-hand."

Ed commented, "I think I understand, John, but I would like to hear why."

John explained. "In societies run by businessmen, we educate the young to secure jobs, to make them good and productive workers as well as free-spending consumers so the businesses have on-going buyers."

"In societies run by authoritarian types, we educate the young to keep order in society, to keep people under control, so they learn their place and stay there."

"In institutional societies, we do not necessarily educate students, but merely pass them through a series of hoops so they earn a certificate at the end. In these systems, we get some students who graduate but cannot read or write."

"Obviously for a society to function, its members must speak a common language, agree to abide by the protocols and rules of that society, and have sufficient skills to take care of themselves and their families, while hopefully contributing to the common wealth of their society. In our literate society, this implies a reasonable mastery of language and numbers because we are a society of the written word and of measures and money. But beyond that, what is important for the students who will learn in Villageton? Will they be engaged in their learning, or bored and angry like your daughter was in Blandville?"

"Good question," Ed commented. "What answers did you bring?"

"When I joined the team of what they call the Village Stewards, I came with more questions than answers. Education is not about bringing answers, it is about finding answers, it is about growing and learning, not packaging and shipping. The problem we face in education is that we encounter complex human beings, called children, not empty buckets that we can fill with processed knowledge and facts. Because children are human beings, they come with all sorts of lives, talents, and experiences that probably began when they were still in the womb. This idea for an assembly line model of education, where we insert the raw child in one end at age six and then spend twelve years subjecting them to the state curriculum, rarely produces the expected product at the other end when in cap and gown we hand them a diploma. The system your daughter railed against is the factory model of education, and while that system produces great Model T Ford cars, it has trouble producing great graduates."

"Yes", interjected Ed, "while she did not use those words, that's her view too."

John continued. "Such a system makes sense in a commuter society. If Mom and Dad go off to work at the office or factory, it becomes most convenient to send the kids off to a school campus since segregation of society is the norm in commuter societies. However in a human-scaled society where people do not leave their community, such segregation would not only be expensive - school campuses cost millions - it's completely misaligned with Villageton life."

He explained. "Before we invented formal school education – which I should add, is a recent invention – children learned by observing and doing. Reading was often taught with a 1:1 student teacher ratio, as an adult read to the child. Watch what happens when you place a toddler in a foreign country. They learn the language, mastering it without a single class or language lab. Why? Because Nature designed children to learn; it's natural, it's what children do."

"The problem a suburb faces is the absence of *daily*. If you dropped a child from Africa or Asia into your Blandville suburb during the work-day, they would never learn English, because there are so few people there and fewer interacting. If you take them to the office, the kid is underfoot, and becomes fidgety because there is nothing to do, nothing to touch. If you let them watch soap operas all day, they will learn vernacular English, but their bodies will not develop naturally. So you send them to a separate place where one teacher tries to create a learning environment for as many as thirty children. In human terms, this is abnormal."

"So what you are saying," Ed observed, "is that while our commuter campus design makes sense in the context of a suburb, it is flawed because the fundamental premise of a suburb is flawed."

John replied. "I am not sure that is exactly what I did say, but I would agree with you that you are probably right in your observation. But in any case, in Villageton, we begin with a completely different experience. If we place the classrooms on the plaza, the first thing that happens occurs outside the classroom. The students are in the middle of life. They are in the thick of it. They see people working in offices and shops. They may take their lunch where the adults eat, and they watch adults interacting. Indeed they may find themselves interacting with the adults, especially since the adults know them – they are neighbors after all."

"One of the first lessons Villageton children learn outside the classroom is not only that the society around them works, but how it works. They hear words they do not know and they ask what they mean. They see successful people, talented people, and they also see damaged people, dysfunctional people and they see how their community deals with them." John explained.

"So when they go into their classes, the teachers find the students sitting before them are naturally more ready to learn, provided the subject matter is relevant and not packaged in a way that is contrary to the reality they experience right outside the door in Villageton."

Ed cocked his head and then said, "I'm not sure I follow you on that one."

John explained. "An example of misaligned learning might be a teacher who insists on teaching arithmetic by hand when everyone in Villageton uses a calculator or a computer. To engage the student, a Villageton teacher instead may let them first do the work on a computer but select a laptop with a weak battery and a mislaid charger. The teacher sets the expectation that finding the right calculation has a time deadline. When the laptop quits, the student must revert to a pencil, a pad of paper and their brain. At that point doing arithmetic by hand becomes relevant. When the student understands the danger of a black-box society – where one does not understand anything except how to press buttons that display answers – then the learning is realigned with the outside experience."

"Got it." Ed said. "Please go on with explaining the Villageton difference."

John complied. "With segregated education, we not only separated students from society on school campuses, we also arbitrarily separated them by date of birth, grading them not by aptitude or interest, but age. This serves what I call the interests of administrivia, but has very little to do with serving the child."

"If we look at small communities where all the grade 1 to 12 students fill a one-room school house, we find no handicap when those students graduate. Indeed in many cases a one-room schoolhouse education is superior, and I speak from experience having taught in one. The reasons are obvious. First, the teacher usually has fewer total students, and the older students help the young. Second, the students learn at their own pace, since all ages are present in the same room."

"However, the separation of school between primary and secondary has value. Studies of brain development show that about the time we end primary school and move students on to secondary, the brain reorganizes itself to shift from dependency on adults to dependency on self. The reason some systems have a middle or junior high school can be seen as reflecting the age when the brain is breaking down. The student may say 'I feel like I am losing my mind,' and their parents would probably agree. In traditional societies, these phases, which also coincided with the onset of puberty, were marked by rites of passage."

Ed laughed. "I sure wish you had put that in the Time article. It would have given me a great come-back to my daughter's constant harangue. Sorry, I am being flippant. So how did you transform these observations into a school design?"

John chuckled and continued. "After the Villageton founders talked over these ideas, they decided the young ones would have classrooms on their own plaza, with students going to the same rooms every day in their own village. This gave them a sense of home, of familiar surroundings where they were with the same adults most of the time. In most of the villages of five-hundred people there would be an average of about fifty students in that age group. Due to the savings in capital costs, the Village Organizing Company was able to negotiate for a permanent student teacher ratio of 12:1, meaning we needed four classrooms per plaza."

"The first teachers helped design the classrooms, and they proposed an unusual arrangement where the four classrooms were in a single building, built around a common shared room, with sliding walls, so any teacher could monitor any other classroom when the wall was opened. If a teacher needed a conventional room, they closed the wall. In addition, the side walls where the teacher put up posters, learning aids and the children's work had a pocket design. At the end of class, all work would slide away, and the room was available for community use."

"That's good in theory, but how do adults sit in children's chairs?" Ed asked.

"Good question", John replied. "They designed multi-purpose furniture. It serves the needs of students during school, but is usable by adults after hours. This meant the neat rows of small desks and chairs had no place. Children are remarkably flexible, and do far better with more flexible furniture design. So they built collapsible trestle tables and benches with different height stands, and they used floor mats and other innovative designs humans used for centuries before the 20th."

"Of course," he explained, "not all the school-day stays in the classroom. Most days the children have an expedition, where they explore other villages. In a population of 10,000 it is surprising how many different experiences they can have. This outing proves to be one of the most popular parts of the day even if it is little more than a walk along the streets or in the Greenbelt."

"When the children come of age around 13, the whole town becomes their campus. We have about 1,000 teenage children on average, so we created three cluster programs for them. I prefer to use the word *program* instead of *school* to avoid the encumbrances and expectations implied with the latter," John added.

"In effect, each of these programs has its own anchor – a large meeting space where the day begins. The day officially begins with the general meeting, but in fact it begins about 45 minutes earlier with a socialization time when students and teachers gather with the youth equivalent of morning tea at the café. Everyone has their own cup that they keep clean, and we provide free, non-sugared, non-caffeinated hot and cold drinks. Usually one team of students would make and bring morning breads to go with the drinks. In this interactive electronic era, some of the teachers always bring their old-fashioned morning newspapers to the gathering, and leave them on tables for students to read."

"That's interesting," Ed interjected. "From what I read and hear, most schools feel they are not up-to-date unless every student, or at least every classroom is equipped with the latest electronic gadgetry. What is your feeling on that?"

John thought about it and replied. "Computer technology is with us, and it will play an increasingly important role as time goes on. But it is probably over-promoted by vested interest trying to sell their machinery, and it still lacks the aesthetic of real paper. There is a great pleasure in spreading out and reading the morning newspaper, a pleasure that a glass screen cannot match. And, if you spill tea and breadcrumbs on the paper it won't jam up or start sparking. Books don't need batteries, and I fear for a world when all books are only stored in a hard drive somewhere. But in any case, we do not make the decision. The students pick up the paper and read it, so they must regard it with value."

"As a lover of books, John, I must agree with their regard, and am heartened to hear of it," Ed replied, "but do continue describing the programs."

"The meeting rooms use long tables, and students tend to circulate; it can get noisy even though the room has sound absorbent surfaces. When it is time to begin the formal day, someone stands up on the stage and calls for attention. In the beginning of the year, the convener is a teacher, but soon the job is taken over by students who learn how to run a meeting, keep it interesting and accomplish the intended purpose. Sometimes they arrange for an inspirational speaker, something easy to do in a culture as enriched as Villageton," John explained.

"Then teachers collect their first class and they go off to a classroom, a workplace or another location where learning is to occur. The state provides a general curriculum, and as part of the public school system, it is followed. However, *how* it is followed becomes part of the students' learning. The first assignment the students have is to lay out their coursework for the term. We make them responsible for their own learning. There are many ways to learn the same subject, and by engaging students they not only have a higher commitment to learning the subject matter, they learn how to learn."

"How do you juggle that one?" Ed asked.

John answered, "we, they, try to use real life as much as possible. Thus, in studying the arts and sciences we sometimes use classrooms in the guild halls and generally try to engage guild members in the courses. For applied courses, we use apprenticeships after school, to mix theory with practice. In teaching history, we find the elders most helpful. They tend to have had better educations in history, and their early memories now qualify as history. When I tell students about my building airfields in World War II, or the night during the London Blitz when a buzz bomb dropped in the middle of my parents home, the questions are delightful as they can't believe anyone can be so old and still alive." John laughed.

"One class of history students is learning the skill of historian, recording and then confirming oral histories of the elders. They find it revealing how granny tells an absolute story of the past, only to find it impossible – that she created a sequence of events in her mind not supported by historical evidence. That class later went on to study the speeches of former President Ronald Reagan to analyze the influence of movies rather than history on what the President said. In the third term, this evolved into a study of news, to examine the apparent gap between what happened, and how it was reported in the media."

"But enough of me nattering on about it. Let's ask a parent, since one of them happens to be sitting here, having come in while we were speaking, to have a cup of coffee." John stood up and called to a middle aged man sitting at another table. "Francis, do you have a moment? We have a visitor interested in Villageton's education program. Perhaps you could give Ed the parent's view."

# The Parent's View

Francis introduced himself and said "With seven children, from a 9 year old girl to a 22 year old boy, now doing his master's degree, I suppose I am an expert parent. We moved to Villageton when the oldest was 14, so we have experienced both the transition from conventional public education for the older children to immersion from day one for the younger."

"While I would expect that John here spoke about quality education and the learning experience; for parents I would say the number one concern before they move to a place like this is safety. Suburban life, where we moved from, is boring for most children. Left to their own devices, they get into trouble, and every parent worries about getting that call from the hospital or the police about a party that got out of hand, a car crash or a drug overdose that produced permanent damage or worse. In some communities, the glorification of gang activity in music and video is producing levels of vandalism and violence unknown in prior generations. Watch some of the videos your kids watch, and you will be shocked at the violence, the crudity, and the almost sociopathic lack of kindness. They present sex kitten role model for girls and angry violent role models for boys, appealing to the basest urges. This sells product, but at what cost?"

Ed agreed, telling Francis about his grandson glued to television.

Francis acknowledged Ed's story and then he continued with his story. "In most cases today, both parents have to work. They entrust their children to the schools where in large measure what occurs in the classroom and on the playground is happening peer to peer. Neither parents nor the community have much influence, indeed for the most part they do not know what goes on. Overworked teachers with large classes sometimes have less effect than television, movies and computer games which pander to urges, seeking out the lowest common denominator. The children's experience is of a world that comes to them rather than a world where their parents have much say. Concerned parents feel a sense of helplessness. Others are too busy to notice."

"When we moved to Villageton, it was like moving from a war zone to a land of peace except we had no idea we were previously living in a war zone since it was all we knew. We were given both the gift of time and of proximity. It was more than safe, it was good. It *is* good."

"How so?" Ed asked.

"For a start," Francis replied, "as you have seen there are no cars in Villageton, which means children spill out into the streets, meeting each other and forming friendships – sorting themselves out. They travel in groups, little ones following the bigger ones, as they explore their territory, play ball in the street and visit each other's homes. Because we have so many children, our home tends to become one of the more popular gathering points. We wired our intranet with an automatic speaker phone in the living room, which is on the ground floor, so other parents could buzz it and ask if their child was with us. It works like a neighborhood intercom system."

"At first all the parents were fairly protective, but within a few months they realized the town had thousands of adults all keeping an eye on the kids. If someone scraped a knee, someone put on a bandaid, wiped the tears and all was better. Because we have the intranet, if it was more serious, the parent would hear in moments they were needed," Francis explained.

"That's a fascinating combination of old time community and new technology" Ed observed.

"That's a good way to put it," Francis said. "And that's just talking about the community part. The formal schooling was an eye-opener both for our children and for us, as parents. Our oldest has always been a good student, but our next child found school boring. Skeptical going to school here the first day, he came home so excited he could hardly keep his words straight as he gave us a blow by blow narrative of everything that happened. For a start, his teachers not only knew his name, but something about him, and he said they were really interested in him. The class sizes were so much smaller than his old school, and the way they studied was completely different. He said to me that instead of handing out text books, the teachers first asked the kids how they would put together a course that would meet the state curriculum and still be interesting. He said he never knew there was a state curriculum... he figured the teachers just decided what they would teach. So they spent the balance of that class looking at the state curriculum and talking about how to learn it without getting bored."

"What a wonderful story," Ed commented. "Was this the same for the rest of your children?"

"The experience for our youngest children was different," Francis answered. "They had never been in another system. For them, there was no undoing of the damage. They never learned the ditties about hating school, hating class and hating the teachers. Ever notice how often we use the word *hate* in day to day talking? Our kids use it a lot less since we moved to Villageton."

"Class size here is smaller, and in the first six years, most of the teachers prefer to use team teaching. This means they leave the classroom wall open and cluster some of the children not rigidly by age, but by interest. During the day some of the children from two or three different age groups will gather with one teacher when working on a particular subject. It works brilliantly."

"It sounds, Francis, like you are an exceptional parent," Ed observed, "that your children would have turned out OK no matter where they went to school."

"That may be true, Ed," Francis replied, "but imagine what world I leave to my children if their peers do not get the same level of parental interest or support. We create losers when they are young, and society pays for it later."

"Can you say more about that?" Ed asked.

"Sure. Let me tell you a story that happened when we lived in the suburbs. Once when I had a week off from work and all our children were in public schools, I asked to sit in on classes. For a full week I sat in the back corner of different classes and said nothing. I observed that most of the teachers taught the front two or three rows, and the students in the back row were completely detached; hardly listening, not learning much. My children always were in the front two rows, but I paid more attention to the ones in the back."

"Afterwards I asked about this. Those teachers willing to answer said the kids not interested in learning get put in the back. They minimally pass to move through the system. Most drop out as soon as it is legal. When they grow up many end up as losers in society, eroding society not contributing to it. In the meantime they tend to corrupt the school environment, and become the origin of most of the adverse peer pressure and negative tension within the school. There was one teacher who told me he could spot the future criminals in his class, and had been teaching long enough to be able to prove it. Frankly, I thought it was a crime to allow that teacher to continue in his profession, although I said nothing."

"I asked to meet some of these students, and I found all knew their rank in the school hierarchy. A few were dull, unaware and yet happy with themselves; for whatever reasons, their brains worked at minimum power, and they did not have a clue what the teacher was talking about. They needed to be in hands-on training not dumped in the back of an academic class. Others were stunningly intelligent, sharp and highly critical of the system. Many were angry and came from damaged families. All were aware they were classed as losers by the school. Most could tell me precisely when the system branded them as losers; one said it was in second grade when he despised the teacher and said so. After that their record dictates where they are directed, and they lost any interest in school. When I asked what education they would do well in, they had clear, do-able answers. When I raised this with the department heads, it was new information, they had no idea, and I think for those particular students, it resulted in a reassessment that benefited them. But overall, that educational system produces winners and losers, where the losers bring the whole system down to a lower level than necessary."

"Got it," Ed said. "Please go on about education here in Villageton."

Francis complied. "Most Villageton parents would agree Villageton education is outstanding. Our children are more articulate, discerning, and self-starting. Overall they show more confidence. Their life experiences are greater because we no longer surround them in a womb of protection. They look forward to becoming adults since they see them all around. When they do they become better adults. When they apply for college or university we see higher admissions to their first choice. Admissions officers commented in the Villageton Press, our local weekly newspaper, that Villageton graduates tend to be more mature and very clear about what they expect to get out of their higher education."

"Not all children are university bound, and for those not, Villageton offers apprenticeships. In the secondary program, some students gravitate toward the industrial park or businesses run on the plazas and primary streets. The business people know them, and many begin with entry-level, part-time jobs on weekends or during school vacation. Then at one point the students get to select from apprenticeship opportunities offered by the business. The teachers focus on the understanding and theory, while the apprenticeship focuses on the doing."

"Finally, we appreciate that there are opportunities here for those children who want to live in Villageton as adults. In so many places, the children leave due to lack of opportunity or affordability. Buying a home in most family communities is out of reach for young adults. Here, it's not so. The youth zone offers affordable solo housing for first time buyers. Instead of paying rent, they build equity."

Ed commented, "This is so different from the experience of my family or people I know. For the most part, children move far away to find jobs. My kids live thousands of miles away, but Blandville does not have enough attraction to bring them back even if they could. There's nothing there. Even the town where I grew up has changed so much that everything I knew as a child is gone. It now looks like everywhere else, with so much sameness."

Francis agreed. "That's what makes this place so special. If I had to sum up life here, I would say it offers many of the qualities in life I knew as a child such as freedom, safety and community while offering many additional qualities I would have loved to have experienced. Life is so interesting for children in Villageton. So many things happen, so many different things going on at the same time."

"From a parent's perspective, we are involved with our children's education. We see them walking from one class to another. As parents, we are welcome to visit the classes at any time, and because they are so convenient, you will find at any time in any class one or two parents sitting in and observing. New teachers find it unnerving for a few days, but after that they love it, and frequently call upon the parents to participate in the lesson."

"Tell me about that," Ed asked.

"OK. The other day, I was talking with one of the high school teachers, who said the curriculum required three days on Native Americans, and it happened that one of the parents sitting in the room was part Indian. His mother was half Navaho and half Hopi. The curriculum had a fairly two dimensional politically correct narrative about how the bad white man had stolen their land and exploited the first peoples, which certainly is not what I was taught when Indian studies were about Manifest Destiny and Custer's Last Stand. The curriculum had a pamphlet the students had to read, and the teacher called upon one of the parents in the room, Len, to give his thoughts on it. Len is a quiet man, but as he began to tell his story the whole character of the course changed."

"Len spoke to the curriculum pamphlet on how whites used alcohol as a tool for conquest, but then talked about how the new alcohol-serving tribe-owned casino on the reservation at Churchrock caused huge controversy. He said it is a federal crime to possess alcohol on Navajo land. He spoke how his mother's people are prone to alcoholism, and he described the terrible impact it has on their culture."

"Len then went on to describe what happens when two cultures that took thousands of years of years to develop on different continents then meet. As he was also half European ancestry, he gave a far more informed view of how that clash looked from both sides, in which he romanticized neither. Len's daughter, who was in the class, later said she had never heard her father talk about these things, and she was deeply moved. The teacher said his only regret was not having a video camera on, since she felt whoever wrote the state curriculum needed to come out of their ivory tower and reality-check their work."

"Good luck," Ed said. "Having worked in a bureaucracy all my life, I can assure you the organization defines its own reality. I remember reading a paper written by the National Institute of Health, that said that organizational conversations are controlled by deciding who gets to talk about what to whom, how time and money is allocated, and how rewards and perks get distributed. The conversations within the organization are shaped by these controls until they become their reality. Which raises an interesting question here. What is the organizational structure of the schools?"

John looked like he was ready to answer this one, but Francis spoke first. "In light of what you just described, I can see why our educational system works so well. The organizational framework of Villageton schools is unusual. Officially, it complies with all the state regulations, but in practice we integrate it with the community. Parents and interested members of the community serve on advisory boards. Each village has its own board. We have official principals, but in practice they are really *Principal Teachers* meaning they focus far more on learning than what John calls *administrivia*. Because we have the intranet that links the whole town with data, audio and video, the required administrative information is paperless. Scanners record when students come in and out of classes, tracking where they are expected to be at all times. Instead of running a separate school office, we found it saved money to contract all the paperwork to the Villageton administration. This frees the principals and senior managers to focus on teaching and learning. From what you just described, this has the effect of separating the educational conversations from the financial controls. The teachers are wholly focused on learning, with no administrator power-tripping."

"This use of technology fascinates me, Francis." Ed said. "May I hear more?"

"Sure. In addition to the practice of welcoming parents into any class, each classroom has a large telepresence screen with a video camera and microphones. This enables long-distance learning, and Villageton establishes working relationships with experts around the world. When an age 9-12 class studied Africa, the teacher organized a telepresence link with a primary school in Kenya through someone they knew there. They managed to secure sponsorship so this Kenyan town that only has a generator for electricity was able to secure a satellite broadband link for the school. For our students, it made the curriculum section on Africa real, and we hear for that town, it is a huge boon. Among other things, the doctor there uses it to consult with medical experts in England where he can video the patient and work out diagnosis and treatment on line."

"We also use telepresence locally, and it proves especially helpful for teacher peer support and evaluation. If a teacher encounters difficulty, they will ask their support team to tune in via telepresence. In this way they can record the class and the teacher can then get together with the team to analyze what's happening, and how to address it better. With parent and students' permission, some of these tapes were edited into instructional videos that teachers' colleges use in their coursework. As you can imagine this results in the top graduates of those colleges applying to teach here, which makes it a win-win."

As Francis finished that thought, Ed could hear the bells of the town's clock tower chiming, and Francis said, "Ed, I suppose I could keep talking for hours, but if you are taking a tour of Villageton, there are many other things to see. Coffee break is just over for me, and it's getting on time for me to get back to my office. It's been a pleasure, lady and gentlemen."

"Francis, John," Ed replied, "your stories about education in Villageton fascinate me, and if there is one thing I would like to do, it is to see if my son and his family can move here. I have no idea how they could do it, given their financial position is akin to a train wreck about to happen, and they would need to find jobs, but if it meant my grandchildren could grow up in an environment like this, it would be such a blessing."

"I visited them recently, and found my grandson plugged into the television every free hour of his day. I expect soon he will graduate to computer games, and probably by the time he is in high school they will have invented a brain cap with headphones and goggles, so you can live in a fantasy computer generated world and only stop to attend to bodily functions. I fear it will be worse for my granddaughter as her life from the moment she was weaned and put on formula is nine hours a day in day-care. These kids know so little real human contact; it's so abnormal, except my son tells me everyone he knows raises their kids this way."

"You have inspired me and given me hope. Thank you both." Ed said "And thank you Richard, for your fascinating tour of your village. It is brilliant, and I mean that literally as well as figuratively."

# Passion

As Michael, Ed and Sophia left and continued their stroll thru Villageton, they passed through an arched gate sculpted with a profusion of ten-petal flowers and round fruits on spiraling vines. Ed noted the intricate carvings, wondering if they were done by an artist or computer carved from a photograph of real life. "This is a very beautiful village gate," Ed commented to Sophia. "What will be my pleasure this time?" he asked, enjoying this transition that truly felt as if he was travelling from one country to another.

"With luck," Sophia replied, "we may find the answer to your question with Andrew, the village coordinator, who about this time of day is usually at his favorite Café de Chocalat in the plaza enjoying his afternoon cup of coffee and a chocolate croissant – often with friends, neighbors or his family. But if I may give the short answer, Andrew wanted to create a village where all the residents were true citizens, meaning they had already discovered their purpose in life and were living it with passion and success."

Had Sophia given this answer at the beginning of their tour, Ed thought to himself, he probably would have grunted politely and in his mind made some sort of dismissive value judgment about such a purpose. However, he noted the extent to which his mind had become more elastic and open from meeting the people of Villageton on this lovely sunny day. "Then I hope we shall be lucky, for I look forward to learning more." Ed said to both Sophia and Michael.

As they walked into the plaza, Ed immediately noticed the exceptional architecture. The 12-sided plaza with its covered walkway around its perimeter supported by columns connected by arches, slightly reminded him of the courtyards of medieval monasteries but with a radiant kind of... *vibration* was the word that came to him, a light and joyful vibration. The two and three storied buildings seemed to be reaching for the sky while feeling grounded at the same time. He saw the effect was created by perfectly balanced attributes... long and high windows, clear lines and perfect symmetry were balanced by arched openings, rounded balconies, intricate stucco details and warm colors. The warm terra-cotta plaza floor and the tree in the middle of it gave this village a feeling of a courtyard in Tuscany.

Across the plaza in the afternoon sunshine, Ed's first sensation alerted him by scent rather than sight to the café where Sophia hoped to find Andrew. The wafting aroma of chocolate and fresh roasted coffee drifted around him, stirring a long-forgotten memory from his young days in his year abroad studying architecture in Florence. Sophia led them toward a table with a tall man with striking blue eyes, enjoying a freshly baked croissant and café latte.

Sophia greeted them. "Andrew, may I introduce you to a visitor to Villageton? This is Ed Rice, and Michael brought him here for the day. I have been giving him a tour, and he is intrigued and inquisitive about everything in Villageton. Would you have a minute to share with him about the concept of your village?" asked Sophia.

"Hi Sophia and Ed, yes absolutely it would be my pleasure," replied Andrew inviting them to take a seat with a gesture. "Michael my friend, it is good to see you again."

"Wow, this plaza feels very well thought out." Ed opened the conversation.

"Yes," replied Andrew, "we did give it a lot of thought and we had a truly extraordinary architect to support us. He is from an old aristocratic family in Austria. So he is well rooted in tradition and the ancient knowledge of energy-flow through architecture, and at the same time he is a modern person reaching for the future. What makes his work unique is that he is capable of bridging past and future in a harmonious and beautiful way."

"Very remarkable indeed", agreed Ed, "Sophie mentioned your village theme being one where you attracted people who live their purpose. What exactly do you mean by that?"

"Well you see I have travelled the whole world for decades and lived in many different places and I have found that even though places and cultures seem to be different on the surface, there were certain aspects that were universally true. One such aspect of human behavior is that most people at least at some point in their lives have a dream or a vision for their life but only very few actually manage to live it. Most people get caught up in making a living to pay the bills. What that does is it kills joy and passion rather quickly. That's even true for those who pursuit a career if the career is based on the wrong motivation, such as making lots of money or becoming powerful. So the result is our modern society with a high standard of living and a low level of joyful creativity and plain enjoyment of living. Most people are caught in the rat race." Andrew explained.

Ed had always heard people refer to the rat race, but never thought much about it. Now, sitting in this beautiful plaza where people truly were enjoying what Morgan called the Good Life, he appreciated the distinction. "I am following you," he said to

Andrew.

Andrew smiled and continued. "Since we were starting with a fresh slate here at Villageton I wanted to take advantage of that and attract a different sort of people to my village... people who had already found their calling in life and lived it with passion and in a successful way. You see, when someone has found their vocation they behave totally differently from someone who is a doing a job to pay the rent. Someone who lives their purpose in life does that with a sense of pride and dignity which spills over into their product or service, consequently rendering much more value to their customers."

"Isn't that the privilege of a small number of people who have pleasant jobs?" Ed asked, thinking about the vast number of complainers he encountered in his long career working in Blandville.

"No," Andrew replied. "In fact, it doesn't matter what line of work they are into. I began scouting for my village business people while traveling. The first one was a marvelous hair dresser who is really a therapist in disguise. She makes people feel well about themselves by cutting their hair and raising their awareness about issues camouflaged in the chit-chat she has with her customers while she works. We also have a baker like that. To him, making all kinds of great tasting breads is an art form that he excels in while at the same time he considers the ability to feed people a privilege and great service to his community. So his breads are not only loaded with healthy and nutritious substances but more importantly with love and devotion."

Then..." Andrew pointed to a small shop on the plaza, "we have the dress maker over there who is a truly outstanding artist and just like the hair dresser she transforms people's emotional issues by creating these outrageous dresses and suits for people which make them feel special and unique. I could go on for hours about the different entrepreneurs and artists here but also about the great majority of our citizens who might do *normal* things like raising kids, being teachers or working in the administration of Villageton. None of them are normal because they all love what they do and they do it with all their heart and soul. That's why we get such outstanding results here in this village. This place is humming and buzzing with joyful success and no stress."

Ed digested this answer for a moment, and considered that it answered his question about people living their purpose – although he realized after he asked the question, that he met very few people in his career that had done so. Most people were either caught up in the politics or pressure of their work, or they worked through it the way Michael Henderson had talked about his days as a commuter – having driven through it and arriving and being unable to recall the journey. He thought about his own career, and suddenly got the impression that a great deal of it had been as if he was sleepwalking. Punctuated by moments of joy, such as the birth of his children or special holidays, he realized a great deal of his life looked as if he lived it in a fog.

"Your answer truly is impressive, Andrew", Ed said. "May I ask, what did you choose as your Guild Hall?"

Andrew beamed. "The Guild Hall became my main project. I have always been disappointed with mediocrity of our modern society and so over the years I have developed quite a bit of passion for supporting people in uncovering and living their greatest potential. Our Guild Hall is a place of higher learning where we joyfully unfold our human potential. The guild provides leading edge resources and technologies to recognize, stimulate, train and master our natural gifts. It is designed to cater to the differing needs of all age groups, to bring about mastery on the physical, emotional, mental and spiritual level. By doing that we assist people in finding their true purpose in life which is the purpose of this village." concluded Andrew. "And," he continued, looking at the clock tower, "I have the pleasure of giving lectures there from time to time, and if I don't leave you now, I may be late for the one I am supposed to give in a few minutes."

Ed and the others stood up to go, and Ed asked "One more question, if I may? I noted the beautiful flowers and fruits carved on your village gate. What are they?"

"Passion fruit." Andrew answered with a twinkle in his eye.

## THE VILLAGE AS UNIVERSITY

As they left Andrew's plaza, Sophia suggested "Let's go to my village next. It has the university abroad program where I study and live. You will also enjoy the Travellers Inn there. In my humble opinion it is the best such inn in Villageton, and it certainly is the most popular. Rooms are fully booked and the hall downstairs is a great place to meet people and hear stories. My Sociology specialization is in American Studies, and I probably learn more in the Travellers Inn than I do in classes."

As they walked into the next plaza, Ed, a lover of books, stopped in front of Callback, the college plaza bookstore, feeling both the architect's desire to do a sketch of the archetypal book store and the book collector's great tug to go in, get lost in books for the rest of the day, and emerge with a box full of used books that he would have no place to store in his room at Heathcliff Manor. Sophia noted this, and said "This bookstore proves it is still possible to run a successful book business in the internet era where the on-line giants demand high publisher discounts that undercut the traditional book store."

"Would you like to meet the owner?" Sophia asked. "Martin used to be a corporate executive in something called the Boomer Project, but when he moved here he started the book store. He is an interesting man and probably Villageton's foremost expert in the baby boom."

"I would," replied Ed, "but let us sit outside for a moment so I can sketch the front. It is so much what a bookstore should look like."

When Ed had finished his sketch and showed it to Sophia and Michael, they went in. The front door had an old fashioned bell on it that jingled as they opened it. Inside it was a book lover's heaven and Ed again felt the tug to browse. But Sophia brought him over to its proprietor, Martin, and after making introductions invited Martin to tell his story and give Ed his views on life, liberty and Villageton.

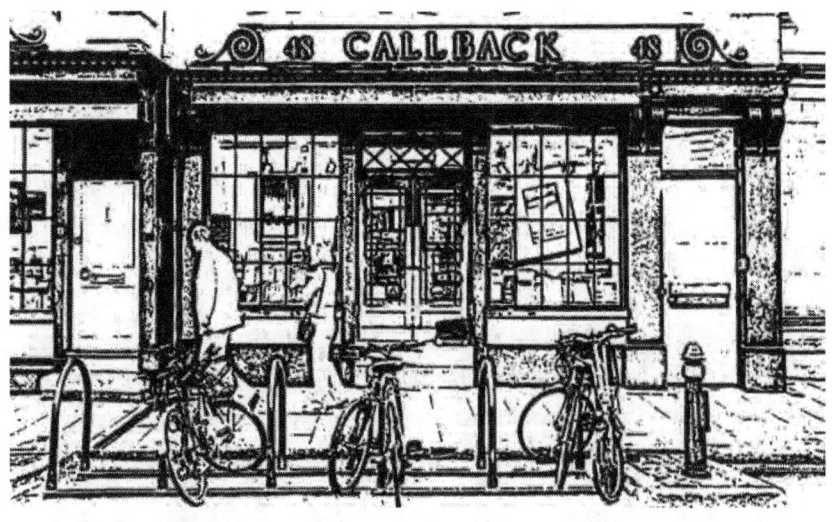

# Chapter 10

# The Baby Boomer's Story

Martin began to tell Ed his story. "I was born in 1951. That puts me on the older end of the middle of the baby boom scale that officially runs from 1946 to 1964. In almost every stage of my life it's been crowded. I recall a high school classroom when there were so many of us in class that my desk was squeezed in the doorway. When the bell rang, I had to drag it into the hallway to let the other students out. When I graduated and applied to colleges, their admissions were flooded with too many of us – a condition made worse by lots of guys seeking deferments to avoid being drafted for Vietnam. Looking for a job was brutal, too many applicants. My first job out of college was making floating docks, my second was selling motorcycles. It took me five years to get a job where the college degree meant something, and then they required I go back and get a master's. When it came time to buy my first home I found all my peers were in the market and house prices had skyrocketed due to increased demand."

"When we were born, it seems parents suddenly discovered babies as Dr. Spock wrote the definitive book on *Baby and Child Care*. Where previous generations focused on discipline and not spoiling children, Spock advocated treating babies and children as individuals. It must have worked, because I am strong in the individuality department, but a bit weak on discipline. *The Peter Pan Generation*, my stern grandmother disapprovingly called it; the kids who never grow up. Guilty as charged, only my wrinkles betray me," Martin joked.

"Yup," Ed interjected. "My wife and I read that book religiously, and certainly I have to say my daughter never grew up."

Martin laughed and then continued. "When we hit puberty, the universe discovered youth... flower children, sexual liberation compliments of the pill and Playboy. For a hormone-charged teenager it could not have come at a better time. We marked the end of our childhood by consigning the gray Eisenhower years to the dust bin. The Kennedys ushered in 1960's with style and class. For many boomers, the '60's became their defining moment; many still live that bright, shining 1960's ethos. It is safe to say that in every stage of their lives, baby boomers redefine the expectations and the rules."

"Kennedy's inaugural speech inspired a whole generation to be of service:"

*And so, my fellow Americans: ask not what your country can do for you - ask what you can do for your country. My fellow citizens of the world: ask not what America will do for you, but what together we can do for the freedom of man.*

"To be honest with you," Morgan commented, "I was only nine when I watched that speech on a black and white television with rabbit ears. I remember seeing it, but whether I was inspired by the speech at the time, or by its constant repetition during my teen years is hard to say; but the message stuck. Where the previous generation were serious grown-ups by the time they were 20, we remained idealistic."

"The trauma of Kennedy's assassination seared that generation in a way hard to imagine now. No one had been murdered like that before; not in our lifetime. Gunfire in Dallas ripped apart a dream world of elegance, style and youth in a matter of moments. With Johnson's swearing in on the plane back to Washington, the good life seemed to die. Mind you, we were too young to be partisan; it was not about liberal or conservative. They called it Camelot, and I would say that fairly captures the mood of the time. When Kennedy was killed the roundtable was broken, chivalry died, innocence lost forever."

"If this seems mythical and rose tinted, it was. I remember nuclear attack drills where everyone in class would get under their desks when the warning bells and sirens rang. Under Kennedy we had the Cuban missile crisis and as kids we really feared the sky would light up with a burning ball and torch the buildings and trees into oblivion as we flashed into nothingness. One of our neighbors put in an underground bomb shelter, and I remember climbing down into it with its special air filters, cot beds, food stock, and essentials packed into a very small concrete tomb. They manufactured fear differently in those days."

"I appreciate your saying that, Martin," Ed interjected. "Too often lately I hear baby boomers speaking nostalgically about their youth, and yet as I remember it, there were many problems and challenges then."

"You're right, Ed." Martin replied. "But despite those downers, we were young. We invented hippies and a whole new genre of music, both English and American. We went off to war a divided nation, in what might be described as a civil war between generations; baby boomers versus the establishment, aka their parents. *Don't trust anyone over 30* – I still don't," he laughed. "It was probably the first war fought as vigorously in the media as on the ground. Those of us who fought came home not as war heroes like our fathers from World War II, but to a mixed reception of a nation divided. An awful lot of the images from those times were more prevalent in the media than in real life, but we believed the media's mirror. We were the great myth-makers."

Ed smiled at this comment. "I could not have thought of a better way to put it, Martin. The great myth-makers. I like that one."

"But, Ed, if there is one single defining element about baby boomers, the one that is non-debatable, it's the numbers. As the baby boom progresses through every stage of life, we are like the elephant swallowed by the python – a big bump moving from mouth to tail. Look at the media now. No longer is youth celebrated; now it has discovered aging. Why? Because we dominate, our numbers call the beast's attention."

"Today," Martin continued, "we are at our peak earnings, the peak of power and the peak of our wealth. Analysts say that part of the reason for the long economic boom that extended all the way up to 2007 can be explained by the Baby Boom. We bought homes and drove the prices up. We invested in stocks, directly through mutual funds, or indirectly through investments made by our pension funds. We bought, prices went up. Overall, it's been a great run; a generation where every year brought more prosperity than the year prior; that is, until recently."

"The great crash that began in July 2007 when the mortgage-backed securities began to come unstuck and then spread to the global financial systems may have done us a favor. From what I can tell, its causes were systemic, not demographic. At its root, we find greedy people, failed regulatory systems and corrupt minds. The next economic storm promises to be worse, unless we change direction and reinvent concepts like retirement. Ed, have you ever heard of the Comptroller General's report on the unfunded liability of the US Government?"

Ed replied, "No, Martin I confess it has not been on my must-read list."

Martin smiled and explained. "By the end of 2007, the unfunded liability of the US government was $52 trillion, of which $41 trillion was to pay for retiring Baby Boomers in Social Security and Medicare... pensions and medical care. To put this in perspective, the Comptroller General noted that the total net worth of all Americans... the net value of their savings, investments and homes was $58 trillion. After the 2008-9 bailouts and the dropping value of homes and stock, it's very possible those numbers are now reversed. America's liability for the Baby Boomer care is huge and unfunded. Unfunded means they have no source for the cash to pay the Social Security and

Medicare costs when baby boomers begin to retire. $41 trillion is unthinkably large."

"You're right about that one Martin," Ed said. "$41 trillion is mind-boggling."

Martin continued. "The numbers are crushingly simple. We do not have enough next generation taxpayers or workers to provide us with the same systems we provided for our parents. It gets worse. In our free market system, the value of stock and of homes is determined by supply and demand. The stock market saw a large increase in demand as baby boomers invested in stock. What happens when they reach the age where they need to cash in their investments to fund retirement? The prices will go down because for every eight Baby Boomers, there are seven next generation buyers. Not only will the boomer's stock go down, their pension funds will see their equity decline: no money, no pension."

"Same problem with housing." Martin went on. "What happens when they need to sell their family home and move to a retirement village somewhere? With seven buyers for every eight sellers we will have a game of musical chairs, only it's not one loser and seven safe. In real estate, all will suffer. At the same time, just as when I was in high school sitting in the desk in the doorway, demand for retirement homes will shoot up, although not so much as we might project if boomers lose their asset base."

"Unlike the crash that began in 2007, the base of this looming financial disaster is demographic... too many people. If we lived in a Stalinist USSR, there would be an easy solution for us – wipe out 20 million of us through war, disease or starvation. But this is a democracy, and we will have a whole lot of political clout all the way until the end. We vote and we will demand to continue to live with the comforts to which we have become accustomed. Given the impossibility of this expectation, something is going to break – either us or the system. And of course, that is not the only crisis facing us. This one is just the status quo about to become a major crisis. So how do we respond?" Martin asked.

"Do we print more money, thinking this is how we will find the $41 trillion for the boomers? Do we instead focus on Climate Change as the latest crisis and turn all attention on going green? "Do we continue to build suburbs to sell cars to save Detroit? Which crisis should we react to? The point is that if we want to provide for our future and not break, we need a Plan B." Martin said.

"Martin, that's not a pretty picture you are painting," observed Ed, "and as both my children are baby boomers, it is a worry. Both of them are living in the present and doing very little planning for the future."

Martin replied. "Ed, my generation needs to find a new plan, and we need to find it now. We are living longer. We cannot count on retiring at age 60 or 65 like our parents. In fact, we probably need to toss the idea of retirement in the trash, or to recycle it into a very different concept. I prefer the term *settled work*. We may not need to work like we do now, especially as for the most part our children are now grown and no longer dependent on us, but we will need to keep working. Settled work means we work less, work at what we love, and we move slower."

The option of a retirement home will become more difficult as many more will be seeking beds. Beyond that problem however, is the fact that many baby boomers put their parents in retirement homes, or retirement villages as they often now are called, and hated it.

"Tell me about it, Martin," Ed commented. "That's where I am going today."

"I hope you don't find me insensitive in talking this way, Ed."

"Not at all. I suppose from what you are saying, I should be grateful I can still find an open bed," Ed replied.

Martin continued. "My father and mother chose to go to a retirement village when they felt they could no longer cope in their old home. The private company promoted it as fairly upscale and it did have some nice amenities, although the cost was stunning – goodbye inheritance. My mother did OK, keeping herself busy, but for my father the enforced unimportance proved difficult. He believed every person is here on earth for a purpose, and that old people are the elders who have the time and a lifetime of experience to give back. He felt something was wrong with the idea of elders being neatly packed away with their talent and time being wasted. He observed how many of the other people living there began to act like teenagers again, who-was-not-talking-to-who sort of stuff. He looked forward to my visits so he could provide me with his analysis of the social construct of the retirement village. He convinced me to make certain I would find a better alternative when my time came. As you can see, I did."

"In terms of health, we need to keep ourselves in better shape, and unless something changes, we may find certain health services no longer offered to us, unless we have savings set aside to pay for it. When we need nursing care, we must find a less costly way. The isolation of a nursing home is awful."

"When my father finally had to be moved into one, I found visits to be painful which seemed selfish considering that he had to suffer it 24 hours a day. We pack old people in overheated institutional buildings with nothing to do other than watch TV or play games. We bring in therapists to keep their minds somewhat active. The smells can be offensive, especially the ammonia used to clean up accidents. The sounds can be loud and distressing, from those in pain, those suffering senility and the background noise of overly-loud televisions watched by the partially deaf. My children hated to visit grandpa, saying the people were creepy and the place stank. When they did visit, all the other patients whose minds were alert would crowd in as so few children come to visit. Yes, the Sunday-school choir would visit and sing, but the elders needed more. They needed life not a show."

"In most cases the staff are poorly paid and overworked, and my father continually complained how they talked to him like a child when his mind functioned clearly. He had a semi-private room, no locks, little privacy, and people stole what few possessions he had left; some say it was underpaid staff, others blamed unstable patients. My father, in his usual dispassionate clarity, reported that his psychological state suffered not from his age, but the environment of the nursing home. It was an awful way to die, especially for such a fine man."

Ed looked at Martin with kindness. "He sounds like a good man, and I am sorry to hear both he and you had to go through such a sad ending."

"Yes, he was, and you are right, it was hard on both of us. But unless we do something, it will be worse for baby boomers. While I vowed I would not go the route my parents went, I realized vowing is not enough; I needed a plan and I needed to start now, not wait until my wife and I were lucky enough to move to Sun & Fun Retirement Village where we would shrivel up like old prunes.

Ed asked him, "I see you here, so I see that you made the move, but how did it happen? What's the rest of your story?"

"I use the internet a lot," Martin answered, "and I subscribed to some web sites that feature interesting ideas about habitat. One day I read a review of a book called *How to Build a Village* that had a section called 'If you are a baby boomer worried about when you retire.' Yup, that's me. I went to villageforum.com and they had a preview I could read on line. Read the website, ordered the book, and read the book from cover to cover. I then went back to the web site, signed up saying I was interested and waited to see what would happen."

"They sent me an email welcoming me, and since I had selected a project already in the pipeline, I was contacted by what they call a Village Steward who asked me which particular village was of the greatest interest to me and my family. Talk about being a kid in a candy store, there were twenty different choices, twenty-one actually if you count the town square with its posh mansions – not my cup of tea – and each village offered a very different character."

"We picked the village where Sophia lives because I always enjoyed being around college students. They are beyond the awkward stage of teenagers, but still have the idealism and passion of youth and I love the impromptu debates in the café. With our own kids at the moving-out, moving-on stage, we need young people around to keep us young in body and spirit."

"Yes, I would have to say the few hours I have spent with Sophia touring Villageton has certainly made me feel younger," Ed quipped. This time it was Sophia who blushed.

Martin winked at her and continued his story. "We chose a home site close to the plaza, about 50 yards away, on one of the quieter back streets. It's actually two homes in one building. The Village Organizing Company has several designs for what they call elder-housing, so on the ground floor, we built an elder home with its own entrance. Then in the rest of the building we designed a large home for our current lifestyle. We have a lifetime collection of furniture, art, mementos and what our kids would call junk; we were not ready to get rid of it. Even though there are only two of us, we have several extra rooms for visiting friends, children, and perhaps one day soon, grandchildren. We designed the guest rooms with privacy, so we can take in paying visitors during the festivals that they hold here several times a year."

"We rent the elder home out to a lovely old lady who keeps it in spotless condition and who is an absolute hoot. If I ever find I am becoming a bit low, I knock on her door with a tea bag, and within minutes she has me in stitches with the stories of her life. I keep telling her she should have an internet video show – something they produce at the filmmakers village, but she's not interested."

"We are planning ahead. When that time comes when we slow down, and the big house is too much for us, we have an agreement with one of our children, who now lives over in the youth zone, that we will move into the elder home below and sell the building to her. Instead of a mortgage she will pay us a monthly pension sufficient to meet our needs, and when we die, it's hers free and clear... provided, of course, she doesn't bump us off to get it early." Martin laughed. "We have some friends who made similar arrangements only not with relatives. Instead they enter into a formal arms length contract with a young family that could probably not get such good terms on the open market. Both parties win."

"So is it safe to assume you expect there will be no Social Security and no private pension when you can no longer work?" Ed asked.

"I've crunched the numbers, Ed, and either the income tax will have to go up to 70%, or science will have to invent the elixir of youth. Social security and pensions won't disappear, but it will be miserable for those without any Plan B," Martin replied. "I will be delighted if they solve the problem, but I sure don't plan to bet my life on it. I can't go it alone, but 10,000 people can create a society where we take care of our own. That's what we have done here, and what I recommend others do as well. If they don't do it by 2018, it will probably be too late."

"But that is dwelling on the negative side, the fear-of-the-future stuff, and if there is one thing I am sure of, you can't build a community in response to fear. I used to work in the advertising business, where we probably knew more about the baby boom than anyone. I advised businesses that needed to know how Boomers think, what they value, and how to position their business to be of service. I enjoyed the work, but the travel was a killer. I could have moved the business here, but I finally began to read my own advice. If I was going to change my life so I had more time for what Morgan calls the four pillars of conviviality, citizenship, art & intellect, and spirit, then it was time to stop living to work."

"I've always enjoyed books, and I saw the need for a great new and used book store in Villageton. Used books are the most fun. Many of the people who live in Villageton move here with substantial collections of books they no longer read. I take them in and put a 10% commission on consignment. It runs more like a library as I see the same books cycle many times. I don't earn as much as I did in my previous career, but I sure enjoy life a lot more, and the day-to-day cost of living is significantly lower."

At this mention of books Ed winced, and told the story of how he sold his lifetime collection of books using an on-line auction where the whole lot was put on at a no-reserve $1 start, where it drew only one bid.

"That's the danger of the internet and its instant nature," Martin responded. Here your books would wait for someone who wanted one of them and was prepared to pay a fair price. That's exactly what the book seller who paid a dollar for them will do. Also, he will list them on book web sites, including the big ones that allow resellers to list their current catalog. Sorry to hear about your loss, Ed, I would have been happy to take the whole lot here on consignment, and they probably would have not stayed here long. When we get a private collection in, I send a notice out to subscribers in Villageton, and some of the books get sold directly out of the shipping boxes. We changed our unpacking procedures to allow the regulars to help unpack. We get free labor, and they get first pickings.

"Oh well, lesson learned" sighed Ed. "If I may return to the baby boomer topic... if I were to talk with my son and daughter, how would you summarize both the problem and how Villageton addresses it?"

Martin thought for a moment, then said, "The challenge is too many boomers, not enough next-gen workers and different expectations about entitlements than prior generations. The numbers don't add up, and something is going to break. Relying on national solutions runs huge risk. If they don't get it right, our generation – your kids and their children – will suffer."

"Village-towns like this one give people a higher level of control over their own lives. They secure that control by bringing together enough people to build a strong local economy, but not so many people that the community becomes bureaucratic. It needs to be a comprehensive community, not solely a village for baby boomers. Boomers should plan to reinvent their elder years, where they remain active, involved and if possible have a plan to convert a lifetime of assets, most particularly their home, into a lifetime pension."

"Well, enough of me," Martin concluded. "While you visit this plaza, permit me to suggest you stop by the Travellers Inn. You will never want to stay in a motel again. Oh, and Sophia, I think the front desk has the urban landscape book you ordered. It just came in. We found it at a specialty used bookstore in Connecticut."

# Chapter 11

# The Politician's Story

The Travellers Inn was unmistakable; from the outside it was large and long with tall, welcoming ground-floor windows and wide balconies on the upper floors suitable for sitting, reading or people-watching. Sophia commented that while it was fun all the time, in the winter it had a roaring fire going – one of the few buildings allowed an open wood fire, due to pollution regulations. "To comply they installed an industrial scrubber system. They don't need the fireplace for heat but somehow it's important for human beings; takes us back to our camp fire or cave dwelling days." Sophia said.

Ed held the massive door for Sophia as they walked in. Huge, Ed thought to himself. No other way to describe it, but huge. The tables and benches were hewn out of thick logs; mostly long tables with a hearth big enough to roast a bull. Near the walls smaller tables provided space for people who wanted to talk privately. Near the hearth, a few well worn leather library chairs provided seating for those wishing to read or chat.

Sophia explained the long tables encourage people to mingle, and locals would frequently come in to meet visitors and hear their stories. "In winter they fly a special flag outside to signal a *Bard Night* when a local or travelling story teller would sit in the bard's chair by the fire. Those evenings tend to be packed, and it is the only time everyone sitting here is quiet."

"The Travellers Inn brews its own beer, both alcoholic and ginger, and for those avoiding processed sugar, alcohol or caffeine, they make a medieval drink out of pomegranates, cloves, mint, ginger and various roots and herbs with honey that actually tastes lovely," she told Ed and Michael.

Ed said he was game to try something new, or ancient as it were, and he bought drinks for all of them. He paid at the counter and Sophia pointed to the table where they would sit.

As they sat down, a loud, clear voice rang out "Sophia darling, how's my favorite Slovenian princess?" Looking over, Sophia said, "Ed, what luck. Let me introduce you to Sarah Walker, the Mayor of Villageton, and no, I am not a princess. Sarah, Ed is a visitor and I am showing him around. He used to be the head planner in Blandville."

Sarah held out her hand and greeted Ed. "Actually, I'm not officially the Mayor, I am the Chief Executive Officer of the Villageton Council, but since it is an elected position, and VTC is the governance body for the community, people call me the Mayor. I used to be one of the elected representatives for the county that had to approve and rezone so Villageton could be built, and I thought it was such a great idea that I moved in. Then everyone thought I was such a great person that they elected me CEO, and I've done such a great job – or I'm so stupid that no one else wants the job – that I've kept it ever since."

Sarah belted out another one of her deep belly laughs, and Ed warmed to her immediately. This woman had charisma by the bucketful. "What's it like being Mayor, or CEO, and how hard was it to learn the job?" Ed asked.

"It's a hoot. I have never enjoyed work so much as I do here. I work my butt off, but its great work. I love it, I love the people who I work with, and I love this place. Learning the job was great too, since no one had ever done it before, there were no shoes to fill, good thing too, if you look at my feet, you see they're big."

## Becoming a Politician

"Seriously though, I probably do have a lot of experience. I was born in the cotton country of the Bootheel of Missouri in a little town that had no running water, the streets were not paved, and when it rained hard we used boards to walk from the front door to the gravel road. No one had much money, but the community was strong and the people caring. I was a little girl when our little place incorporated itself as a fourth class city. We had about 700 people, and except for a few volunteer workers, everyone was black and dirt poor."

"In the early 1970's the Federal Government started giving out grants to poor towns, and our mayor went to Washington to say he was mayor of the third poorest city in America. I don't know if it was true, but it worked like magic and he came home with a $300,000 grant to put in water lines. Our elected officials had not been in office long, but they sure learned the art of corruption fast. They tried to get through a resolution that would have let them and their buddies into that federal hog trough even before the money had cleared the bank."

"What they didn't reckon on however, were a group of staunch ladies, including my mother who took me along to watch. My mama waited until they were ready to put the resolution, and then she stood up, stared the mayor down, and said "Now, David, you do right." The mayor looked up at mama, and he started that old country talk, "What you talking about Robbie, I'm just taking a vote; it's my job." Mama stood up again, and this time like cold steel she said it again. "David, you stop that nonsense now, I'm not going to tell you again, you do right!". Well this went on for about five minutes and she did tell him again while the other councillors got more and more fidgety with those women standing behind my mama staring them down. When the mayor finally banged down the gavel and insisted on taking a vote, he could not get it passed. He tried again the next meeting, but he could not get those councillors passed my mama glaring at them like an old hawk eyeing chickens in the coop. In the end, they did it right and honest. My mama never told those councillors how to vote, or even what "right" meant, she just laid it on the line. I could not have been more than seven years old then, but that was the night I decided to go into politics."

"It was certainly easier for me than for my mama's generation. She used to pack a loaded revolver under the drivers seat. One time when some good ol' boys tried to run her off the road she pulled it out; aiming over shoulder, she put a few holes in their radiator. After that they left her alone, but it was not an easy life she had. There were ten of us children; my dad was not well most of our growing up. He got injured bad in the cotton fields when I was a baby and was home most of the time. But for me that was a good thing, because he drilled me on my school homework. When he felt they were not teaching me enough, he brought home books from the church library that were donated by a white church up in St. Louis, and we would read those together."

"I was the only one in town to go to college and when I graduated, mama made me swear I would not come back home. "Nothing here for you girl, you go out into the world and make your family proud." So I did. After I graduated from the state university, I went up to Chicago and I started a business making and selling hair-care products. I did well, and I found I had enough time to get involved with city politics up there. Huewee, was that an education! Mama's eyes would've popped right out of her head staring down those politicians to do right." Sarah let out another great laugh.

"I got married to a lovely man who worked up there. He had a big family down here, and we just did not feel Chicago was a good place for us to raise a family. So I sold my business, we moved down, had two lovely girls, and I started a new business here. My husband continued to work as a freelance journalist switching to rural and agriculture reports, and we settled down to enjoy a right comfortable down-home existence. I took up singing in the church choir and joined the Rotary Club. Actually, I was the first woman to join that chapter and four years later they elected me club president. They must have liked the way I ran the club because a group of them put my name forward to be a representative for the County Council and shock of shocks, I won. Until then I had been a party worker, not an elected representative. The biggest surprise was that it was not the same political party I had worked with in Chicago. They changed my colors!"

## Approving Villageton

"In my second term, I read about this 10,000 person Village Organizing Company, as they called it, looking for a site to build a billion dollar town with its own local economy that would bring in thousands of new jobs, generate hundreds of millions of dollars in new revenue in the region, and have no adverse environmental or social impact. I think I was on the phone to them about ten seconds after I finished reading."

"I have to tell you, I can be one tough negotiator, and like my mama, I'm always looking for the snake in the grass, but this one was the genuine article. So I took it back to the county and bluntly told them they would be insane not to do everything in their power to land this one. I told them how wonderful it was, how important it was, and it seemed like they were half asleep until I said "one billion dollars". Man, it was like I had tossed viagra in their teapot. As soon as I started talking money, their eyes opened wide, and I had to tell one of them to close his mouth before he started drooling."

Ed found himself laughing, as Sarah so accurately painted a picture so close to his own experiences working with the Blandville Council.

"They voted to form a special committee to investigate it, and made me the head – I had less seniority than everyone else on the committee, but I suppose they figured it would be hard work, and I had opened my mouth first. As it turned out the hardest part was getting the staff to understand that as elected officials we made policy and they carried it out."

"The staff had their own ways of approving rezoning for subdivisions, and they loved taking years to make plans and then insist everything fit within their plan. This idea for Villageton was so far out of their box that it could have been from another planet. So I called in the head of planning – he held a similar position to yours at Blandville, Ed – and on the whiteboard I drew a three column list."

"I had him write all the principles the planning department set out for future development... economic, environmental, social and cultural, on the left side. Then in the middle column, I listed the effects should we approve Villageton and asked the planning head to add in any adverse impact. He could list none. I then pointed to the third column and asked him to put in the impact of another suburban subdivision, commercial boulevard with big box stores, shopping mall, office and industrial park. That third column was part of his existing beloved plan. Under that column I asked him to identify all the effects, both positive and negative. He had to concede Villageton came out far closer to the planning principles."

"I have to say, the Villageton people were sharp negotiators. Had they bought land and then approached us for rezoning, my planning department would have been in the drivers seat, and they would have tied it up for years. By turning the process upside down – first finding the buyers, then looking for a cooperative jurisdiction and only then looking for the right land, it was a political proposition first, voter-taxpayer issue second, and a bureaucratic one, dead last."

"Our planning director kept insisting we had an official plan and had to stick with it. I finally got it through his stubborn head, that a plan is what the elected officials adopt. If it is in the interest of the people that the plan be changed, the whole point of representative democracy is empowering the policy makers to change the plan. If a proposal was counter to the principles of planning, I told him he might have a good argument, but at the bottom line he was just acting too much like a paper-loving bureaucrat and not enough like a planner. Oh, that got his goat, and I was afraid I had gone too far. His face turned bright red, his left ear started twitching, and I was sorely afraid flames were going to come out of his nose. But then he cracked, smiled and said I was probably right, and after that we took out the proposal and got to work."

Ed shook his head and grinned. He was enjoying this story, especially because he felt like a fly on the wall watching it, not the poor planner in the hot seat.

"As you probably have heard, the Village Organizing Company or VOC, as they called it, proposed something called Dynamic Engagement. They analyzed the whole rezoning and subdivision approval process, and concluded that over 90% of the elapsed calendar time was either down time - doing nothing, or cycle time - where paperwork gets kicked back to the other side. Of the remaining 10%, a lot of time is poorly used because there is a contest between the developer and the planning and approving officials. The developer sees the approvers as inefficient, unreasonable bureaucrats, and the approvers see the developer as driven purely by *pecuniary interest*

– I love that phrase – where they seek to externalize costs that the taxpayer has to then pick up. Unlike a developer, the VOC's brief included *effects* – both good effects and adverse impacts. What this means is the VOC's job is not only to generate profits, but to examine the effects of each part of a proposed development to make sure there are no adverse effects, or if some are unavoidable, that the adverse part is properly mitigated."

At this description, Ed began to figure the planner's hot seat just caught fire.

"Given that Villageton has no commuters, no outbound stream of cars every day, the biggest problem with new development vanishes – no traffic. In fact, what little increased traffic there is, is from our county folks going to Villageton because they love it. The Greenbelt not only ticks the environment boxes, but it provides a huge buffer zone, so the Not In My Back Yard crowd has nothing to complain about. All they see in their backyards are trees and fields of flowers. The nearest neighbors neither see lights nor hear Villageton noise, because the village walls and the greenbelt around it absorb it all. Villageton does its own schooling, treats its own sewage, recycles all its own solid waste and paves its own streets. As a matter of law, within Villageton the systems are privately owned, a bit like the pedestrian 'streets' in an enclosed shopping mall. Once built, our building permit department has no additional work, because except for remodelling, everything was constructed at the beginning. This also meant only one year of intense construction, and thereafter no builders' delivery trucks, or other construction-related vehicle traffic on our county roads."

"I have to tell you the most amazing part came from our citizens. We have the usual group of complainers, aging hippies, under-employed greenies, university types and activist lawyers who oppose almost every development proposal that hits the region. When they heard about this one, they contacted the Village Forum, set up an eight day tour, got their people in front of every newspaper, radio and TV reporter, set up meetings with every elected and appointed official they could find, and held public meetings every night, with the Village Stewards, as they are called, as the guest speakers. The usual opponents became some of the strongest supporters, making for some very unusual bedfellows when the issue became public. It's a rare day when Rotary members and greenies agree on a proposed development. For the Rotary meeting I ordered helium balloons in the shape of pink pigs."

Having been to a few Rotary meetings in his day, Ed chuckled at the flying pig reference, then said, "I see how the idea appeals to business people and environmentalists. It makes me wonder why more developers don't take this approach. But do go on."

## The Farmers Who Feed Villageton... Every Day, Forever

"The other influential group in the county was the farmers. As a woman politician from Chicago, they did not hold a lot of respect for me, figuring I did not know much about farming and the problems they faced. The VOC made it clear we needed to get the farmers on board, not so much to allow Villageton to be built, but to assure a permanent food source."

"Without Villageton, our farmland was too far away to merit rezoning. But once a billion dollar development comes here with its own mega million dollar economic engine – especially with its own industrial park – investors and developers would be here in a flash, pressuring the county to let them convert those farms into more housing, shopping and industrial land. The VOC said we could expect proposals and schemes to imitate Villageton's design, but for the wrong reasons; plans that would create all sorts of new problems for us."

"Instead of relying on the county to promise to not rezone, the VOC went direct to the farmers with a two part proposal. One, they sought long-term contracts with individual farms to feed 10,000 villagers every day for as long as Villageton exists. In doing so, they offered to solve the problems farmers face today. Two, they offered to buy the development rights from those farmers, giving them an instant cash injection to enable them to reduce debt."

"The price farmers are getting for food is going down. For example, farmers growing nectarines get 4¢ a pound, but in the supermarket consumers pay $1.99. In two cans of tomato paste selling for 98¢, the tomato growers get nine cents. In almost every food product the farmer becomes a price taker, not a price setter. In 1950, the USDA says the average farmer in America earned 44% of the price paid by the consumer. By 2006, this had dropped to 19%. In Capitalism 101, when over 80% is taken by the middleman, the opportunity to save money going after the fat in the bloated middle is ripe, if you will pardon my mixed metaphors."

"I love your metaphors, Sarah," Ed commented, "and appreciate your insight."

Sarah thanked him and continued. "From the farmer's perspective the middleman has become a monopoly, and to stay in business the farmer must stay in debt, and constantly invest in ways to increase yield – extracting more food from the same amount of land. In many cases they do this through chemicals on the land, injections of hormones and drugs into animals and concentrations on monoculture foods."

"From the consumer standpoint, this means the nutritional value of our food drops, we ingest many of the chemicals and drugs the FDA declares as safe, and we increasingly expose our country to the risk of an agricultural pandemic where a new virus or bacteria could wipe out a monoculture crop like the potato famine that struck Ireland in the 1840's."

"The VOC gives the local farmers a choice, whereas previously they faced a monopoly that keeps turning the screws tighter. In our case, it offered contracts at about 45% of the supermarket price, provided the farmers back off on yield to eliminate the need for chemicals, drugs and hormones, and they deliver the food to Villageton's freight depot."

"This meant the farmers needed to learn new methods and plant a wider range of crops. The VOC also specified heritage foods that taste far better but that the agrisystem dropped because they don't travel well. All farmers who accepted the contracts became part of Villageton's intranet, meaning they get to participate in other money-saving benefits of Villageton. Finally Villageton and the farmers run a joint venture making alcohol fuel, compost and fertilizer from its sewage, organic trash and farm cuttings. This further removes those farmers' dependency on the price of oil and keeps local money turning locally."

"The second part of the proposal addressed development rights. The VOC buys them for Villageton in a special trust that means the farms can never be developed for housing, commercial or industrial use. The farms will remain farms and Villageton is assured of a permanent food source. Some farmers took the cash to pay off the bank. Others chose to accept an alternative plan where the VOC offered at a substantial discount either homes for the farmers' children – those who moved to the city, and could never return here to the county because of lack of opportunity – or elder housing for the farmer when they retired."

"When all this was put forth to the farmers, the response was surprisingly positive. Most farmers are smart businessmen who love their work, and increasingly resent the extent to which banks and middlemen tell them how they must run their business. They looked for hooks in the offer, and concluded they were dealing with straight up people seeking to align their interests with Villageton's. I have to say in the process, they came to respect me as well. "Not bad for a city girl," was probably the best compliment I was going to get out of them, but from a conservative farmer that was good. It was only later when we became friends, that I told them how I grew up working summers in the cotton fields."

## Zoning and Plan Approval

"So when it came to rezoning, the usual obstacles were eliminated. Next we negotiated tax concessions. Usually when a billion dollar corporation moves in, they want all sorts of tax credits for the first years. Not Villageton. Instead the VOC sought to negotiate fair taxes for services they would use, but no taxes for services Villageton would provide internally, like sewage or recycling. They required this be in the form of a contract to remain in effect as long as Villageton exists. Given the projected quarter billion dollars a year in new income earned by 6,000 workers in the community, this seemed reasonable. Finally, Villageton wanted equal say on any future resolutions that would have an impact on them to prevent "gotcha" politics after the town was built. This caused some consternation among my elected colleagues, but when the lawyers finished hammering out the language, they saw it was a fair request and not one easily abused. It was another form of the checks and balances they brought to the table."

"Once we agreed to all that in principle – and I should note that four other jurisdictions also agreed, all competing for the same village-town – the land search began. Brother, that was a zoo, I tell you. Every land banker, property investor and overheated farmer sick with money fever turned up in their Sunday best. However, the VOC knew its business. It needed at least 500 acres of land, with about 150 relatively flat acres in the middle so they could use huge wheeled-cranes moving down the street to build the homes. They wanted to use marginal land, and refused to consider the best farm land. Proximity to a rail line was a plus, even if no passenger trains ran on it anymore, and it needed to be within two hours of a major or feeder airport. It was essential that Telepresence quality broadband could be brought to the land."

"Finally, decision day came, and we won. Huewee, we had a party that night, I tell you. After that, everything happened so fast it made our heads swim. They conditionally purchased the land, the three month Dynamic Engagement process began, and they took about a year to build the roads, put in the infrastructure, the motorpool, industrial park and freight depot. They also commissioned manufacturing the huge cranes, each one of which would pop out two houses a day."

## Construction

"When those cranes arrived, the real work began. Four-thousand homes, one-thousand workplaces, plus public buildings all went up in twelve months. Bulk material came in by rail car. The cranes were mobile factories erecting the walls of a three story building in a day. There were no subcontractors at all. Everyone on the site was on a full-time contract for a year, and many lived in the dormitories built as temporary housing in the motorpool. In fact we asked the VOC to build the worker's toilets and kitchens as permanent so at any time the motorpool can be converted into Civil Defense housing in case of a county or state emergency."

"Very smart," Ed said. "Someone was thinking ahead."

"Actually, we were remembering Katrina." Sarah replied. "Anyway, the job site ran 24 hours a day, seven days a week. The cranes had roofs and lights so rain or shine, construction continued. By not using subcontractors, every worker understood their job was to help everyone else. If a plumber needed a hand with pipes, the electrician helped. Anyone who said *that's not my job*, discovered they were right, as they were sent packing. Morale was high, and the dorm-resident workers loved it, as they had no rent, no distractions, worked the maximum allowable hours and saved lots of money."

"They built a whole village at one time. They had twenty villages to build, and ten rigs to build them. This meant that some villages were finished earlier. Where it was safe, they allowed people to move in early. Remember, most of us were paying a construction loan, which is why VOC completed construction in 12 months. Residents whose income was not based on local-to-local could move in early. What I mean by this is someone running a bookstore, that needs a 5,000 population to be profitable, would not be able to move in, even if their building was ready. But someone running an internet hair products business could."

"Finally, opening day arrived. The streets were swept clean, the traffic posts installed and about 8,000 people showed up in the Town square. Instead of cutting a ribbon, they broke a bottle of champagne on the Town Hall. That was at noon, and by one p.m. while many had already moved in, it was wild as a few thousand brought in final furniture. Everything had been pre-planned and scheduled so there was no problem with the electric delivery vehicles, and of course many people had already met during the Dynamic Engagement so they got along. But even the best plans can't go like clockwork. Thankfully, the weather was beautiful, and everyone was in good spirits. Except for one piano that got loose going up the stairs and ending up rolling into the middle of the plaza, it went well and we all survived opening day."

"The next three months were wild. Imagine, a whole town pops up, offering a quality of life so much higher than what most of the residents knew in their previous life. Everyone had the same experience. I wager the most common word spoken in those three months was "Wow". I make a habit of listening to the words people use, and before I moved to Villageton, I noticed how common it is for folks to use the word "hate", in complaining. In those first three months, I hardly heard it, and instead I heard the word *love*, as in *I loved my walk this morning just at sunrise, when everyone was still asleep*. I also heard a lot less profanity, especially from the young. They became kinder, more considerate, if you can imagine that." Ed shook his head in astonishment.

"Now, of course, we all accept this life as normal, and it's only when we go out into what we call the outside world, that we remember the life we used to live."

Sarah put her hand on Ed's arm and said "Darling, I forgot to warn you. Ask me a question and I'll tell you a story. You asked me what it was like being the mayor, and learning the ropes, and I take down my photograph album on the bookshelf and insist on showing you every picture. You must be bored silly."

### RACE VS TRIBE

Ed protested, "Not at all Sarah, I'm fascinated, and especially wondering how I would have handled you, if you had been on my town council. I probably would have blown smoke out my ears. You're right about planners protecting turf, and how sometimes we forget that making policy is not our job. If I can ask you to take down another picture album, perhaps one more painful, tell me about racism. Is there any racism in Villageton? From what I have seen walking the streets, there are villages with people of all colors, and then these ethnic villages where people cluster by ancestry."

Sarah got a mischievous look in her eye, but then it appeared the more serious side of her took control, and she chose to answer it straight. "Again, I'm going to answer with reference to the past. When people use the word racism, they use it to cover two very different stories. Where I grew up, we had southern racism. Not far from where I grew up lived the mother of the last black man to be publicly lynched in the state. In 1942, Cleo Wright broke into a home, stabbed a white woman and was arrested that night. In the police car, he pulled another knife from his boot and stabbed the marshal. The marshal fought back and shot him four times. By the next morning, a mob of about 500 white people gathered outside the jail including some of the town's most prominent citizens. They forced their way into the jail, dragged Wright out, tied him upside down to the bumper of a car and hauled him to the black part of town where they set him on fire. Hours later a city dump truck picked up the remains."

"Racism in the south was personal. It was more about class than anything, and a lot of it had to do with class control. At the top you had the white establishment, then the white middle class, and at the bottom, the poor white trash. That bottom class had very little opportunity, a poor education and a lot of anger. Anger is never a good thing in a community, but with blacks living nearby, the establishment encouraged that anger to be directed at the blacks rather than at the establishment. On a day-to-day basis relations were cordial, as long as blacks understood their place. When Cleo stabbed that white woman, he was fair game for mob violence because he broke the code of southern racism."

"When I moved to Chicago, I met a very different kind of racism. It was more like separate realities. Whites and blacks had their own worlds; when they met, there was more fear than class code. As a well-dressed, successful black woman, I had to be early for business meetings because I could not count on a taxi stopping. Walking into a white-run store my husband would encounter suspicion. There is no word for it, this constant pressure. I never tried to put a name to it until I flew to New Zealand on business and had meetings with white people there. They treated me normally, and I realized there was a pressure missing from those interactions. I could get a cab, go into a store, or greet people on the street, and not feel that kind of pressure that is normal in our world, but not in yours."

"A lot of racism is about control and about fear. Villageton is strong on freedom, meaning people get to live their lives without other people trying to control them all the time. Yes, we have social controls, but it's more like *get out of my face*, than telling people how to live. Apparently, early on, someone looked up the root of the word freedom and found it was the same root as the word friend. You hear that story mentioned frequently here, since true friendship is the one relationship where controlling others has no place."

"As for fear, it comes again from control. People who feel powerless tend to be the ones who commit violence. In Villageton we have very little fear because everyone knows everyone else in their own village, and over time the villages all get to know each other. Opportunity here is not controlled or doled out to one class or another. Villageton runs its own local economy, it offers plenty of opportunity to everyone at every stage of their lives. People given opportunity do not prey on other people."

"So, to answer your question, we don't have racism, but we do have tribal identity, the pride that comes from sharing a common ancestry. Thanks to genetics, I know what part of Africa most of my ancestors come from, and it turns out there are about twenty other people here who come from the same ancestry. We got together and formed an informal club, learned about our connection to the old world, and filled in the gaps. I now tell my daughters those stories as well as the stories of life under slavery and the struggle to attain equal rights."

"I also make a point of telling those stories in mixed company, sometimes in the winter, sitting around the fire over there in the leather chairs. I do it for a reason. It makes each of us a real, complex person. Racism is about two-dimensional cutouts, not real people. When you first met me, Ed, I used my brassy voice and loud laugh to break through any two dimensions, and within seconds you saw a human being, not a black woman. You did not see my age, or my gender or my race, you saw Sarah Walker, the CEO mayor, and I felt you warm up to me."

"My goal is to get Villageton to the same state that I found in New Zealand, where people see the color of my skin, but judge me on how I present myself, rather than talking to their own preconceptions. If I had to put it on a scale of one to ten, where ten is New Zealand, and one was my childhood in the Bootheel, I would say Villageton is a nine. We're getting there, and it's good."

"Now, listen darling, we could go on this way all day, but I need to pick my babies up from school, and besides you need to meet more people. You will find that everyone in Villageton has their own story, and they have so many different views of reality. I never cease to be amazed when I shut up and listen to other people's stories. What I love about this place is its ability to bring them all together with enough privacy and space that they keep their differences. I'm off, big kiss, and yes Sophia, you really are a princess."

By this time Ed was getting used to these grand exits, so he downed the rest of his medieval drink –which was wonderful – and said to Sophia, "Where to next?"

"There is someone who I just saw walking over to the Travellers Inn's sun-room I want you to meet. He is a very special man who made a big difference in this country, and provided inspiration that helped make Villageton happen," Sophia replied.

They walked across the large bustling great room and through a portal into a bright, smaller room bathed in warm sunlight. The walls were whitewash, made of an adobe style brick with soft edges. The furniture looked comfortable in a western style, and at a table sat an older gentleman wearing an open shirt and cardigan sweater. He looked up, saw Sophia walking in, smiled and waved, signalling her over.

# Chapter 12

# Stewart Udall - The Conservationist

"Stewart" Sophia said to him after warmly greeting him, "I want to introduce you to a man on a journey, who is visiting Villageton today, and learning about what is possible when good people work together. This is Ed Rice, a retired town planner from Blandville. Ed, may I introduce you to Stewart Udall?"

Before Ed could express surprise, Stewart beckoned the three of them to join him at his table. Sophia explained to Ed that Stewart was somewhat hard of hearing, and she then asked Stewart if he would mind telling both a bit about his life and the message he wrote to his grandchildren.

Stewart began. "I am 89 years of age, going on 90 and I was born in the small town of St, Johns, Arizona near Holbrook and Winslow. We grew up in the country. For the first 18 years of my life, my home was on the Colorado plateau, 60 miles from the railroad. I grew up in cattle country and I grew up where there were irrigation canals and people raised hay and other products. My early experience was the early years of the Great Depression, and I learned how people coped with a depression. You bought flour and beans and sugar, and that was mostly what you had. In small towns like mine, you had very little crime and people were good neighbors. One of the great advantages, in my view, of small and middle-sized towns is that neighbors are concerned about their neighborhoods. Small communities are very intolerant of crime, and the neighbors looked after the kids as they carried on around town. The old people were honored for their age and for the fact they had lived good lives and they had taken care of their community needs. In the small town where I lived, medicine was different because it was an earlier era. One of the reasons I have lived so long is antibiotics were not available. If you got a disease you either died or you fought it off and survived."

"We relied on public transport, and there is a great lesson to go back and study how we solved the transportation problems during the Depression and then on into the war. I saw Southern California before the war when I was on a football team that went over to Southern California. It was a series of garden cities, small cities surrounded by gardens that were connected by fast trains to the other parts of Southern California. They called them Red Ball trains, but after the war the automobile industry conspired to eliminate them. That was my background, my first part of my life." Stewart said.

"The next big thing that happened in my life was that after Pearl Harbor I volunteered for the Army Air Force. I saw the war from the air; I was a gunner on bombers flying out of Italy. We were going after oil because there was only one big oil field that was not in Germany, and that was an area called Ploiesti in Romania. We bombed that several times trying to cut off their supplies, because oil was very important during the war," he explained.

"Under Roosevelt, we would make one step forward and then one step back as he tried to get the economy going. Most people today don't realize the depression lasted eleven years. We got out of the Depression when the Pearl Harbor attack occurred – when we realized we were in a global war and we had to convert our economy. They shut down all the automobile factories in Detroit and they converted them to making tanks... the bombers that I flew on were made in Detroit by one of the automobile companies. The United States had an abundance of oil and because we had technological knowledge, we built ships and tanks and airplanes and so on. The British were broke and we supplied the equipment that won the war. That gave us faith in technology and it also gave us faith in education."

"When the war ended, I studied law in Tucson, Arizona. I met my wife then and married her. The GI Bill was a wonderful program. It gave people like me $75 a month – with a wife and two children you learned to get by on it. About seven years after I married her, in 1954, I was elected to Congress. I served for three terms. Then Kennedy picked me to be the first Arizonian to serve in the President's Cabinet. I was the only Westerner in the Cabinet under Kennedy. As Secretary of the Interior, I thought I had the best job in the country. Kennedy was highly intelligent. He surrounded himself with people who wanted to do new things, wanted to improve the country and he was just starting to do things when he was assassinated. But it was a joy to work with him and the idea of creating wilderness, creating new national parks, new open space, improve natural wildlife refuges. We were doing all those things under Presidents Kennedy and Johnson."

"When Rachel Carson came along and wrote *Silent Spring* in 1962, that was such a powerful book that people started to call the conservation movement the environmental movement and the United States became the leader in this transformation to this new phase of action."

"When I was in Congress, I voted for the interstate highway program – I was amazed when I look back – there was never any discussion about whether we had enough petroleum or natural gas to adopt what I call a one-person-one-car transportation system. But we went ahead and did it. After I left my post in the Cabinet, in the early 1970s I was one of the first people that saw that this wasn't going to work – that we didn't have, and the world didn't have, sufficient petroleum that everybody could convert to automobiles. And so after I was in the Cabinet, I wrote books. I did a lot of speaking and I was, in effect, a spokesman for the environmental movement." Stewart concluded.

Ed then asked him, "Earlier today, I met a man named Morgan in the visitors' center and he quoted a message you wrote to your grandchildren. He said you voted for the Interstate Highway Act as a freshman Congressman, and later saw that as a colossal error. Would you say more about that?"

Stewart smiled sadly and then explained. "I was 34 years of age when I was elected to Congress. And I had a wife and four children then, and as a junior congressman of course, I had very little influence but I recall that Albert Gore from Tennessee, a Senator, was the sponsor of the Interstate Highway program. I did not participate in the debate, there were very few questions asked. *Where was this leading us? Did we have enough petroleum to last not a hundred years?*"

"The proponents of the Interstate Highway System said this was to be the American system of transportation. The railroads will just slowly fade out. There was very little debate at all, and no debate on how much oil there was in the United States of America. During World War Two, we had been the nation that supplied most of the oil for the European war effort and the effort against the Japanese, so there was a kind of an aura that we have unlimited oil and this is a good idea."

"The reason that I wrote the letter to my grandchildren was that I wanted to prepare them, to say to them, your lives are going to be different from the lives your parents have lived. You are living now through what I call the end of the petroleum age. This is the end of the dream that my generation started out with in the 1950's when we passed the Interstate Highway Program; that we were going to be an automobile culture. Our assumptions were wrong. I realized that afterwards. I began to speak out soon after I left office because of predictions made by a petroleum geologist who became famous – his name was King Hubbert, he was a friend of mine. Geologists in the geological surveys said 'Oh, there's plenty of oil; we'll never run out of oil; new fields of oil will be discovered' and so we needn't worry about that.' Well I wrote an article for the Atlantic Monthly in 1970 – eighteen months before the Arab embargo really hit us between the eyes and said "Hey, you've got to question, ask questions about whether you made the right decisions and whether you can go ahead."

Ed was listening carefully. "It's remarkable to hear what you are saying. You were an eyewitness... no, even more than an eyewitness, you were a participant in that historic vote that changed America and that is changing the world, and yet there was no debate about the potential consequences. The decisions were based on an aura of optimism."

"Yes," Stewart replied. "The war gave us faith in oil and faith in technology. I am not negative about technology. But this country, at that time, and later in the time of the space program, we thought technology would solve all of our problems. No reason to worry about technology because technology is growing. We see now that that was a huge mistake."

"One of the favorite sayings of the people in the space program was *today's science fiction is tomorrow's reality*. What a false misleading statement that was!" Stewart laughed. "And they said *well if we run out of petroleum or other mineral assets and so on, we'll mine the moon, we'll go to other planets*. What a huge mistake that was. This country had a final burst of optimism after the space program. We had to open the door, in effect to raiding other planets, mining the moon, manipulating the earth's weather from space platforms, exporting polluting industries to asteroids, mounting shuttle trips to other planets, constructing colonies somewhere in outer space to serve as *backup stations* for earth's inhabitants, and discovering vast new sources of energy in the event that earth's fossil fuels were depleted. Experts described a future where resources would be available for unlimited growth. The Secretary General of the United Nations, proclaimed, *It is no longer resources that limit decisions; it is the decisions that make the resources.*" I look back on the 1970s when the space program succeeded as a period when our country lost its bearings and we were sold on the idea that technology would solve all of the problems."

"It is fascinating that Al Gore Junior became the leading advocate of saying we've gone too far and we are going to have to have different priorities as far as transportation and oil are concerned. It has been a fascinating period for someone who went to Congress when he was 34, and now I come out and I am advising my children that they are inheriting a different world. Their world is 'Think small, drive small, walk a lot, build transportation systems that encourage people to walk, break up your cities into smaller parts,' and that's the way you are going to solve the problem that the United States has today."

"We, in effect, threw out our railroads that carried everything during the war, and we said after the war *we don't need you anymore* and we kept a few of the mainline railroads, but we're going to have to turn back, we're going to have to change our ideas on transportation. We're going to have to have communities that have good public transportation; it's already starting and this is vital. We're going to have to build new kinds of communities with populations of a thousand, two thousand, ten thousand, twenty thousand maybe. People are going to walk to work. Our cities are going to have to be smaller, with walk-able destinations, and our energy systems for travel and transportation in cities are going to have to rely on new functioning solutions to transportation problems." Stewart concluded.

"As I have met you in this ten thousand population community," Ed asked, "it seems the kind of new community you are calling for is coming into being. How did you get involved with VillageTowns?"

"In 2009" Stewart answered, "I released a public letter to my grandchildren that was published in the High Country News, and it attracted considerable attention. I received a letter from an American living in New Zealand, who asked if he could come visit and interview me. I read his book on building VillageTowns and agreed. I gave copies of the book to my son and nephew who are serving in the US Senate, and I agreed to become Chairman Emeritus of the Village Forum. At my age, that means lending your name to support the idea. The idea represented the kind of thinking we need if we are to meet the challenges that face us... thinking that is positive, that sees the challenges as a way to improve life, based on caring, sharing and mutual cooperation. It honors the values I knew when I lived in that small town on the Colorado Plateau, while taking advantage of the good things technology has to offer."

Seeing that Stewart's caregiver had brought his lunch into the room, Ed then asked, "At your age, you are truly a senior statesman. If there was a message you were to say to the younger generation of the world, what would it be?"

Stewart thought, then said, "The larger message I want to deliver in my 89th year to the people of this little planet is that we're all in trouble, maybe everywhere except where the Maori and New Zealanders are a wonderful example for all of us to look at. But don't play petty politics. There are some good leaders, there are some good countries, there are some bad leaders and some countries that are not doing what they should do. Support the leaders that are ready to point a new way for us to build new kinds of smaller cities. Think small, think walking and not traveling in an automobile or some other kind of vehicle. This is a great moment of history, and the people who are going to help develop solutions to these big problems are the people that are in favor of change. Don't be afraid of big change. Our mistakes are so great that we have to make great changes in order to resolve them. I wish you well, all of you. I wish you well."

Sophia reached out and held Stewart's hands. "Thank you, Stewart. As one of that new generation, I take your words to heart. I appreciate how much you have done."

Ed and Michael also thanked him, and Stewart said goodbye as his aide, Karina brought his lunch to the table in that warm, sunlit room.

As they walked out, Sophia said to Ed, "Before I came to America, I was under the impression the great dynasty families of American politics were very partisan, loved by some and hated by others. In meeting Stewart and learning about his family, I found a very different kind of dynasty. One passionately devoted to public service; humble and kind. He once told me of a comment made by the Speaker of the House, Sam Rayburn: *We elect one president at a time, and whoever he happens to be, I want him to be a successful president.* There are not many countries where that view of politics holds sway, yet I learned that is how the Udall family views public service. I was also impressed to learn – although not from Stewart, I had to look it up – that the eastern most point by travel in the United States in the Virgin Islands is named Point Udall, in honor of Stewart, and in 1987 Congress honored the work of his brother Congressman Morris Udall by naming the western most point in the USA, in Guam as Point Udall. How fitting to honor a family that loves Nature, sunrises and sunsets."

"Sophia," Ed said, "What an extraordinary day this is becoming. I don't think my head has been so filled in a long time, and at the same time, my heart is feeling an optimism I have not known since I was a young man in the 1950's. I am younger than Stewart, but not by much, and I remember how positive we felt as a nation. Meeting and listening to him reminds me of those days, makes me aware of how dark and sad our time now has become, yet in that darkness, I feel hope. And as we are again walking... what's next?"

"As Stewart is a man of the outdoors, I thought I would take you to the Greenbelt outside the walls", she replied.

# Chapter 13

## The Many Faces of the Greenbelt

As they walked out Ed showed them his sketch of Stewart and an earlier sketch he made of the Traveller's Inn.

"Ed," Sophia asked. "How do you do that? You were completely focused on Sarah, I saw that, but at the same time you were doing a sketch."

Ed replied. "I don't know. I've done it all my life. Perhaps Miha explained it best early today when he talked about the left brain and right brain working. I draw with my left hand, and somehow I can listen and draw at the same time. It came in very handy in Council planning sessions when we would be discussing the rezoning, because I could draw out what they were discussing. Pity our subject matter in Blandville was not imaginative."

Sophia smiled to herself as they walked to the Greenbelt. She thought Ed was looking younger than when she had met him earlier in the day – softer, happier.

Sophia began to explain what was to come next. "We are heading toward the quietest end of Villageton, furthest away from the industrial park and the youth zone. On this side of Villageton, the wall is not adobe, but a living wall like the ancient hedgerows in England. It marks the boundary beyond which development shall not happen, and at the same time keeps toddlers and senile elders from wandering too far. The wall also discourages village cats and dogs from plundering the greenbelt."

As they went though the hedgerow gate, Ed found he caught his breath, as in front of him was the most exquisite field of flowers he had ever seen in his life. Soft breezes kept it moving and he could hear the drone of millions of bees in pollen heaven. In the far distance on a slight hill he could see a cemetery, with only a few grave stones, which made some sense given the young age of Villageton.

Sophia explained. "The primary purpose of this field is to be. Remember those romantic movies where the heroine is seen running through such a field? Why don't we have this in real life? Here we do." They walked on paths through the flowers and Ed felt a peace that had eluded him for so long he could not remember, and then it came to him. He was five years old, hiding under a green bush on a warm summer day with golden-green sunlight streaming through the leaves. The joy he felt at that moment was perhaps the purest memory of his life.

At the edge of the field, a forest rose up and Sophia explained it long predated the development. "One of the reasons for selecting this land was this ancient woods that generations of farmers never cut, but preserved. It now is a scientific reserve, but I am hoping my professor, Elisabet, is here, because she will let us in."

Elisabet was and Elisabet did. Her forest was as magnificent in its own way as the field of flowers, although far older. Its silence was profound, broken only by bird song. It had a high canopy of mixed hardwood, cypress and pine with rich undergrowth where old trees fell, opening the forest floor to sunlight.

"What a magnificent place to work!" Ed said as Sophia introduced them and asked Elisabet to explain to Ed about her work.

Dr. Elisabet Sahtouris greeted Ed and began. "My biological research looks at cooperation between species in mature forests. In the 20th century, government and business embraced Darwin because his scientific/theoretical observations served their purposes. As it turns out, survival of the fittest is not the only way of Nature. In a mature ecosystem, plants and animals are intricately and cooperatively interwoven. If the 20th century was a time of intense competition for resources where the fittest – or in our case, the fattest cats with the shrewdest lawyers – took as much of Nature as they could dig, cut or transform, then the 21st century needs to take its cue from more recent biology that shows cooperation becomes essential for long-term survival."

Ed took this in, and then observed, "I've often wondered why Darwin's science has been cited for so long when most other science gets superseded. So what you are saying is that Darwin's science was exploited by business leaders to justify predation, and our relationship with Nature is out of whack, to use an unscientific term."

Elisabet smiled and replied, "An excellent term, actually. For example, it is said that for every physical ailment that afflicts humanity, Nature has provided a cure that may be found in plants or in the earth. Yet in our haste to conquer, we bulldoze over those gifts and we destroy the indigenous tribes who already found some of those cures. In the 21st century, business is finally listening to what has been learned in biology and how it can be adapted for humans. Our technology has always copied Nature—after all there was nothing else by which to be inspired—we wove like spiders, flew like birds, tunneled like moles and developed radar like bats and invented computers that work like brains, as I wrote in my book *EarthDance: Living Systems in Evolution*. My friend the science writer Janine Benyus gave new meaning to the term 'biomimicry' that had referred to species mimicking each other by showing that human inventions imitating how Nature actually works—rather than how we thought it worked—produce excellent results."

"In my own work on evolution," Elisabet continued, "the Eureka moment came when I realized that Darwinian competition was only the first stage of a species' learning curve that then goes on to mature cooperation as the economic cost-effectiveness and security benefits of collaboration become apparent through trial and error. Interesting to note that in the Soviet Union, evolution biology was taught through the work of Kropotkin, whose theory was rooted in cooperation as observed in Nature. If you put the two theories together, as I did, you see the whole picture, the sequence. Oddly, ecologists recognize Type I *pioneer* ecosystems in which species are primarily competitive and Type III *climax* ecosystems in which species are primarily cooperative without seeing this learning curve I find so obvious. The reason it is missed is that western science is based on assumptions about Nature that make it impossible to see its inherent intelligence, and thus its capacity for species learning or maturation at any size level from bacteria to mammoths."

"Remember the first photograph taken from space of planet Earth?" Elisabet asked. "In that context, human beings are as much a part of Earth as our own body cells are part of us. And just as most of us move from a feisty, competitive adolescence to a more mature cooperative citizen stage, so did the most ancient bacteria, who had Earth to themselves the first half of its evolution – going through the same process of hostile competition before evolving communities with a division of labor. These communities evolved as nucleated cells that became the only kind of cell other than bacterial ever to evolve; they worked so well. In the next round of the maturation curve, these new communal cells went through a long creative competitive phase before learning the advantages of cooperation and forming multi-celled creatures. So we ourselves are communities of cells that are themselves communities!"

Ed chuckled at this reference to adolescents. "So what you are saying is that our contemporary civilization is like a bunch of pimply-faced, hormone-raging teenagers just beginning to transition to the more civilized state that comes when they begin to grow up? I like that analogy, and it is a comforting thought that our society is at least growing in the right direction."

Elisabet laughed, liking Ed's optimism. "Looking at the biology of Earth from that perspective, we can see the huge importance of communities as the mature stages of evolution at all size levels and recognize globalization as the latest maturation process for humans. At present we are half still in feisty competition and half in our future cooperative mode. We can keep friendly forms of competition such as sports, design or music competitions to drive our creativity without having to waste resources on warfare or exploiting each other."

"When I look at the complex cooperative patterns such as found in this ancient forest," she continued, "I too am optimistic about humanity's future. In biology, the simultaneous flowering of whole new ecosystems as well as the most intense growth periods, happened in response to crises such as great extinctions due to dramatic climate changes. Nature is very conservative when things work well and radically creative when they don't work. As I look at Villageton, I see a natural evolution coming out of the chaos of the last 400 years or so. It is consistent with my findings in the natural world of biology," Elisabet concluded.

"I see we caught you in the middle of your work, Elisabet, so if it is permitted to walk through this glorious woods, I would be most grateful." Ed said.

"Please do, Ed; and Sophia, as you walk Ed and Michael through the forest, point out how some of the plants have developed interdependent relationships with other plants, animals, birds and insects, and try to relate it to the biology of human beings."

They bid Elisabet thanks, leaving her to continue writing in her notebook under a canopy of rich and ancient life; leaving Ed with a lot to think about and the perfect place to do so.

The three of them, Ed, Sophia and Michael, walked through the ancient forest. When Sophia finished the science tour, they came to a sign that marked the boundary between the reserve and a woods with walking and equestrian paths. The trees were younger. They looked to Ed like second growth, and soft paths provided recreation use. They walked through this preserve passing exercise stations where people jog, then use other muscles as part of their workout. "This sure beats going to the gym," Sophia said.

Ed joked, "Why do I feel like we are in the Wizard of Oz walking down the yellow brick road? Sophia, there's no question that you are Dorothy, and after today, I'm probably the tin man, but how about you, Michael?"

Michael grinned and said "I'm happy to be Toto, but if you need a lion, I can play that part as well." Sophia did not understand so Ed found himself explaining the archetypal American story, the first movie his parents ever took him to see.

"There is no place like home," Sophia repeated. "Yes, I like that very much."

They walked into open land with productive gardens. Sophia pointed out a handsome building in the middle of it, and Ed said he had understood there was no construction allowed outside the walls. Sophia explained that certain buildings that were part of the greenbelt experience were built, but their purposes are limited to education or application. "The building in the middle of the gardens has private and shared tool storage and a large meeting room that is used mostly by the high school students studying permaculture. They have a similar building on the equestrian grounds for those students passionate about horses. They store the tack and hold classes in the same building," Sophia said.

They walked through more parts of the greenbelt, finally walking past the Industrial Park that Ed realized was built into a hill, so that from the road, it looked like a large grass field that was actually the roof of about 50 acres of building. Finally, they came to a part of the greenbelt Ed had wanted to see, the waste treatment plant. What he saw surprised him. It looked like one massive moonshine still.

## Alcohol Production and Permaculture

Sophia found David, its engineer who explained to Ed that distilling alcohol as a fuel, rather than to drink means its final product need only run a tractor, not taste like a single malt whisky. "We start with nutrient-enriched water, also known as semi-treated sewage, that causes certain plants to grow superfast. We then harvest those water plants, grind them up into mash and brew them into alcohol. We then put the residual into a soup of a bacteria that cleans heavy metals. We also add ground-up fish that eat sewage. After the bacteria has cleaned this soup, it is dried and packaged as safe farm fertilizer. We do not sell the alcohol or fertilizer; instead it is delivered to the farmers who grow Villageton's food. The farmers co-own this plant, and they bring in all their organic cuttings as well, so in effect they grow their own fuel and fertilizer instead of depending on the global prices for petroleum. Villageton residents do not pay for waste disposal since their sewage and organic waste are valuable raw materials."

"Brilliant" Ed exclaimed. "But while that addresses sewage and organic waste, how do you dispose of inorganic solid waste like packaging and things that break?"

## Solid Waste Avoidance and Recycling

"Probably the most important part to that answer is the buying club," David answered. "While citizens may buy anything they want from any vendor in the world, as part of the Villageton corporation, we operate a wholesale buying group. It regularly surveys what our citizens need to buy, which it then posts on our Intranet to determine how many people may want to buy such a product. Based on that projected volume purchase, it then contacts vendors to get prices, but it also analyzes their vendors' products in terms of its durability, packaging and recyclability once it becomes trash. In the case of large orders, it will negotiate for packaging that can be recycled, or turned into another useful product. This is not a new idea. It is said that Henry Ford demanded his suppliers ship car parts using a specific quality of timber that he then used in building the Model T. In our case, we try to specify more generic packaging that can be most easily turned into energy, compost or new products."

"What sort of products do you make?" Ed asked.

"Let me take you over to the Industrial Park and show you some," David replied. As they walked through a recycling area that was part of the Greenbelt, David explained that each home had separate containers for waste collection. "We designed all the homes so they face the front or rear street in a way that waste products drop directly from the house into the recycling containers... sort of like a hole in the kitchen counter, although more sophisticated." David explained. "Glass, paper, metal and plastics go into these slots and they are collected up from special access doors on the outside. Food is handled differently. Kitchen sinks have their own grinders and plumbing. Food waste travels in a grey-water slurry mix to the plant where the nutrient value is used as part of our permaculture system. We had originally thought of collecting food scraps in the bins, but this requires regular cleaning of the containers."

"What do you do with glass? Ed asked, aware of the volume of day-to day trash that Blandville had to manage. He was looking at a large pile of glass outside the wall of the Industrial Park. "That seems like an awful lot of glass for a 10,000 population town."

David laughed and explained as they entered the Industrial Park. "We bought a system from a company in Santa Fe, *Earthstone International*, that figured out how to replicate what goes on inside a volcano when it produces volcanic aggregate we find so useful. The system turns ordinary glass into building materials, cleaning and abrasive products and so on. However, for it to be cost effective, it needs to serve a minimum population of about 70,000. So we went to the County and proposed that we handle their recycling. In the end, they were happy employing us to do the curbside collections in the rest of the county, which we do using alternative-fuel trucks. It provides jobs for locals and removes those types of packaging from their waste stream."

"In fact, most of the recycling raw material you see here comes from the County." David continued. "In Villageton, we use far less packaging material. For a start, every home has a chilled, locking food box next to the mailbox. Food that comes from the surrounding farms is delivered in reusable plastic bins we make from recycled plastic bottles and bags. Liquids come in stronger glass bottles, just like the old-time milk bottles that were used many times."

"None of this is new," David said. "As I am sure you remember, Ed, when we were kids, bottles were returnable for a deposit, and the milkman always took away the empties when delivering milk. We stopped doing that when accountants worked out that they could externalize disposal costs. It is not cheaper to use throw-away packaging, but it is more profitable, because someone else has to pay the cost... either in trash collection and disposal or in litter. I read that there is about 100 million tons of plastic floating in a huge part of the Pacific Ocean called the Plastic Vortex. The companies that made that plastic do not need to account for it, so they made profits – they externalized the cost. However, someone will need to pay for it, either by cleaning it up, or by suffering the consequences when the plastics break down into small enough particles that fish eat it instead of food."

"So the first thing we do," explained David, "is to avoid. If we don't need to buy packaging, we avoid having the problem in the first case. In the case of things that break, we try to address this at the purchasing phase, so things purchased last longer and can be repaired. This is especially important in the electronics industries where complex products are designed not to last decades, but only a few years."

"I would be interested to hear how you deal with that," Ed said.

"In a word, *smartly*," David replied. "Let me give you some examples. While everyone is free to buy as many televisions as they want, including those massive home theater models, isolated TV watching tends to have a long-term social impact. So on most plazas we have a digital TV theater. It is very similar to the old fashioned movie theater except that the room does not have to be dark, and we have several different rooms so not everyone has to watch the same show. Unlike movie theaters, we have comfortable sofas to sit on, and they are designed so people can talk about what they have seen. That is the social aspect of it. From a waste disposal view, however, the equipment we buy is industrial quality, meaning it is designed to be repaired."

"We do the same thing with the Intranet video displays that are standard in every building," David continued. "While people may feel free to buy whatever display they want, through our buying group, we identified top quality units that are easily repairable and upgradable, which means less trash. For the units that do break, they go on the parts shelf because most are the same make. We employ an electronic genius who loves tinkering and keeping equipment running. It provides him a job, it saves villagers lots of money and it keeps electronics from entering the trash stream."

Ed thought about this for a moment, then asked "What about tools, digital cameras, kitchen gadgets and toys, to name but a few types of trash people toss out?"

"Good question," David answered, "and I am sure you would be disappointed if we did not have an answer. "With children's toys, we have a toy library and most families are happy to use that. The library also has a resale area where people can drop off their old toys as a donation and the library cleans, repairs and resells them. Here in the Industrial Park we have a tool room where citizens can rent tools – anything from a hammer to a hydraulic press. They can even book them over the intranet, and the local delivery drivers will pick them up from here and deliver them to the locking dry goods mail box each building has as a standard design feature. Electronic devices, like digital cameras are part of the inventory of the Guild Halls. The inventory is paid by the initial development, and each hall has its own system for providing access. With things like the digital camera example, we buy professional gear. The difference between a $500 DSLR and a $2,500 one is not just better quality photos, but also its durability and repairability. The professional's tool is made to be fixed, the cheap unit is disposable. The media guild hall not only provides very low cost use of the professional camera, they also provide instruction classes so our citizens become better photographers. As for kitchen gadgets, it's a similar answer. We try to encourage buying industrial quality machines, the tool room includes a catering section that any citizen can access – including tables and dishes, and we have a machine repair service."

"Impressive," Ed observed. "And I should have expected no less, given the extent to which the VOC examined the issues before Villageton was built. But what do you do when avoidance is not possible, when you end up with what in Blandville was good old fashioned trash? Do you have a landfill for what is left?"

David replied in mock horror. "OMG, he has uttered the forbidden *L-word*." The others laughed at David's theatrics. "No, we don't bury trash here. In fact, we have no trash here, only surplus raw material. Most of what you call trash has energy value, nutrient value or raw material value. We avoid hopelessly toxic trash – don't buy it, and the rest we have systems to break it into its useful components and use them accordingly. Plastics can be remanufactured or their energy can be converted into fuel. Metals are easy, they are far more refined than ore, so the only question is whether we use them locally or pack and ship them off to volume recyclers. Perhaps one of the largest non-household trash sources is construction material. Obviously, when one builds from a single bulk material – concrete, and builds everything at one time, that is eliminated. We even recycle old shoes, although you may have noticed many villagers wear shoes designed to be resoled. We have some outstanding cobblers in Villageton, and while their prices may seem higher than bargain warehouse shoes, their shoes last for years, decades even, not months. While this was encouraged for local consumption, it now seems they have a strong visitor and internet following."

By this time, they were walking through what looked like a manufacturing zone, some with clean, high-technology production, and others with machine shops with more basic manufacturing. Ed asked David if he had the time to point out what they were looking at.

## The Industrial Park

"Happy to do so, Ed" David said. "One of the privileges of being the Trash Czar is that it looks like I am working when I am walking through here with visitors. In fact, I am always keeping an eye out for what is going on, both to see if the manufacturers are producing surplus materials we can use, and at the same time potentially having a need for stuff we have in inventory. But mostly, I pay my way here so well that no one minds how I use my time; it's a dream job, really."

"I forgot to ask, David," Ed broke in. "Who do you work for?"

"Originally," he answered, "I worked for the Villageton Council in their utility department, as they projected solid and liquid waste disposal as an expense to be charged to the citizens; the same as you have in Blandville, no doubt. However, we began to turn a profit, and when it became apparent that this was a permanent state of affairs, Villageton set up a subsidiary for-profit corporation, and I am the boss. I also oversee the joint venture we run with the farmers that produces their fuel and fertilizer. The accountants and lawyers said it would be better to run it as a joint venture so the farmers are not buying fuel from us, but making it themselves for their own use."

"Thanks for that," Ed said. "Apologies for interrupting. So tell me about the Industrial Park. What do you make here? How does it work?"

"When Villageton was in its development phase, we encouraged prospective business leaders to have a look at moving their businesses here. It offered them both a lifestyle and a nearby business location. The recruitment drive worked and almost every business in the Industrial Park is privately owned," David explained. Some companies own their own facilities, other buildings are leased by private investors. The Freight Depot is connected to the Industrial Park, so we do not need truck-sized roads inside the industrial park. Instead we have rail tracks and small electric delivery vehicles. In our case we were lucky to be near an existing rail line, so we laid a spur track to go directly to the freight depot, and our electric tugs tow single railcars directly into the Industrial Park. We do enough volume now that we have an outbound shipping railcar that fills every day with postal and courier delivery boxes. Most of the workers live in Villageton, and we discourage commuters coming in from the outside by how we structure parking costs in the motorpool. The buildings themselves were designed with a fixed standard in terms of roof height so that walls can be easily moved and affixed – a bit like the concrete highway barriers they set up when doing a construction project. It's all under a single turf-covered roof... on top of it are sports fields."

As David was explaining this, they walked by a window and door factory that was obviously doing a lot of business. Ed noted the manufacturing seemed a curious combination of mass production and custom bespoke. He asked David about it.

"This company, and two others like it, opened for business before the first home was built in Villageton. In this way, their first customer base was from 4,000 new homes to go up in 12 months. That enabled them to pay for their tooling, set up their mass production and secure good wholesale contracts for raw materials, not to mention earning a tidy profit to relieve the normal pressure on a startup. However, the Villageton Business Advisory Group – part of our Villageton Council corporation – made sure they also were planning ahead for the day when all the orders would be filled. So from the very beginning, funds were invested in both retail and wholesale marketing on a global basis. These doors and windows fit a niche-market. They are energy super-efficient, made to last for at least a century, with exquisite details that dress both the building and the streetscape. As such, the future-orders book began to fill up while the three companies were busy supplying Villageton's needs. When opening day approached and no further doors and windows would be needed, these local factories began to work on their national and international orders. They keep prices fair, and we hear that all three have orders more than 12 months out. They are structured to fill internet orders within weeks, while supplying the wholesale buyers on longer term contracts. I should mention that the first of our villages that the VOC built was the village for the Industrial Park workers. It was constructed at the same time as the Industrial Park so we could provide worker-housing for the companies making the components for Villageton." David concluded.

"What else do you make here?" Ed asked.

"Hmm," David pondered. "That would be quite a list; we have almost fifty acres of manufacturing space. We probably have a disproportionately high representation of environmental companies, and also of leading-technology development, which makes sense given the number of inventors and entrepreneurs Villageton attracted. There are several prototype development companies that bring products to manufacturing stage, but large scale manufacturing is difficult to do in America, given the difference in offshore manufacturing costs – we pay our people more and run closed-loop businesses that do not pollute. Having said that, there are a number of products that could be sourced elsewhere, but our citizens committed to support their local manufacture. They decided that it would be a mistake to deplete our tooling and skill base that would render us dependent on offshore suppliers for essential products."

Ed pressed for more detail, asking "Can you give me an example of that?"

"Sure," David replied. "Villageton uses electricity for most of its energy. While we harvest energy from wind, solar and hydro, we cannot afford to waste it. So we make an electric motor that uses about one quarter the electricity of a conventional motor. We also make our own solar panels here. In much of this work we focus on prototyping and testing, but we also make sure we do the old fashioned manufacturing. We probably earn more from the patent licenses than the products, but knowing how to make things remains important in our economy. It also provides apprenticeships for our young people so they do not suffer a black box mentality."

"I have a hunch that I know what you mean by a black-box mentality, but to be sure, would you explain it to me?" Ed asked.

"Sure." David said. "When I was a kid, you could take apart a telephone and understand how it works. Today, all you will see is a circuit board and some buttons. Inside that circuit board is smart software, but you can't understand how it works unless you can reverse engineer the programs. So kids grow up today pressing buttons but having no idea why they work. Here, our young people who have an interest in such things can apprentice in businesses that actually make the stuff, so when they go on to study advanced engineering, for example, they have real experiences to draw on. For them it is not a *black box* but a device they can design, modify or repair."

As they were talking, they came to a space filled with old cars, some classics and some just old and cheap. There were about twenty young men working on the cars, and Ed remembered Sophia telling him about the automotive workshop. He asked her if this was the place, and she confirmed it was. David explained. "Sometimes people are surprised to see this in Villageton, given our car-free policy. However, we do run a motorpool and we are most pragmatic about car use. In essence we eliminate a quarter million miles of driving a day - based on the US average of 35 miles per day per person, but we are not anti-car per se. Cars are not bad, it's how we use cars in this country that is shortsighted and unintelligent."

"The automobile is a brilliant piece of engineering, and for a particular type of young person, mostly male, it is a source of passion. They probably spend more time working on them than they do driving them, and most were converted to alcohol as a fuel because it is cheaper given that we make it ourselves. When we set up Villageton, the founders decided to allocate part of the industrial park for public use, a bit like we did with the artist guild halls. The youth who run this program had to form a club to assure they would run it responsibly and care for the equipment. Not far from Villageton there is an old racetrack and the club made arrangements to revive its use. This has had an added benefit for the whole county, as previously they had a real problem with bored teenagers replicating street racing they saw on videos like *Fast and Furious*. Now most of them go to the track under the sponsorship of the Villageton Car Club and the club has an associate membership for kids who live in the country."

Ed saw they were coming toward the end of the Industrial Zone, and he asked David if they were not overly imposing on his hospitality. David replied that he had enjoyed giving the tour, but would need to get back to work. They thanked him, and Sophia resumed as tour guide; she saw it was now time for Ed and Michael to depart.

# Chapter 14

# The Last Chapter - The time is now

The sun hung late in the afternoon sky as Sophia, Ed and Michael walked back to the Visitor Center, where Sophia was to leave them. As they reached it, Sophia said to Ed, "I hope you have enjoyed your tour today of Villageton, Ed."

"Enjoyed is too weak a word, Sophia." Ed replied. "It ranks as one of the finest days of my life, such a remarkable punctuation between a sad ending to my life in Blandville that I closed this morning and the sad future I expect awaits me in Heathcliff Manor this evening. I shall cherish today for the rest of my life, and am eternally grateful for the friendship and kindness you extended to me today."

Sophia blushed, gave him a soft kiss on the cheek, and a hug to Michael, and then she turned away to not show the mixed feelings of sadness and compassion she felt for Ed, as he departed with Michael to resume the track of his life.

As Ed and Michael walked back to the car, Ed turned to him and asked, "I have one final question, Michael. I'm a professional architect and urban planner. You could not have driven more that two hours from Blandville. Villageton is phenomenal. Why is it that I have never heard of this place?"

Michael looked at him and spoke. "Ed, that is a difficult question to answer without my answer sounding like a ghost story. Since you studied the classics, let me try it this way, going back to Plato. In discussing what is real, Plato, or perhaps I should say, Plato's character and real-life mentor, Socrates spoke of four different planes of reality. For example, Socrates would speak about a wheel and ask what is the most real wheel? You and I would agree that a wheel on a car or wagon is more real than a picture of a wheel. Socrates would agree, but then he would introduce two other higher planes of reality that he would assert are even more real that the physical. He suggested that what we might call the blueprint of the wheel, the knowledge of how to build one, is more real than the one we sit on. If you don't know how to build one, you will never have one."

"Then Socrates goes one plane higher; what he calls the "form" of a wheel. This is the conception or very idea of "wheel". If we lack a word for wheel, because we never thought of it, then we can never think of a wheel, much less design, build or use it to ride in a wheeled vehicle. So this gives us four planes of reality. The two highest, *intelligible* realities are the form, then the blueprint, the lower two existing in the *visible* realms, the physical plane and the lowest being the image."

"For example, the Aztec and Inca advanced civilizations in Central and South America did not conceive of carts on wheels; they lacked the *form* for cart wheel. This was not for lack of imagination, but lack of draught animals to pull them – donkeys, horses and oxen came with the Spanish. The form of the wheel probably came to some early inventor in Europe or Asia after they dragged stick-frames on the dirt behind horses or oxen, and came up with the wheel to reduce the friction. At the highest level of reality, the form "wheel" came into the mind of an inventor, who then worked out the details, probably first in their mind, then through sketches in the sand, and trial & error, until a working model finally existed in physical reality."

"Ed, if you can accept these higher planes of reality as... real and more real, then I may be able to give you an answer. So permit me to try."

"In coming to Villageton you arrived to the highest plane of Socrates' reality – the idea that forms the possibility of a VillageTown. Having walked through it, seen the form of Villageton and accepted that it works, you explored the next lower level of reality, how to build your village within Villageton. Today you heard from people who have mastered or written the design, the blueprints, the plans that put the pieces together. Based on your professional knowledge, you see that it will work, or at least despite trying hard – and yes, we all could hear your mind working at full tilt – you were unable to find a reason why it would not. It made sense to you, and you liked it."

"As for the reason you have not heard of Villageton even though you are about a two hour drive from Blandville, the answer I am about to give you will be very difficult for a time-and-space-oriented western mind to hold. It would be much easier for me to give this answer if you came from an older culture, even perhaps an indigenous culture that still remembers who they are and have a very different understanding of the true nature of reality. But let me try this as well."

"It is because on the physical plane, the only plane that uses time and space, Villageton exists not in the present, but in the future. It exists here, on this land you walk, but like past Plato's Athens that once was, but is now gone, future Villageton will be here soon, but is now not yet."

"Now, in your present, here and now, you have a choice. You can go back to your plan, and in two more hours, you and I will arrive at Heathcliff Manor where you will die as you planned – in seven years, just as your savings run out. Or, you can acknowledge that you have plenty of life left in you, and that you are needed to help make this Villageton move from the upper two planes of reality to the lower two – to make it what you would call real. You will help it to built itself, and then it will be featured in the architectural magazines where it will win awards and accolades from your peers... although I suspect you will no longer subscribe to or read those magazines anymore, because in the hierarchy of reality they are the least real."

"If you choose the latter life, we will drive instead to a small, single floor home in a village that time forgot. It was built by pioneering Quakers long ago and later inhabited by industrious German immigrants who supplied products to the surrounding farms. Constructed long before cars changed the landscape of this country, somehow urban renewal never got there. It looks the same today as it did when it was built except cars try to park on the narrow main street which has a 20 mile per hour speed limit. You will have access to what you need to live, and presuming you kept your laptop, you can plug into broadband. More importantly, some of the Village Forum people working on Villageton live there – in fact, the first person you met in Villageton, Agnes, is one of the Village Stewards. You may take up dancing once again. The Stewards have an office in one of the old buildings over the old Post Office, and they could use someone with the skills of a town planner to help make Villageton a physical reality. You will not need to drive, and the walking should keep you fit. The vacant home was built for an earlier time; it's a real split log cabin with chinked walls with two rooms that serve as a good model for the solo person's housing in Villageton."

"If you chose this direction, you will find you feel as vigorous and alive as you did when you first finished your studies and set out to change the world. Only this time, you will have learned the importance of setting aside much of the hubris taught in your profession... for example, the architect is *not* the artist with a blank canvas doing a design to win accolades in architecture magazine, but there to enable the people who will actually live in the design have it both serve their needs and give them a place they come to love."

"Ed, make no mistake about it. You are needed. You have a lifetime experience of how wrong we can get it. You were on your way to the ultimate reward of such a lifetime... seven years waiting to die, hoping death would take you swiftly and not dump you in a nursing home... alone, away from family, with no true community to support you, among people there to serve only because they are paid to do so, living amid lost souls as abandoned as you."

"You know how bad suburban sprawl is, I saw you counting the car dealers, fast food outlets, big-box stores selling products with the shortest distance between factory and the landfill and all the other lonely commercial and residential buildings that make Blandville what it is. I heard how you felt betrayed by yourself, and I sensed how you wished you had a chance to do it over again."

"As you have heard, you can build Villageton in three years. If you stick to your seven-year plan remaining on Earth, that gives you four years to enjoy what you saw today. However, if you choose to build your Village, I predict you will live a much longer life, a more fulfilled one, and when you die, you will have lived the Good Life."

"It's up to you. The time to decide is now."

## This is Not a Drill

No matter what your age or profession; no matter what your stage in life, or where you are going, you are, or can be, Ed Rice. In reading this book, you can allow it to be a fantasy, a dream you think about as you continue on your day to day life. You may continue presuming things will continue pretty much as they are now, keeping yourself busy and hoping things will get better for you.

Or you can take the message about freedom to heart. Things are not going to continue pretty much the same as they are now, and we face some very stormy times ahead. The clouds are there for all to see, and a few will begin to make plans now to find shelter. Many people see those clouds, but most of the ideas on what to do are reactive. Green architecture is a response to climate change, not what to do about the soon-to-retire baby boom. Bank-bailouts are a response to an economic crisis that could have crashed the monetary system, not the safety concerns of parents of school-age children. Systems are so big that people feel they have little control over their own lives anymore.

Crisis means turning point, not necessarily disaster. The turning point facing us now is not about the environment, the economy or energy, it is social. It is about the freedom to pursue life, liberty and happiness. How we choose to respond to the environmental, economic and energy crises will determine the level of freedom you and I and future generations will enjoy. You and I cannot change the world; it's too big and too complex. However, you and I and others can change our world. It's local.

To do that, we need a framework, and we need permission. Permission from whom? That's the funny thing about freedom, it means permission from ourselves. The idea of the Village-Town is a framework. It's not the only one, but it is a workable one. More importantly, it's an initiative, it's happening, it's a real activity you can join to really make it happen for you... in any country or state. This is not a drill.

If you want to explore more, go to *villageforum.com* where you can read what is happening. You can watch videos of Village Stewards, volunteers who are putting their time into helping make it happen. You can buy the books *How to Build a Village* and *VillageTowns - the next step* that set out the details showing how to do it. And if you like the idea, enroll. It's the first step to living in a VillageTown.

The key is people. When the critical mass is reached, what they call the tipping point of people ready to form a VillageTown, it will begin. It's affordable, it's doable and it can be done within three years. It's up to you.

## Build your Village

*Life Liberty Happiness* sets out the vision and some of the principles. The next step is to read *How to Build a Village* ISBN 978-0-473-12188-4, that provides the framework to build a VillageTown, and *Villagetowns - the Next Step* ISBN 978-0-958-2868-8-6 when you are ready to become involved  Both books can be found at www.villageforum.com, or ordered from bookstores or online.

Crisis means turning point, not necessarily disaster. The turning point facing us now is not about energy, the environment or the economy, it is social. It is about the freedom to pursue life, liberty, happiness. How we choose to respond to the fear-based issues of our age, be it terrorism or what we call *Pogwec* (the threat of Peak Oil Global Warming Economic Collapse) will determine the level of freedom we and future generations will enjoy. Few ordinary people can change the world; it's too big and too complex. However, we can change our world. It's local. To do so, we must act as citizens, not consumers.

We propose this can be done by building VillageTowns.

# Checklist for the Stewards and Future Citizens of a VillageTown

## Organizational - How to do it

- ☑ The Stewards *name* the VillageTown project
- ☑ Fund the Village Organizing Company *VOC*
- ☑ VOC appoints a Town Coordinator - a "*TC*"
- ☑ The TC recruits 20 Village Coordinators *VCs*
- ☑ The VCs enrol & engage the future villagers
- ☑ VOC as corporation negotiates for zoned site
- ☑ VOC oversees building the VillageTown
- ☑ VOC gives deeds to buyers & pays investors
- ☑ VOC morphs into VillageTown Council
- ☑ VillageTown citizens move in & begin life

## Characteristics of Country-Town type

- ☑ About 500 acres (or more) total land
- ☑ 150 acre urban core of 20 villages & 1 center
- ☑ Each village has a different look, feel & flavor
- ☑ Each village has its own plaza & arts guildhall
- ☑ Live, work, play, shop all within 10 min. walk
- ☑ Micro-zoned to balance public and private
- ☑ Urban core surrounded by 300 acre greenbelt
- ☑ 50 acre Industrial Park outside village walls
- ☑ No cars within the village walls - slow pace
- ☑ Motorpool to park private & rental cars
- ☑ Located within 1 to 2 hours of a major airport

## Economic - The foundation of living

- ☑ A diverse, robust, durable local economy
- ☑ Not dependent on the regional economy
- ☑ Provides the foundation for *the Good Life*
- ☑ 80% sell local to local, 20% sell local to global
- ☑ Walk-to Industrial Park – local manufacture
- ☑ Contracts with local farmers to feed citizens
- ☑ Access to global networks & transport
- ☑ Local-to-global *Telepresence* businesses
- ☑ Intentional support for local to local business
- ☑ Permanently affordable, costs less to live well
- ☑ Parallel market real estate - affordable housing
- ☑ Economic protection from global fiscal crises
- ☑ Minimum exposure to skyrocketing oil price

## Social and Culture - The Good Life

- ☑ Provides for *the Good Life* which includes:
- • Conviviality, fun, never boring, *slow food*
- • Citizenship, liberty within ones society
- • Intellectual and artistic growth & mastery
- • Spiritual development & fulfillment
- ☑ Socially enriched with variety & stimulation
- ☑ Culturally enriched with ongoing creativity
- ☑ Artist Guild Halls to support Creative Class
- ☑ Multiple villages designed by their citizens
- ☑ Surrounding region welcomes VillageTown
- ☑ A safe & stimulating place to raise children
- ☑ Children learn well, many role models
- ☑ A place for single persons & the single life
- ☑ Affordable first housing, a youth zone
- ☑ Supportive of families, less stress, more time
- ☑ Actively promotes healthy food & exercise
- ☑ A better plan for aging Baby Boomers
- ☑ A place for elders & infirm in the community

## Physical Environment

- ☑ 20 villages with plazas plus larger town square
- ☑ Beautiful, timeless architecture & streetscape
- ☑ Careful balance of private and public spaces
- ☑ Pedestrian streets & footpaths, human-scaled
- ☑ Quiet by design, acoustically sealed homes
- ☑ No cars, trucks or loud fans, compressors, etc.
- ☑ Fireproof buildings, no *design by firetruck*
- ☑ Good, healthy and diverse supply of food
- ☑ Greenbelt to provide real access to Nature

## Natural Environment

- ☑ Designed to tread lightly on Earth
- ☑ Designed & built to last for centuries
- ☑ Not a perpetual construction site
- ☑ Non-toxic, healthy environment
- ☑ Pollutants minimized, mitigated and recycled
- ☑ Wholesale buying club to reduce packaging
- ☑ Greenbelt forests, fields of flowers, cemetery

# About this Book – About the Vision

I went to the USA in June 2009 for two weeks just after doing a TED talk in Australia. Two coasts, six states, seventeen meetings all in 14 days. A month later I started writing a new book. I had not intended to write this book; it demanded to be written. The first book I wrote took eighteen months. This one wrote itself in 25 days.

I returned from the USA profoundly disturbed by what I had seen and heard. When I got home I was flattened by what I thought was the flu, except none of the normal symptoms. For two weeks I could not get out of bed. I wonder if it was not detoxing from the alien diet of too much un-nourishing food. The forced break was most helpful, as all I could do was think – to reflect on what I experienced visiting America in 2009.

Since 1997 when I moved my family from Connecticut to New Zealand, the USA drastically reshaped itself, an explosion of sprawl... suburban housing, McMansions, commercial strips and malls, office and industrial parks, all surrounded by massive swathes of black paving. From East Coast to West and the heartland in the middle, the new suburban landscape was uniform and indistinguishable. Whether it was Cerillos Road off the freeway in Santa Fe, New Mexico or Plank Road off the freeway in Fredericksburg, Virginia, it was the same impersonal blandness – the same stores, the same brands, the same motels and the same food that was astonishingly bad, laden with fats, sugars and salts. Even local accents blanded, especially among the young, as regional dialect gave way to a new TV, teen-video accent derivative of *valley girls* and *surfer boys*. I noted the vocabulary of many people I met – they used fewer words with less precise meaning, peppered with profanities and meaningless filler words. I saw more people seeking identity through brands. Even politics sounded more branded than principled as divisiveness, fear and vilification supplanted reasoned debate about the rightness of leadership in decision-making and action. I found the presence of media to be overwhelming and yet vacuous.

I saw the cracks in the American Dream – shopping malls with numerous vacancies, office buildings displaying "for lease" banners in place of company names, whole streets of weed-infested uncut lawns fronting unsold, peeling and molding new homes next to half-finished buildings with wooden studs exposed to the weather. Visiting shopping malls, I found it sad to see the physical condition of the people and how parents related to their children in those stores - children grasping, parents berating or bribing – no joy. On the obesity of Americans, one host commented that despite their size, they are nutritionally starving.

Many of the people I visited were aware of it, hated it, but felt powerless in the face of it. "We all know what we want, we just don't how to do it," said one. Listening to people I heard sadness, fear, anger, frustration and worry. It was not just a worry about an economic downturn – such cycles come and go. Rather it was a deeper sense of something terribly wrong. It permeated most conversations. It felt as if life was closing in, its systems failing. I sensed people felt imprisoned by these very systems that they and their parents helped to build. I met people who felt their lives were successful, and heard a sense of "is this it?"

– that the reward for their success proved empty. For those struggling to get by, there was an underlying feeling of desperation amid first-world affluence. Life felt hollow.

I witnessed relentless pressures especially on families with young children. Reliance on TV was huge, creating zombie-like kids. As I explored this, I found in many cases it showed a high correlation with rootlessness. In New Zealand, the Maori people define their connection to land with the term *Tangata Whenua* which literally means *people of the land*. In their language, the word *whenua* not only means land, it also means placenta – the first source of nourishment in life. From Maori I learned the importance of connecting land to community. In Maori, people do not own land; land owns people. When society seeks identity through brands and media rather than land and people, something goes terribly wrong.

It was not all bad. While I saw many changes that saddened me, the fundamental character of Americans gave hope. Countries pass on their myths and myths carry power. America's myth came at its founding: the idea that citizens gather in taverns or on the village green, come together, make decisions for the good of community and country, and carry them out. Individual Americans still carry that sense of empowerment; everywhere I went, I met individuals working hard to make life better. Instead of printing presses, they use the internet. Instead of meeting in taverns and travellers inns, they host visitors in cafes, private homes or workplaces. In two weeks I visited the homes and offices of right wing Republicans, left wing Democrats, environmentalists, architects, artists, actors, inventors, entrepreneurs, planners, scholars, teachers, developers, investors, policy analysts, builders, authors, chefs, publicists, farmers, business executives, hunters, publishers, famous people and ordinary folk. In almost every one of those visits, I witnessed a sense of capacity – if we turn our mind to it, we can do it. This sense of capacity, consciousness and inventiveness is America's greatest asset.

On my tour, 89 year old Steward Udall and his assistant Karina invited me for lunch in Stewart's home in Santa Fe. After driving through mile after mile of life-depleting, commoditized land in New Mexico, Maryland, Virginia, Arizona and Southern California, it revitalized to hear a man deeply anchored to land and public service. Stewart is a Westerner from a time when that meant something. He grew up in a small western town, and dedicated his life to restoring and protecting the nation's land, air and waters. He spoke of the Depression, saying his generation worked through it by strengthening their families and communities, committing themselves to a better future especially through the education of their children. "Small communities valued education, and they taxed themselves to pay for it.", he said. "*They taxed themselves*" is such a different view of citizenship than found today in suburbia. Stewart's body was getting old, but the spirit he radiated was solid, and when he spoke about family and community, he provided the antidote to the new dulled America.

Two weeks later, fighting off whatever bug I caught in America, I pondered what could have caused such erosion in the American character. Why the blandness? Why the sense that so many places now looked and felt like everywhere else? The easy answer says that everyone wants to make a buck, and once a formula is worked out, everyone repeats it. But America has always been a capitalist country; everyone has always wanted to make a buck. It had to be more complicated than that.

Gradually a theme emerged. We no longer call people citizens; we call them consumers. Citizenship is firstly a relationship to land. Secondly it is a relationship to other people... family, community, state and nation – in that order. It is about serving the public interest, protecting both society and civilization for current and future generations. When we stopped asking people to be citizens, and instead developed a new role called consumer, we did more than create a fatter business climate. We redefined what it means to be human and in doing so we isolated people, replacing identity with brands and relationships with media.

Now consumption is beginning to bite back. Consumption is based on the flawed assumption that resources are infinite; that we can safely consume at an ever increasing rate asking Nature to deal with increasing concentrations of our detritus. Stewart talked about the pivotal vote in Congress in 1956 when America committed itself to burning petroleum to drive the American future. He called it the myth of superabundance. Nature took millions of years to make resources we deplete in less than a hundred; some used as energy, the rest pumped as exhaust that makes a chemical soup that turns our skies dirty brown. But beyond the environmental impact, the intentional separation of destinations so people must drive has a more sinister effect. It systematically breaks down family and community.

Consumption – the activity that defines a consumer – makes a lot of money. It drives the economy to ever increasing heights, but in doing so, it seems people feel unhappier, less free and less alive. Visiting America in June, I got this sense many people were postponing life.

In his cameo in this book, Michael Henderson wrote *"I think much of our typical western lifestyle has resulted in delaying such sensual gratification. We work hard, often in places we don't like, to earn enough money to eventually take the vacation or buy the dream home or getaway place that makes our lives feel richer or more complete. The village offers us the opportunity to reverse that process and begin, enjoy and end each day with a place and lifestyle that nurtures the soul. Why would we want to wait twenty years to experience that?"*

Consumerism exists in parallel with another ism – Corporatism. Corporations are neutral; a way of organizing people to increase wealth, and they proved most effective. However, corporations define their purpose as:

(1) make profits for their stockholders,
(2) provide jobs for their employees and
(3) provide goods and services for their customers.

In other words, their sole purpose for existence is monetized. As a result they view people solely in terms of profit; over time they develop sophisticated systems to maximize those profits. Citizenship, family and community don't fit in this equation, thus as an unintentional side effect those defining elements of human civilization become collateral damage.

How do we reverse this trend?

Radicals say "Destroy the corporations" which strikes me as both unrealistic and fraught with its own dangers... like who fills the vacuum? The radicals? No thanks.

As I explored the question, it seemed to me the smarter approach is not to fight corporations, but to join them... or to be more precise, to form corporations whose stockholders are citizens defined by a common locality, and as citizens, demand more of their own corporation than profits on detached investments... form a corporation that invests in, provides for and is owned by citizens who define themselves geographically – by their town.

If this sounds similar to *government of the people, for the people by the people*, except swapping government for corporation, it's because, since the end of World War II, corporate power strengthened while government power declined. Don't fight it, take advantage of it. Corporate clout is purchasing power. Combine citizens' purchasing power through corporate power.

This conclusion surprised me. I did not expect it. I doubt if I would make a good political theoretician, as the idea of building a community using corporate law does not fit neatly in anyone's continuum of left wing to right wing. Environmentalists love the idea of VillageTowns because they tread lightly on Nature. But so do Conservatives who believe in market forces. Liberals like the caring aspect especially for the elderly and the young, but recently I was most surprised to see ideas in my first book quoted by a staunch Libertarian who feels government interferes in people's lives. I'll leave it to someone else to work out the political theory. I've never trusted left or right wing theory; to me it mostly seems to be fancy words dressing a way to grab more power over others. In my view, leadership is either about service or the heady experience of wielding power over others. I prefer the former.

What drives me is a sense of what will make life better – we are evolving as a human race as we expand our conscious capacity to think and act. But we also come up with some awful ideas that spawn terrible problems, appalling messes and huge suffering. This idea of VillageTowns came about by identifying those challenges and then seeing how we could not only avoid them but enable citizens to create a physical environment that fulfills, that stimulates, that gives them the space to pursue what they love. The key is that <u>they</u> do the creating, not <u>me</u>. Utopias are places where one person decides what is best. It never works. Set up the framework, but let the future citizens decide what they need... and what they love.

My brain is not big enough to hold global-sized issues, so I work on ideas that are human-scaled. I can imagine calling together twenty people, each with a dream for their own kind of village – 20 people each of whom can attract 200 families to their vision. 20 villages x 200 families = the 4,000 homes of one VillageTown. I can imagine local governments welcoming the idea of a $1 billion development without the usual problems. It's a small vision, much smaller than the War on Poverty, War on Drugs, War on Terror or the latest War on Carbon. Unlike those titanic campaigns, this one is an idea that can be done by ordinary people, rich and poor, in any country where there is peace and reasonable access to water, technology, and long distance transport. I want to be involved in the first few VillageTowns, but after that I hope lots of developers like the idea and for the good, it changes how they do business.

The purpose of this book is to spread the idea faster and further. If you like the idea, spread it widely. Find others who like it, come together. Offer to help at *villageforum.com*. To help funding, buy the books; buy them by the case and give them to everyone you know. Propose the sites for the first VillageTowns. Get involved. Build your Village.

*CLAUDE LEWENZ*

# Twelve Principles for a VillageTown

1. We build for the Good Life. When a community has established a self-supporting economy, the purpose of its continuance is to enable its people to enjoy *the good life*, generally understood as *conviviality, citizenship, artistic creativity, intellectual growth* and *spiritual experience*. Thomas Jefferson expressed this as *Life, Liberty and the Pursuit of Happiness*. For each person, and in different times, the balance of these pursuits will be different. Design the foundation as a strong local economy, build for the good life.

2. It's cheaper to save a dollar than earn one. Work smart. Will you live to work, or work to live? Create a framework for a local economy that is diverse, self-creating, self-informing, self-regulating, transformational, reciprocal, empowering, balanced, responsive and protective. Understand the difference between free trade / free markets and rigged trade / rigged markets and test the facts rather than listen to the spin. Own your bank.

3. It's your money. It's your life. Look not to national or global systems for the answers. They are too big and too vulnerable to manipulation by special interests. Look after your own food, homes, community, employment, your young and your elderly. Seek to work in harmony with large systems, but keep them out of your family life and out of your purse.

4. It's your home, your village, your town; assert yourself. You will live with the results long after the architects and builders go on to their next job. Architecture and the physical environment provide the framework and stage to pursue the good life. Beyond architecture's utilitarian purpose of protection from climate and hazards, well-designed built and cultivated spaces exist to provide connection, stimulation, production, contentment, hospitality and daily delight. Beauty, harmony, utility, efficiency, durability, authenticity, character and timelessness are all valuable attributes. Also, the contrast provided by walk-to places with diverse character is important to combat boredom and make life more interesting. Build for your life.

5. Communities can be human-scaled or machine-scaled, but not both. If you build for cars on your streets, people, especially the young, the old and the frail, are secondary. Cars and trucks cannot be domesticated. Keep them outside the local transport area. Machines extend the power of human beings and have great utility. But they are no replacement for face-to-face human contact in a civilized community that values the good life. Telepresence may be key to the economy, but walk to the café afterwards.

6. Proximity creates community. Move destinations, not people. The closer the destination, the stronger the community. The more supportive of all ages and stages in life, the better and healthier the community. It is of especial importance to provide proximity of elders to children, for this is how the wisdom of culture is handed down, and how parents can get a break from the pressures of parenting. Education works well

when children combine school learning with life observation and participation. Build classrooms in each village, not in a segregated campus.

7. Food and water are the basics of life. Know your farmers, know your food. Conviviality embraces food and drink; make it nourishing, healthy, flavorful and delightful. Control and protect your food sources. Grow for quality, not for yield. Avoid food produced by organizations whose pecuniary interest is not aligned with your culinary interest.

8. Freedom is important. Use design to shape behavior rather than rules to enforce it. Build a free community where rule-making is limited to enabling people to get along with each other, rather than tell people how they must live. Caring is important. Maintain the physical environment and public spaces, keep the peace and preserve civility, care for weaker members of society, and protect the public good. Govern locally using checks and balances – if governing law prohibits this, use corporate law; but remember that democracy and the marketplace are not the same. Ask your people to act like citizens, not behave like consumers.

9. Cultural enrichment keeps society awake and alive. Intentionally provide for the creative class. Protect their ways of life, and preserve their platforms for creativity. Plan and pay to avoid gentrification. Creativity breathes life into a community.

10. In environmental matters, refuse to engage in what accountants calls *negative externality*. Do not subject Nature to increased concentrations of substances extracted from the earth's crust.
Do not subject Nature to increased concentrations of substances produced by society.
Do not subject Nature to degradation by physical means.
Sustainable architecture and design is smart, but do not make it a bragging point.
Design for efficiency, but without sacrificing joy or the good life.
Do not build a community based on fear-mongering or negatives such as peak oil, global warming or economic collapse (POGWEC). Build on positives; build for the good life.

11. People need a balance of public and private space. Build soundproof walls. Designate quieter zones. Design private space within homes. Construct lesser-walked paths and public buildings and outdoor places where one can be alone. Provide access to real Nature, not solely manicured gardens or parks. Design homes with courtyards and sanctuaries as well as public plazas and pedestrian streets. Provide for sacred architecture.

12. VillageTowns are not for everyone, nor are they intended to be. They are intended to be the ultimate tangible investment – investing in that which affects you, your family and your friends on a day-to-day basis. If you love the idea, build your village.

# How to Build your Village

How do you build a VillageTown? We have set up an organization and some businesses to help make the first ones happen. We separated the organization - the Village Forum (villageforum.com) from the companies, the Village Organizing Company (VOC) for each VillageTown and the parent company, which we call the VillageTowns Company (called the Company). We created this separation because no matter how good the intentions, history shows that without checks and balances, good people make bad decisions. If the power is spread out, in effect creating on-going reality-checks, bad decisions are hard to make and harder to implement. The Village Forum has members and Stewards, volunteers who take a more active role in the Forum. All Forum roles are unpaid.

If you want to live in a VillageTown, join the Village Forum. If you want to lead in the building of a VillageTown, contact the Company and propose to become involved. Involvement includes three stages, each which is likely to take a year. They are Start Up, Implementation, Construction.

1. **Start Up** - The organization of the project.
    a. Propose to The Company a project in a particular country, state and region.
    b. If accepted, the Stewards and The Company jointly "name" the project, generally calling it a VOC for village organizing company, followed by three letters of the nearest major airport. So a project in Northern California might be named VOC-SFO.
    c. The Company confirms business assumptions necessary to raise first stage capital and raise funds. This includes checking with potential host local governments and local experts to confirm such a project might be considered. So localities are "locked up", either for conservation reasons or by a network of vested interests that effectively keep others out.
    d. The Company puts together a business case required to seek Stage 1 funding. This funding pays for the preparatory work and securing the Stage 2 funds required to make it happen. If Stage 1 funding cannot be secured the project stops, to be started when funds arrive.
    e. With funding secured, the Company establishes a Village Organizing Company (VOC).
    f. The Company also provides separate and adequate funding to the Village Forum to employ staff to advocate for the forum members who will express interest and eventually buy into their village. This establishes the checks and balances between the forum and the VOC. While the relationship is expected to be cooperative, the advocacy is put in place to assure it remains so.
    g. VOC recruits the Town Coordinator and the 20 Village Coordinators
    h. The village coordinators define the central theme of their villages and begin to enrol interested individuals and families who also join the arms-length Village Forum. At this point, the enrollment is an expression of interest, meaning there is no financial or legal commitment, but a sincere intent and proof they can afford it. As they learn more, and become both more involved and more confident in the process, they will gradually make commitment steps that lead to buying a home and possibly a work place or space in the industrial park.
    i. When the enrolment reaches a critical mass, the future villagers are asked to make a written commitment that empowers the VOC to search for the land and negotiate terms with

potential host local governments. Only those serious about moving toward buying a home in the VillageTown make this commitment. The individual or family must also confirm their intended purchase budget that forms the basis of collective purchasing power.

    j. The VOC then uses this collective purchasing power to negotiate with several competing local governments, of which one will be selected to host the VillageTown.

    k. Parallel to this active search process, another part of the VOC will focus on drafting corporate and legal documents that accompany title to buildings, engineering specifications to build the infrastructure and public facilities in Stage 2, and banking.

2. **Implementation** - Securing the land, preparing the site, design, financing
    a. Secure Stage 2 financing
    b. Secure land - preferably on a conditional purchase with delayed (but higher) payment
    c. Dynamic Engagement design process to secure all approvals and subdivision
    d. Build roads, plazas, infrastructure, public buildings necessary for State 3 construction
    e. Establish bank to process mortgages and market securities
    f. Order tooling, mobile factories and construction materials
    g. Establish local secondary manufacturing of housing components, possibly building part of the Industrial Park to house these manufacturers
    h. Negotiate rights and contracts with farmers to feed VillageTown
    i. Build Stage 3 manufacturing plant and systems
    j. Establish the banking capacity to fund construction of all mortgaged properties and letters of credit for all properties paid for by other means.
    k. VOC contracts with one or several Village Building Companies (VBC) who work at arms length doing the actual construction. Funding provides for progress payments on individual homes when milestones are met, with profits earned on successful completion.

3. **Construction** - Build the villages, finish the project
    a. Staged construction financing managed by the bank subject to approved inspections
    b. Build exterior-finished lock-up shells of all buildings, with completion village by village sequenced to allow early villages to be occupied safely while construction continues in other villages
    c. Interior finishing, activate and hook up all utilities
    d. When heavy equipment departs, pave streets with final surface materials
    e. Finish, remove tooling, clean and prepare for move-in.
    f. Village Forum appoint citizen "establishment board" to begin transfer of powers from VOC to VillageTown Council Corporation (VTC)
    g. VOC contract employees notified of termination, with some on transition contracts until VTC elections
    h. Title transfer comes with stock certificate in VTC active on VOC completion
    i. Investors paid, surrender stock in VOC, morph into VTC with assets and rights.
    j. Establishment board holds VTC elections
    k. VTC Board and CEO take over. Transition to new hires, Remaining VOC contracts terminate and new staff takes over.
    l. Project Complete

To learn more, contact the Village Forum at **www.villageforum.com**.

www.ingramcontent.com/pod-product-compliance
Lightning Source LLC
Chambersburg PA
CBHW082038230426
43670CB00016B/2698